Forever, Sophia

An Intimate Portrait
by Alan Levy

Baronet Publishing Company, New York

First printing January 1979

ISBN: 0-89437-064-2 paper

Library of Congress Catalog Card Number: 78-71969

Printed in the United States of America

Contents

to Herbert Rosenberg,
who endures

ACKNOWLEDGMENTS

SINCE I DIDN'T MEET SOPHIA until 1969—in the thirty-fifth year
of her life—I have drawn material from times and events at
which I wasn't present from such books as Tony Crawley's *The
Films of Sophia Loren* (Citadel Press, Secaucus, New Jersey,
1976), Donald Zec's *Sophia: An Initmate Biography* (McKay, New
York, 1975), José Luis de Villalonga's *Femmes* (in French: Édi-
tions Stock, 1975), Arturo Lanocita's *Sofia Lorenová* (in Czech:
Orbis, Praha, 1970), and Lilli Kaufmann's and Christiane
Mückenberger's *Filmschauspieler International* (in German:
Henschelverlag, Berlin, 1974); for historical background, such
standard film reference works as *The Liveliest Art: A Panoramic
History of the Movies* by Arthur Knight, *Movies: The History of an
Art and an Institution* by Richard Schickel, *Hollywood and the
Academy Awards* by Nathalie Fredrik, and *The Oxford Compan-
ion to Film*, edited by Liz-Anne Bawden; the magazine journal-
ism of Alberto Moravia in *Show*, Israel Shenker in *The New
York Times* Magazine ("The Name is Ponti, Not Mr. Loren,"
June 6, 1965), Michael Stern in *Cosmopolitan* ("Sophia Loren:
Carlo Ponti's Work of Art," November, 1962), Rex Reed in
Ladies Home Journal ("Sophia Loren: A Contented Aphrodite,"
April 1976; later collected and corrected in *Valentines and Vi-
triol* by Rex Reed, Delacorte, New York, 1977), Joseph Barry,
Sam Blum, Lenore Hershey, and Helen Markel in various
women's magazines, and especially Dora Jane Hamblin in *Life*
and in person—as well as lesser sources too numerous to enu-
merate here.

Wherever possible, outsiders' contributions to this otherwise personal report are acknowledged directly right where they are made, though the crucial roles of Alexandria Hatcher, Herbert Rosenberg, and Shari Steiner are too enormous to be described at all. I am grateful to John A. Flint, Elizabeth Pope Frank, Rosa and Norman Goldfind, Rose Kaplan, Don McKinney, Robert Stein, and Mark Zussman for editorial guidance given along the way, as well as to Elsie Washington for her preliminary research, Charles Zambello and Jean Sincere for their technical assistance, Nino Lo Bello for background materials on *paparazzi* and *fumetti*, for foreground materials on poker and religion as they pertain to Sophia, and, along with his wife Irene, for general help with the Italian language. And to the libraries of the Austrian Film Museum in the Albertina Gallery, Amerika Haus (especially Drs. Roswitha Haller and Günther Anger), American International School (particularly Mrs. Renee Jeschaunig), and the British Council, all in Vienna, as well as to the New York Public Library's research collection of the performing arts at Lincoln Center, I express my gratitude.

Whenever possible, materials not witnessed first-hand were double-checked with Sophia—and indeed a few of my best sources (such as her sister, Maria Mussolini; director John Hough; Peter Ustinov; photographer Tazio Secchiaroli, and agent Luciana Schwarz) were suggested or even set up by Sophia herself, though I have also proceeded independently (contacting Miloš Forman, Oskar Kokoschka, and Dora Jane Hamblin, among others) to an extent that may well be faulted on occasion by Mr. and Mrs. Carlo Ponti themselves.

Within my domicile, the unfailing devotion, encouragement, loyalty, assistance, recollection, and criticism of my wife Valerie and daughters Erika and Monica were invaluable, as were the voracious photo-chasing of Opal von der Diensthütte and the meticulous filing, cataloguing, and other office work of Grimhilde Bauersima.

—White Horse Inn
im Weissen Rössl am Wolfgangsee
St. Wolfgang (Salz Kammergut), Austria
August, 1978

Aldonza

JUST BEFORE THE 1972 SCREEN VERSION of *Man of La Mancha* ended, there was a particularly fine moment when Sophia Loren exhorted a lifeless Peter O'Toole *to dream the impossible dream.* It was sung, as never before, with the fervor of one who has lived an impossible dream.

La Mancha began its life in a Quonset hut on Washington Square. From off-Broadway musical to Broadway hit, from Paris to Prague, from the Theater an der Wien to *státní hudební divadlo,* with Don Quixotes ranging from Richard Kiley and José Ferrer to Josef Meinrad and Jacques Brel, *The Impossible Dream* has always been identified as "the Don's big song." In Arthur Hiller's wooden windmill of a movie, however, when Peter O'Toole "sang" it, dubbed by Simon Gilbert, neither they nor United Artists' eleven million dollars could bring the 132-minute film, or its audience, to life.

On the other hand, as the kitchenmaid Aldonza, Sophia—who in her first major screen appearance back in 1953 had mouthed lyrics for Renata Tebaldi in *Aida*—did her own singing throughout *La Mancha,* which was her first big screen musical. And her small closing reprise of the Don's earlier solo was so much more eloquent than O'Toole/Gilbert's that *The Impossible Dream* is now remembered by millions of moviegoers as "Sophia's song."

Sophia would hope to make more musicals when the right shows come along. "A *Hello, Dolly* or a *Funny Girl* I could never do," she told me, "but that girl from *La Mancha,* Aldonza, her I understand. She had to fight for everything in her life, every crust of bread."

As these words crossed what Irving Penn, the photographer of women, has called "the most beautiful lips in the world," the elegant lady was pouring me tea in her silk-damask-and-frescoed Paris triplex apartment. When I asked Sophia for the fundamental character trait that brought her all this way from a waterfront slum on the Bay of Naples, I might have been feeding her a song cue, for she replied:

"I'm stubborn. When I have something in my head, I've got to go and do it. I'm impatient to do it. I'm very rational: Whatever I specifically want usually isn't the impossible. Whatever I ask of life is something life can give me. I never sought the impossible dream, but from life I sometimes got the impossible dream because I took it step by step, little by little, with patience, too. If you wait for the impossible dream to come true, it won't. But if you work at a little corner of it and then another corner, well, one day you may have the whole mosaic."

Sophia began below the bottom by growing up illegitimate amidst grimy poverty and wartime chaos. And she came to own not only that sumptuous triplex just off the Champs-Elysées, but a fifty-room, fifteen-bathroom, Pompeiian-red villa near Rome, three homes in Geneva and a hotel suite on Central Park South in Manhattan. She was a nobody, a hungry teen-ager hunting for a job and a bit of respectability. Now, her face adorns the cover of *Vogue* and the walls of the Museum of Modern Art. Her films play to packed houses around the world and her glamor remains undimmed as she glides through her mid-forties. Say "Sophia" anywhere today and nobody will wonder whether you mean the capital of Bulgaria. No, people will think of an Italian actress whose first name has become a household word.

"What is Sophia, who is she?" the critic Stanley Kauffmann asked rhetorically in the erudite *New Republic*. "She is sunlight, she is hearty warmth, she is great contentment with simple things. She is song and laughter, dance. She is a free-hearted lover, yet never depraved. The wonder is that although she could not possibly exist, there she is: existing. She is not fake."

As early as 1962 *Time* was embroidering her genealogy thusly: "She has rewritten the canons of beauty. A daughter of the Bay of Naples, she has within her the blood of the Saracens, Spaniards, Normans, Byzantines, and Greeks. The East appears in her slanting eyes. Her dark brown hair is a bazaar of rare silk. . . . In her impish, ribald Neapolitan laughter, she epitomizes the *Capriccio Italien* that Tchaikovsky must have had in mind. Lord Byron, in her honor, probably sits up in his grave about once a week and rededicates his homage to 'Italia! oh Italia! thou who hast the fatal gift of beauty.' *Vogue* Magazine once fell to its skinny knees and abjectedly admitted: 'After Loren, bones are boring.' "

In his handsomely detailed coffee-table book, *The Films of Sophia Loren,* British cinéaste Tony Crawley writes:

With her voluptuous shape—a face and frame she admits to be 'a unity of irregularities'; legs that talk; Etruscan eyes that sigh; and all-over Vesuvian contours, only out-deafened in their clarion call to arms by the over-generous appeal to the senses when the complete equipment is viewed in vision of motion—she is most definitely, definitively, Italian: Neapolitan! As for style . . . ah! If only they could bottle it! She is truly gifted in all facets of the kind of stellar Style already trickling out of screen fashion when she was an extra, and which she, alone among the postwar superlegends, continues to impart—in her own incandescent, shimmering way.

Her feet, though, have rarely strayed far from the ground. She may well be the stuff that superlative dreams are made of; she may be at once both fantasy and reality. Yet she knows her roots. From first to last in a career of sparkling enjoyment, rich in Neapolitan laughter and tears, Sophia Loren has remained *La diva popolana.* A star of the people, for the people, and by the people.

Even in the lavender lyrics of Rex Reed—" 'Well,' she said,

her Gioconda smile erupting into a sulphurous Vesuvius of laughter as she led me to the door, 'nobody's perfect.' "—Sophia endures as:

> . . . one of the few film queens of international stature. For an ugly duckling whose chin was too short and whose mouth was too big, with the neck of a swan and bosoms like pumpkins, she has emerged as beautiful as Aphrodite rising from the Aegean. For an actress who began as one of 10,000 slave-girl extras in *Quo Vadis?*—with no talent, no training and no range—she has developed into an Oscar-winning artist of the first rank. She has sung duets with Noël Coward, dined with Queen Elizabeth, and shooed President Tito of Yugoslavia out of her kitchen for sticking his finger in her spaghetti sauce. Elizabeth Taylor credits her for saving her marriage to Richard Burton. [sic] She has beaten Taylor, Burton, and another friend, Peter O'Toole, at both scrabble and poker.

Amidst all this purple prose one can barely perceive the film-fledgling peering blankly over Deborah Kerr's shoulder in a banquet scene of *Quo Vadis?* (1950) let alone the accomplished actress who, playing a character a dozen years older than herself in *Two Woman* (1961), won the first Academy Award for Best Actress ever given to a foreigner in a foreign-language film.

With more than seventy films to her credit, Sophia Loren possesses not only international fame, but a legend extending far beyond the cinemas of the world. To mark its twentieth year in Italy, the United Nations Food and Agriculture Organization put her on a commemorative coin as Ceres, the Roman goddess of grain—no mean crown for a confirmed Earth Mother and screen Venus.

What not everybody remembers is that Sophia happens to be human, has managed to stay human, and has had to cope with a host of human problems whose solutions most women take for granted. She has had to fight church and state, press and public, her husband's inclinations and her own insecurity just to enjoy what was once supposed to come naturally to a woman:

marriage, children, and a life of her own. Though she has spent much of her life grappling with painful problems others rarely have to face, she has never lost her natural delight and interest in others, down-to-earth sense of values, and sunny Latin warmth, generosity, and humor.

By dint of charm and tenacity, Sophia has won her wars. But the battles stay with her and, if you can see them through her eyes and words, as I have tried to, you can begin to see Sophia as she really is.

I have known Sophia for nearly a decade—since the Spring of 1969. I have visited her nine different times: often with two or three sessions to the visit. We have met in Austria, Switzerland, France, and Italy—and this variety of settings serves to show her life style and spice the action much the way changes of scene can enhance the momentum of a stage play. But the metaphor here, appropriately enough, will be cinematic, with intensive close-ups, vignettes and, wherever revelation and illumination warrant, voice-over analyses by such Sophiologists as Peter Ustinov or Richard Burton, Tazio Secchiaroli or Alberto Moravia.

This, then, is an honest, affectionate look at Sophia over the ups-and-downs of our friendship, with particular emphasis— sometimes critical—on what (and who) made Sophia the way she is now. If sometimes it reads like a love story, it should not be mistaken for an authorized biography, though it is sometimes more intimate than any which will be written. And, as is not the case with any first-person autobiography of Sophia, nothing in *Forever, Sophia* has been censored by Mr. or Mrs. Ponti or anyone else; not one word of it has ever been shown in advance of publication to any of the Pontis or any representative of theirs; nor have I ever been asked to do so.

The best way to portray a personality—and perhaps the most penetrating means when one is a journalist and the other an actress—is to catch her at as many different times in as many different moods of her private life as one can. This I have done.

CHAPTER 1

Sofia Scicolone

"I'm not your lady. I'm not any kind of lady. For a lady has modest and maidenly airs [which] a blind man could see that I lack," Sophia Loren tells Peter O'Toole in *Man of La Mancha,* and then she implores him to look at her, look at her, *God, won't you look at me! Look at the kitchen slut reeking of sweat, born on a dung heap to die on a dung heap. . . .*

If real life wasn't always that bad, it was sometimes worse. Born out of wedlock in Rome on Thursday, September 20, 1934, Sofia Scicolone grew up eight miles from Naples—in the earthquake-prone port of Pozzuoli, once described as the most squalid city in Italy. Since ancient times, volcanic activity has produced noxious fumes and vapors rising from the banks of two nearby lakes, Averno and Lucrino—so much so that early mythics pinpointed the area as a main entrance to Hades. Subterranean gases continue to escape from extinct volcanoes through vents in the vicinity and, in 1922, almost all the fish in Lake Lucrino were killed by sulphuric regurgitations. Today, industry and poverty have helped to pollute Pozzuoli further— and its small but picturesque waterfront on the Bay of Naples, with whitewashed houses and fishermen bringing in catches you'd hesitate to eat, reeks of the residue of trade while the waters, oily and green, spattered with lemon peels, have all the makings of an Italian *insalata* that would take away anyone's appetite.

In one of the two bedrooms of a four-room apartment above

the Capuano vinegar works at Via Solfatara 5, Sophia recalls that "there was one big, big bed where my grandfather, grandmother, aunt and I slept, and a little bed for my mother and kid sister, Maria. My uncle and his wife had the other bedroom."

One day, her mother introduced her to a visiting stranger: "This is your father."

Sofia replied: "He isn't my father. I already have a father."

Her mother said: "No, Sofia. The man you call Papa is your grandfather."

"Well, if he *is* my father, why doesn't he live with us?"

"Maybe he doesn't want to live with us," her mother said gently. Besides, Riccardo Scicolone had a wife in Rome. He had not yet completed his engineering studies, but he'd told Romilda Villani he was in films soon after he'd met her on the street when she was eighteen. Sophia's mother has described the beginning of their romance succinctly in a 1973 interview with Donald Zec: "He saw me in the street and came up behind me. We met again some times, and after three weeks we went to bed together. Then one month and twenty days later I am carrying Sophia. When she is born I do it quickly, easily, like an animal" —in the ward for unmarried mothers of Rome's Clinica Regina Margareta.

Sophia remembers her father, what little she saw of him, quite vividly as "tall, strong, distinguished-looking. He had gray hair and his face was slightly round, with a nose hooked like the beak of a bird. Large hands and feet, but slender wrists and ankles. He always dressed elegantly but quietly—like a gentleman. He had a beautiful smile and a rather haughty expression. And great charm."

She never considered herself illegitimate just because her mother wasn't married to her father. He had, after all, signed a formal statement that Sofia was "the natural issue of Romilda Villani and Riccardo Scicolone," though he balked at doing the same after Maria was born four years later. But Maria was definitely Scicolone's child, too. (When Zec asked Romilda Villani why she'd had a second child by him, she replied: "I was hoping he would marry me. It is the mentality of a small village.")

Fortunately for both girls, their mother was a very strong woman: father figure, mother figure, everything. She was a talented but frustrated would-be actress and musician. Once, she had won a contest to find The Girl Who is Garbo's Double; one of the judges was the playwright Luigi Pirandello. But her superstitious family had forced her to forego the prize that included a first-class ship ticket to New York, train travel to Hollywood, and a screen test there; after all, hadn't Roldolfo Valentino been poisoned to death in America?* A little later, though, with a thousand lire (barely a dollar) in her purse, she had taken off from Pozzuoli to study music in Rome and become a concert pianist—only to return in disgrace a year later with three-month-old Sofia and no husband.

Despite her social difficulties, Romilda Villani gave Sofia and Maria most of the warmth and love they needed. "Unconsciously, though," Sophia says now, "I must have had a problem because I always wanted to be surrounded by men much older than me. Without knowing it, I was always looking for my father." Her real father seldom came down to Pozzuoli from Rome, where he was now a construction engineer raising his own family; "I have two half-brothers," Sophia says succinctly. But, sometimes, yearning for Scicolone, her mother would send him a telegram saying SOFIA SERIOUSLY ILL STOP COME AT ONCE. Now and then, he fell for it but, finding upon arrival that Sofia was perfectly well, he would erupt like Mount Etna situated two hundred miles to the south. And, of course, Sofia wasn't perfectly all right, for everything was backward: at such times, she was made to feel guilty for feeling well. Her good condition was greeted by her father with dismay and anger, rather than relief.

On very rare occasions, Riccardo Scicolone came to visit on his own—without being invited or falsely alarmed. But he seldom stayed long, for he was an outsider, an intruder or, as Sophia put it, "like a donkey at a concert. So he couldn't wait to get away, especially because my people never forgave him for not marrying my mother."

*No, Rudolph Valentino died in 1926 of a ruptured ulcer.

In her childhood (in her lifetime, for that matter!) her father gave her only two presents, but one of them was "what I wanted the most in the world: a car! A little blue toy car with red wheels. The other was a pair of roller skates."

Back in the early 1960s, the Italian novelist Alberto Moravia did a very Freudian analytic interview with Sophia, which is worth citing not just for his observations (Sophia later informed Moravia she found them a trifle warped), but for her own reactions to them at the time. She told Moravia then, as she told me more than a decade later, about the two gifts from her father, and he asked her: "Did you take care of them?"

"Yes, I did take care of them," Sophia replied.

"Usually children don't," Moravia noted.

"Usually children get presents every birthday," said Sophia.

"Did you feel the lack of a father?" Moravia persisted.

"I would have if he hadn't been there at all," Sophia answered. "But he was both there and not there. He was present just enough of the time to make me have complexes."

"What kind of complexes?" Moravia asked.

"My biggest one was that I did not have a normal family."

"Meaning what?"

"Meaning a real father who lived with us and took care of us and worked to support us, and a real mother—"

"Your mother wasn't a real mother?" a surprised Moravia interrupted.

"I would have preferred her not to be so beautiful and to be a real mother instead—the kind they have in Pozzuoli, who are old and even ugly."

"So that even your mother's being beautiful made you feel that your life was abnormal?" Moravia made much (too much, according to Sophia) of the young Sofia's feelings about "being different." Yet Sophia admitted to him that the abnormality of her family circumstances "made me ashamed." Especially at her Catholic Parochial school, "where the other girls could talk about their fathers, but I couldn't." So she used to arrive either at one minute to nine, "when everybody was already in, or at eight o'clock because nobody was there."

Ironically, if her father had any plans for her at all, he wanted her to be a schoolteacher. Sophia had no such ambition, but she thinks now that she turned her reaction to advantage by wanting "to go to work very young so that I could not just tell him but show him that I didn't want to be a schoolteacher. It helped me decide early what I wanted to do."

Alberto Moravia summed up the early Sofia Scicolone as one who, feeling abnormal without family or father, was driven to assert her own personality and find a way of artistic expression that would make her own will prevail. "Success," he told the latter-day Sophia, "was a surrogate for the normality you could never achieve."

My own cross-examination of her childhood took a different tack after she told me about her father's only two gifts. "Did you ever believe in Santa Claus?" I asked her.

Sophia gave an answer that would have delighted every feminist I know: "I liked to believe in her."

"In *her?!*"

"*La Befana,* we call her in Italy. The witch who comes with the presents. She comes from the chimney on the sixth of January—the Day of the Three Kings (Epiphany). In the beginning, I truly believed in her, in being good to please her so she would reward me. Then, growing up, I just pretended to believe."

"What changed your belief?"

"My father came into my life and took over from *La Befana.* Of course, my mother and grandmother always got me something from *La Befana:* a doll bedroom or a kitchenette for my dollhouse or, if there wasn't that much money, maybe just one piece of doll furniture or at least a sock with chocolates."

It was hard to make ends meet for eight people, even though her grandfather worked as a cannonmaker in a munitions factory, her mother gave piano lessons, her uncle was a laborer, and her aunt a typist. Still, until the war, the Villani household had enough to eat: a bread-and-bean soup for breakfast and a substantial supper of "*pasta* with beans, *pasta* with carrots, *pasta* in one form or another—food that was filling. Meat we ate once a week, on Sundays. Sunday was the day of the sacred stew. My grandmother used to get up at six in the morning to make it. The best I've ever eaten in my life." On Sundays, too, the whole family went to Mass at the Church of the Madonna del Carmine and, after the relatives had joined them for the sacred stew, some of the men would play soccer in one of the rooms while the women watched. Then "if we had any money, we went to the movies. If not, then we didn't do anything."

On the twenty-seventh of every month, when Sofia's aunt got paid, Sofia and Maria and Romilda would take the train into Naples and join her for pastry and hot chocolate. They would stay all afternoon and leave for Pozzuoli at eight in the evening.

When I asked Sophia what lessons she had learned from early hardship, she replied:

"Later, you appreciate things more because you didn't have them. But, at the time when you can't buy things or have things that other people have, it's terrible because you don't have any-thing—especially when you're a little baby. Little toys you have to make for yourself—yes, and when you play with a little box for a whole afternoon, you develop much more your fantasy. But you only know this afterward, not when you are experienc-ing it. For instance, buying a pair of shoes was a big holiday. For children today, though, a present isn't clothes and they hate going shopping. So, with clothes, you have to surprise them. Only then do they appreciate such a present from you. Other-wise, they take everything for granted—everything!"

World War II brought poverty and starvation that matured Sofia early. "I've always been old," Sophia told me once. "Suf-fering means maturity, even if you're a baby." (Peter Ustinov is of the opinion that "one of Sophia's attractions for Carlo Ponti is that there's a side to her that has always been old.") She saw her mother go begging for bread and cheese. Once, her mother scavenged a cup of water from an automobile radiator and doled it out to her two daughters, spoonful by spoonful. Sofia stood for hours on breadlines, even when air-raid warnings sounded, because running to a shelter cost you your place in line. She "looked death in the face every day, saw death in the streets when I was six and eight years old. That you live with all your life. The facts of life are that a child who has seen war cannot be compared with a child who doesn't know what war is, except from television."

She told me this over the years and, in early 1976, she elaborated on this subject to Rex Reed:

"I never had enough to eat. At the age of six, I already knew well the meaning of the word deprivation. I was brought up with hunger and fear. My mother tried to provide what she could, but there was nothing around to provide. Everyone was desperate. We lived on sour bread and rainwater.

"Naples was the first bomb target because of the harbor and the railroad stations all around the port. It was really the city that suffered most in Italy. They only bombed Rome once and the Pope stopped it. But we were bombed five times a night in Naples. My earliest memories are of being always hungry and sleepy. . . .

"I've never tried to block out the memories of the past, even though some are painful. I don't understand people who hide from their past. Everything you live through helps to make you the person you are now. I even have nostalgia for the German boys who marched by my house in the mornings on their way to kill people. Such handsome youths with blond hair and blue eyes, pretending to be men. Whoever thought they'd do what they did later on? I didn't know anything about war or politics, so I didn't hate those men. Children don't know how to hate. When you're a baby, you have no social conscience. Also, don't forget, the Germans were not our enemies in the early part of the war. They were supposed to be our friends."

For several months, during the Allied bombings of southern Italy, Sofia and her family spent their nights living in a stinking railroad tunnel, fighting off the rats. In retrospect, however, Sophia recalls this life not with horror, for "in those hours under the tunnel, we felt protected not only because we felt safe from bombs, but because we were all there, huddled up against each other, breathing the same air, trying to take heart and even finding enough space to play and have fun. It seemed to me there, that I had gained an enormous family. . . . Today, I understand that the tunnel, deep down, was the peace and comfort of a child in its mother's womb."

Toward dawn, the tunnel-dwellers would awaken to shouts of warning, for the first train came through at 4:15 A.M. Romilda Villani would take both daughters by the hand and lead them through the countryside to the wood fire of a goatherd who would look at Sofia "with a sort of pity that he might have felt for some poor starved lamb. He would milk one of his goats and hand me a big mug of the warm, frothy milk. I shall never forget the taste. No flavor, no masterpiece of gastronomy will ever give me the confidence, the assurance of well-being that I felt every morning from that foaming mug—even if I went hungry the rest of the day."

Once, toward the end of an elegant four-course lunch at the Villa Ponti, I asked my hostess whether, at that very moment, she could remember what starvation was like.

"Starvation," said Sophia, "is when your stomach is empty and you feel like fainting and anything you look at you'd like to eat—even if it's just the empty table."

"And yet you'd never make a Roman orgy out of eating, would you?"

"I don't like to get sick," she said succinctly. Past privation, however, may account for not only her love of good eating but her use of food nicknames for her friends and intimates: Dr. Christiaan Barnard, the heart surgeon, is *Lasagne Pasticciate*, Marcello Mastroianni is *Cottechino* (crisp pigskin, or crackling), and Carlo Ponti has remarked: "In the ordinary home, when a woman loves a man, she calls him dear, darling, sweetheart. Not Sophia. For dear she calls me *Polpettone* (meat balls) or for very dear, *Peperone* (pepper). But, when she loves me most, she calls me *Suppli* (fried rice ball stuffed with mozzarella)."

The first Allied soldier Sofia saw (in late 1943, shortly after her ninth birthday) was a kilted Scot: "I laughed so hard at a man in a skirt, I got a pain in my stomach." Then came the Americans and "it was a big carnival. They were a symbol of liberty and food." And then there were Moroccan troops, who were known and feared for taking their sex wherever and whenever they could find it—regardless of age, gender, or willingness."

Perhaps because, in her Oscar-winning *Two Women* performance, Sophia Loren and Eleanora Brown, who played her teenaged daughter, were both raped by Moroccans, various readers may think they have heard of Sofia as either victim or streetwalker or both.

"Some girls were raped. I was not," Sophia has insisted. And when Rex Reed confronted her with "those early stories of how she worked as a prostitute on the streets of Naples, seducing GIs for money to buy food," her eyes flashed with anger as she pointed out that she was only nine at the time!

"I was a rather mature child, but I wasn't *that* mature," she told Reed. "In every house, we used to sell drinks to soldiers—to make money. The bars were all closed, so the only way they could buy beer was in people's homes. That was the only contact I had with soldiers. They used to call me Little Chicken. But I liked them very much. They were always very homesick, very unhappy, and very drunk."

Even then, Sofia played second fiddle in the beauty league to her baby sister: "Maria was blonde and fat—and, in Italy, a fat blonde bambina was and is the beginning and end of the world. Everyone told us *she* was very beautiful. I was very jealous of her. I was dark and scrawny: a real scarecrow. I didn't look like much." Sophia's nicknames were *Stecchetto* and *Stuzzicadenti,* which mean Little Stick and Toothpick—and, as a matter of fact, she had a face that was all mouth, and a mouth that was all teeth.

Until she was thirteen. Then, the Toothpick budded into a willow and every stroll down the street became an adventure. One of the first to spot this development was, naturally enough, her gym teacher. He came around to propose marriage to Sofia, but her mother had him "out of the house in two seconds. She told him to go away and take a cold bath."

When Sophia was fourteen, she entered a Queen of the Sea

beauty contest in Naples. She didn't win, but she was one of the twelve runners-up picked as princesses. Her prize money was 25,000 lire (barely $40).

This—plus a few drama lessons—offered enough encouragement for Sofia and her mother to try their luck in Hollywood-on-the-Tiber, as the newly rebuilt Cinecittà complex on the outskirts of Rome was being called now that Metro-Goldwyn-Mayer was there to make *Quo Vadis?,* the first of many multi-million-dollar spectaculars to be filmed in postwar Italy. Seeking work as extras, Romilda and Sofia took the train up to Rome in July of 1949, when the girl was still fourteen.

Upon arrival, her mother called her father to see if he would help them. He wasn't in. So they took their bags directly to Cinecittà. It was a particularly hot summer day on which a couple of the thousands of extras died of sunstroke. So soon after the war, Italians who weren't in the best economic or physical condition had been queuing up from the crack of dawn to try for work in *Quo Vadis?*—and, to add to the agony, Cinecittà's water supply was not yet so good as it should be.

Hundreds of girls and women were anxiously milling around while an assistant director weeded them out. Sofia and Romilda joined the throng and, after a while, Sofia caught his attention. She stepped forward and said her name was Sofia Scicolone. Out of the crowd burst a woman screaming that she and only she had the right to call herself Scicolone; Sofia was "nobody's daughter!" The woman who was looking for work as an extra was Sofia's father's wife.

Later, Signora Scicolone even had her husband call the police because Sofia was a minor, "but since I was accompanied by my mother, there was nothing the police could do to us, so we stayed in Rome." It was all straight out of the grubby neo-realism of Vittorio De Sica, who was making his classic *Bicycle Thieves* and *Shoeshine* around that time for a tiny fraction of MGM's *Quo Vadis?* budget. Years later Sophia would recall that scene at Cinecittà and say to me:

"You can say now that life is like a movie and you can even laugh at such an experience, but when you're a girl of fourteen and it's happening to you, it's terribly painful. I was so ashamed when it happened—with everybody looking at me—that the nightmare was then and there, so I knew nothing worse could happen to me and went on with living."

In this one sees the early essence of Sophia as a survivor: She tends to be the first to pick up the pieces, even when it's her own heart that's broken.

Refusing to let that confrontation scar her for life—or even scare her into retreat—Sofia and her mother not only won walk-on parts in *Quo Vadis?* but were singled out for tiny one- or two-line speaking roles. This big break, however, aborted when they were interviewed by director Mervyn LeRoy, who asked Sofia: "Do you speak any English?"

"Yes," she lied.

"Where did you learn your English?"

"Yes."

How old are you?"

"Yes."

Laughing, LeRoy told his assistants: "Put them in with the slaves."

The work in *Quo Vadis?* lasted two days and Sophia now explains the vacuity of her stare as she peered past Deborah Kerr: "I was trying to see where the camera was."

That was the extent of her acting ability at the time, but the brief encounter with LeRoy taught her the importance of being multilingual. During the uphill struggle that followed, she pacticed French, which had been her best subject in school, and later used her gift of mimicry to perfect it; enrolled in a Latin course, which was a short-lived mistake; took eight months of English lessons from an Irish tutor living in Rome; and soaked up colloquial Spanish while making films on location. Nowadays, she takes a quick refresher in the appropriate tongue before starting any film that isn't in Italian. She performs in Italian, French, English, or Spanish and does her own dubbing. Unlike other actresses, she also spotchecks the Munich dubbing of her films to make sure her German "voice"—which is that of a noted Viennese stage acress, Marion Degler—sounds like her own.

With the 21,000 lire ($33) she earned in *Quo Vadis?*, Romilda

Villani rented a small furnished room for herself and her daughter in an apartment on the Via Cosenza in Rome. Sophia recalls that their landlady was "a real witch. She was sixty years old and she had a lover, a real country bumpkin." When he paid some notice to Sofia, the landlady "became jealous of me. One day she attacked me—grabbed me by the hair and tried to hit me. I got away from her and phoned my father to ask him to help me. Do you know what he answered?"

Her father's reply was: "You two wanted to stay in Rome, didn't you? You're on your own." Then he hung up.

Sofia had contacted her father once before, hoping to buy for her sister, with the money she earned from *Quo Vadis?*, the Scicolone name he had refused Maria at birth. Again he refused. The negotiations ended up costing Sophia Loren two million lire ($3,200), nearly a hundred times her first offer—but a few years later Maria Villani became Maria Scicolone shortly before marriage changed her last name to Mussolini. "Sophia paid for my name," says Maria with infinite gratitude for what she still considers the best gift any big sister ever gave a kid sister.

Feeling "very bitter toward my father" as late as 1962, Sophia told Alberto Moravia that she could never understand why her mother stayed "in love with him for twenty-seven years. She stopped loving him only a couple of months ago." And when Moravia asked Sophia what her father did "to kill such a stubborn love," Sophia confessed: "I don't know."

Once, after Sophia achieved fame, Riccardo Scicolone—by then a successful building contractor—sued his daughter for libeling him in published interviews. But when a magistrate at a preliminary hearing showed skepticism and the Ponti lawyers indicated the defense would be the truth, Scicolone withdrew the action.

"I hated him at the time," Sophia said, recalling that she vowed never to forgive her father for his neglect and money-grubbing. But by early 1976 she was telling Rex Reed: "Now I am older, I have children of my own, I understand more. As time goes by, you learn to forgive and forget. I don't forget easily, but I do forgive. Now my father is old and very ill and very lonely. He sits in dark cinemas and watches my movies. I often wonder what goes through his mind. But it's water under the bridge now." And later that year when Riccardo Scicolone lay dying in Rome, she visited his bedside. She attended his funeral, along with Maria, and burst into tears several times during the service. In her private limousine, Sophia followed her father's coffin to Rome's main cemetery. "Time heals," she says often.

CHAPTER 2

Sofia Lazzaro

REBUFFED BY HER FATHER and reviled by their landlady during those post-*Quo Vadis?* beginnings in Rome of the late 1940s, Sofia Scicolone and her mother moved from furnished room to furnished room.

"For less than two weeks," she recalled, "we stayed with some distant relatives we had in Rome. But they begrudged us even a cup of coffee, so we cleared out and went back to furnished rooms. Once, we slept in a maid's room that was as big as a box."

During those hellish times Sophia recalls that she "worked constantly, with ups and downs, naturally. I remember that once we had five hundred lire (less than a dollar) between us, just about enough to get back to Pozzuoli. My mother was so discouraged she would have liked to give up and go back, but I didn't want to." When Sofia's sister Maria caught typhoid back in Pozzuoli, Romilda did go home—but Sofia stayed on alone in Rome and, when Maria recovered, Romilda returned to Rome.

Soon, Sofia shed the expensive name of Scicolone: too large a mouthful for casting directors to swallow, she was told. Instead, she became Sofia Lazzaro, a name of Biblical derivation suggesting, in this incarnation, that she could either raise or rouse Lazarus from the dead in fewer than the four days it took Jesus to do the job in the New Testament.

Even so, movie jobs were scarce. Sofia Lazzaro turned to the next-best vocation: modeling for *fumetti,* an art form of true-confession and cheap-crime comic strips told in posed photos with melodramatic dialogue in balloons. *Fumetti* look like grainy stills of B-movies you wouldn't pay to see. But for 10,000 lire ($16) a day, Sofia excelled in them for three years, twirling a two-foot phallic eel, being lassoed by Indians, having her bra adjusted by a volunteer fireman, and going to Mass in a skirt so mini that the police confiscated the entire issue.

The *fumetto* is a uniquely Italian phenomenon that has seldom caught on outside Latin cultures, although, oddly enough, a few *fumetti* did turn up a few years ago in a British magazine called *Tit-Bits* and at least one of them, "Man of Her Dreams," featured none other than Sofia Lazzaro as Meg McKenna, who, when I picked up "The Story So Far":

> . . . worked in a little Malta cafe managed by her mother and when she met Lieutenant Jim Blaygrove Meg realized he was the man she had dreamed of all her life. . . . And it looked as though happiness lay ahead for both of them—until Diana Roberts came on the scene. Diana had discovered that Jim was heir to a fortune, even before he knew it himself. She was determined to get both Jim and the money—and stopped at nothing to get her way. By scheming with Manuel, the café owner, and his friend, Alfredo, she managed to get Meg accused of stealing money, and to part Meg and Jim. However, Alice, the other dance hostess at the café, gave the game away. . . . Jim and Meg were reunited. But Manuel had heard Alice talking to Jim, and had warned Alfredo to get rid of Jim—for good! Now CONTINUE:

And, when I did continue, I saw Sofia skulled by a flying bottle and watched her awaken, chastely disheveled and bare shouldered in a hospital bed, and then return home to her room above the café to sleep it off—in the raw, apparently, for when Manuel's son burst into her bedroom to confess the theft she'd been accused of, she pulled a blanket over her chest before sitting up to speak her punch line: "Ricardo—how could you?" Her material, however, couldn't match that of the *fumetto's* heavy, Alfredo, the convent messenger, who knocked the hero cold with his "hamlike fist" and compatible prose: "Take that,

Englishman! Now you will interfere no more!" And that was a
fumetto that was!

One job led to another and, before long, film director Giorgio Bianchi put her behind a beachball in a bikini and gave her a couple of minutes in a movie called *Hearts at Sea*. Sofia went on working in *fumetti* even while appearing virtually unnoticed in such instant forgettables as *The Vote, Bluebeard's Six Wives, I Am the Guerrilla Chief* (starring Silvana Pampanini) for Jolly Films, *Milana Miliardaria* (featuring D. Maggio and the Inter-Napoli soccer team), *The Reluctant Magician,* and *Zorro's Dream.* She even appeared briefly in a Carlo Ponti–Dino De Laurentiis co-production, *Anna,* starring De Laurentiis' protégée, Silvana Mangano, but Sofia was so far in the background that she and Ponti never laid eyes upon each other during the making of *Anna.*

In early 1951, not yet seventeen, Sofia Lazzaro took two $50-a-day movie jobs: first in *The Piano-Tuner Has Arrived,* starring Alberto Sordi, and then in the harem scenes of *It's Him —Yes! Yes!* Virtually the only extant topless photo of Sofia or Sophia dates back to *It's Him—Yes! Yes!* and she has explained that the co-directors, Vittorio Metz and Marcello Marchesi, insisted that she and her harem-mates strip for the sake of the French version. "Besides," she adds, "I was hungry." That was the same year Marilyn Monroe was posing nude for a calendar in Hollywood and her explanation and attitude were much the same as Sophia's—extending even to blushing, giggling, but pardonable pride, years later.* Carlo Ponti, however, takes it less lightly. He is widely known to have suppressed, destroyed, or bought up all modeling shots and movie out-takes of any overexposed early Sofia or later Sophia. As Donald Zec put it: "Rather than allow his beautiful wife to suffer even momentary embarrassment, Carlo would gladly buy General Motors, let

---

*In Paris, 1976, when Sophia signed my British edition of Tony Crawley's filmography, she toyed with the idea of autographing the *It's Him—Yes! Yes!* movie still on page 47 before deciding it was more in keeping with her present image to inscribe her message (*To my dear friend Alan with much love and friendship. Sophia.*) up front—in the book, that is.

alone a roll of negatives." Thus, it came as no surprise (except that it hadn't happened sooner) and unleashed no great man-hunt, though plenty of publicity and reprints, when, late in the summer of 1977, some mysterious stranger or other broke into the Cinecittà Archive and pilfered the naked Sofia footage from *It's Him—Yes! Yes!*

Despite all the credits plus a little notoriety, the roles were small and the pay was less, so Sofia's principal source of income remained *fumetti*—and there was still time to moonlight by entering beauty contests. Having been elected Princess of the Sea in Naples at the age of fourteen, she tried out for Queen of the Adriatic Sirens at sixteen and made it to the finals in Salsomaggiore, where she was voted the consulation prize of Miss Elegance. But it was later in 1951 that she went to watch the Miss Rome beauty contest and fate right out of *fumetti* befell her.

The finals were being conducted in an open-air night club in the Oppian Park overlooking the Colosseum. Sofia had gone there on a rare double date with a girlfriend and two young boys. She recalled, "I was never attracted to boys of my own age. I've always preferred mature men." She told Alberto Moravia that once, in her early teens in Pozzuoli, she had found a seventeen-year-old boy named Manlio attractive—until "one day we took a walk along the highway to Bagnoli. All of a sudden, he took my hand, and I realized he was breathing hard and that his eyes were all bloodshot. All of a sudden, he kissed me on the mouth. I was terrified. I left him in the lurch and ran off like some crazy thing and I never saw him again."

At the Colle Oppio in Rome, the youthful foursome took front-row seats for the beauty contest. The judges sat on a raised platform and one of them was Dr. Carlo Fortunato Pietro Ponti, a rotund, balding Milanese lawyer turned Roman film producer. Sipping a soft drink, Sofia paid Ponti no notice until he sent a friend over to ask if she wanted to enter the contest.

"Why not?" Sofia thought. She now recalls: "I looked at Ponti. He seemed to have a pleasant face, and I said yes. Actually, given the fact that Ponti had singled me out, I was hoping to win first prize. Instead, I came in second."

Life began to imitate bad art when Ponti gave Sofia his card and invited her to call upon him at his office in the Piazza D'Aracoeli the next day. Sofia assumed this was a rerun of a line that, at sixteen, she'd already heard many times: "Men, when they approached me, it was only for one purpose." Still, this one didn't seem to "look at me the way most men did."

For the interview with Ponti, she borrowed a red dress with white polka dots from a friend.

Piazza D'Aracoeli 1 proved to be the stately Palazzo Colonna and, in an upstairs suite, Carlo Ponti sat behind a large antique desk, a pile of scripts, and a handful of trophies, including a Critics' Award for producing *To Live in Peace* (1946), a pioneer picture of the postwar Italian neo-realistic wave that also spawned Roberto Rossellini (*Open City, Paisan*) and De Sica.

To Sophia's surprise, Ponti himself was both businesslike and encouraging. "I saw in Sophia," he said later, "all the best that is Italian: not just Neapolitan gaiety, but a vitality, sensitivity, and sense of rhythm that no Actors' Studio can teach. She was not an actress, she was an artist."

Carlo Ponti himself started out in life wanting to be an artist of an even more creative ilk: an architect. But in Italy it takes longer to become an architect than it does to become a lawyer, so Ponti—born in Magenta, an industrial town not far from Milan, sometime between 1910 and 1913 (the exact date, like an indelicate photo of Sophia, has been carefully blurred)— studied law while working part-time in his father's music publishing house. In 1938, not long after becoming a Doctor of Jurisprudence and beginning to practice law, Ponti was asked by a friend who was leaving Mussolini's Italy to take his place on the board of a film company in Milan. Within a few months, Ponti was its executive vice-president.

By the end of 1939, he had produced six films, the most notable of which was *Piccolo Mondo Antico* (Little Old World), an anti-fascist historic parable that was the first major success of director Mario Soldati, who fifteen years later would direct Sophia's first major success, *Woman of the River.* For making *Piccolo Mondo Antico,* Ponti was arrested and sent to jail for a few days. During the war it was impossible for him to make movies, but he stayed in the business and, as soon as the war was over, he came to Rome and went to work for Lux, the film company for which he made *To Live in Peace* and a dozen other pictures per annum. He claims to have produced Luchino Visconti's first film and added that "there's practically not an Italian director—except the very oldest—who didn't begin with me." At Lux, he insists, "we founded the Italian cinema."

Ponti, who had started out to be an architect, saw himself as one after all: an architect of films. "I like the cinema," he said once, "because you imagine a thing and after awhile you see it. Just like building a house. The director does what I want. I have the ideas.

"For me, the important thing is to create characters. You construct a building from raw materials, and with films you give life to things that don't exist."

In 1950, the year before he met Sofia, Ponti joined forces with Dino De Laurentiis, a small Neapolitan who thinks big. Together, they made such second-rate epics as King Vidor's *War and Peace* (with Henry Fonda, Audrey Hepburn, Mel Ferrer, and Vittorio Gassman) and Mario Camerini's *Ulysses,* as well as smaller but more successful works that included Rossellini's *Europa 51* (starring the director's new wife, Ingrid Bergman) and Fellini's *La Strada* (co-starring Anthony Quinn with the director's wife, Giulietta Masina), which, in 1956, won the first Oscar awarded for Best Foreign Language Film (hitherto, an honorary prize). The Ponti–De Laurentiis partnership lasted seven years, but the two Caesars of the Italian cinema parted because, in Ponti's words, "Dino likes quantity. I like quality." De Laurentiis went on to produce the next year's foreign Oscar winner, Fellini's *Nights of Cabiria* (starring Masina), to film *The Bible* and *Waterloo,* and to build his own Roman studios, Dinocittà.

When Carlo Ponti first met Sophia, he told her he had discovered such stars as Gina Lollobrigida, Alida Valli (in *Piccolo Mondo Antico*), Eleonora Rossi Drago, Lucia Bosè, and even Silvana Mangano (by then Mrs. De Laurentiis). The names he dropped were all female, for he has said: "I don't like actors. I prefer women." He has said that "as a producer, I divide actresses into three classes: those with purely physical appeal, those without beauty but talented, and the rare ones who combine glamor with talent. Sophia began with the pinup and glamor girls but became a member of the select third class."

In a 1965 interview with Israel Shenker—then Time-Life Bureau Chief in Rome, now a New York *Times* cultural lion—Ponti, extolling the early Sofia, took a gratuitous verbal swipe at his wife's first rival:

"It is not a question of beauty. For me, beauty is secondary. Look at Gina Lollobrigida, who made her first seven films with me. When I spoke with Sofia, I understood there was a difference between actress and artist. With an artist, there is no limit to the heights she can reach. You find many actresses, but very few artists. Sophia is an artist. She gives something. She is like a Stradivarius. But even a Stradivarius depends on the person playing it. It is an instrument of sublime quality only in the right hands."

Reaching out for Sofia Lazzaro in 1951, Ponti invited her to make a screen test. "It was terrible," Sophia recalls. "All I did was smile, look profile, full face, that's all. And walk. I thought it was awful." So did the cameraman, who hardly waited until she was out of earshot before telling Ponti: "She is quite impossible to photograph. Too tall. Too big-boned. Too heavy all around. The face is too short. The mouth is too wide. The nose is too long. What do you want of me, miracles?"

Ponti didn't think she was all that bad. He asked Sofia gently: "Would you consider doing something to your nose and maybe losing twenty pounds or so off your weight?"

Vesuvius erupted. Ponti backed off—but he liked the way she fumed and smoldered. He put her under contract; being a minor, Sofia had to send for her mother to sign the pact. And quietly, without any prodding or sharing of confidences, she shed some twenty pounds. But as for the nose bob, she would have none of it—or rather, all of it.

"I have a feeling you could go far," Ponti told her. "But it will not be what you think. It will be very hard work." He sent her to Rome's Experimental Center for Cinematographic Arts to learn more about movies, and found her a speech tutor to cure her thick Neapolitan accent. He cast her in the smallest of fourteen principal parts in *The White Slave Trade* (also peddled as *Girls Marked for Danger*). Sophia played Elvira, a farmer's daughter seduced and sold into big-city prostitution. Her big scene—ninety seconds long—comes when she faints at a marathon dance, is carried into Silvana Pampanini's room, and confesses she is pregant. Legend has it that, witnessing this scene between newcomer and name actress, a member of the crew exclaimed: "*Mamma mia,* she eats up Pampanini!"

From *The White Slave Trade* she went on to bigger and slightly better roles in *Africa Under the Sea* and *We Meet in the Gallery* for other producers; she was on loan from Ponti. These were pictures that would never have left the Mediterranean theatre of distribution, but years later, to cash in on Sophia's fame, they were dubbed into English as second features and late-night TV fare.

On yet another loan, she reached an entirely different public from that of anything that had gone before. This was the title role in the film version of *Aida,* with Sophia in blackface miming the voice of the rather less photogenic Renata Tebaldi. It was a job Lollobrigida had declined, for it was not so much a part as an actor's graveyard. But filmographer Crawley reported that:

> Loren's personality shone through the paint job like an alarm beacon on fire. The film was her first to reach America, where impresario Sol Hurok released it, and Stateside interest in the leading lady was rapid indeed—once it had been established (*a*) she was not an opera singer and (*b*) she was not really black. Even the immortal Cecil B. DeMille was quoted as exclaiming: "Around this girl you could build something really super-colossal!"

And, while *Aida* was just another floridly but stodgily filmed stage-transplant, its special distinction, according to New York *Times* movie critic Bosley Crowther was that "the handsome girl who plays the dark-skinned and regal Aida might just as well be singing the glorious airs that actually come from the throat of Tebaldi and have been synchronized to her lip movements. . . . The advantage is that a fine voice is set to a stunning form and face, which is most gratifying (and unusual) in the operatic realm."

Having drowned in *Africa Under the Sea* (a swimming part, spent mostly in water; Sophia, who couldn't swim, learned on the job) and been beaten to death in *The White Slave Trade*, Sophia recalls that she nearly froze to death in *Aida:* "The filming took place in an unheated studio and, to dispel the clouds of steam coming from my mouth whenever I opened it, a makeup man kept a hair drier pointed at my lips."

Those who knew her then remember how she always knew her lines (and those of her partners, too) and was never late or temperamental—enough in itself to single her out among starlets. Though she had taken to acting "because I wanted to get out of anonymity and become an individual, now I began to enjoy it." She could do before the camera much that she had no opportunity to do—or even try—in life. Finishing one film on a Saturday and starting the next on Monday, she could "change character all the time. For me, acting is like lying on a couch at a psychiatrist's."

Sophia, who had much in life to be insecure about, used to measure her career in tangibles that were later uprooted by her jewel robberies: "After *Quo Vadis?,* the first money I tried to spend for my sister. . . . From *Aida* my mother got our first apartment,* then something else, and so on. What you want first is a house—I mean, a house is a house; you have to have a house to feel that you have roots somewhere—then a car, furs,

---

*Three rooms, kitchen and bath on the Via Ugo Balzani that enabled Maria to come from Pozzuoli to Rome and live with her mother and sister, instead of her grandparents.

clothes, and then jewels! When you learn that these things don't really mean anything for your happiness, you forget such superficialities and do in your life whatever you feel like doing. But when you're still very young, you don't know and you like to spread around everything you can, if you can. It becomes an obsession. Even changing the color of your hair. Every day! Because you are not sure of yourself, you're not secure and you don't know what really counts in your life."

Somewhere during *Africa Under the Sea,* Sofia Lazzaro became So*phi*a Loren. Contrary to the prevailing Pizza Pygmalion legend, it was not Ponti who made this particular name change, but his longtime friend, Goffredo Lombardo, chief of the Titanus film combine that made the film. Lombardo didn't like the name of Lazzaro for an underwater epic (he is supposed to have said it sounded more like a corpse than its resurrection). Thus, in the hope that "Ponti's starlet" might one day amount to "another Marta Toren" (a Swedish actress who was being touted as the next Ingrid Bergman, which she wasn't), Lombardo worked his way through the alphabet—from Boren to Horen to Koren before stopping at Loren—and then refined her first name's *f* to *ph* while he was at it.

The rest of the Pygmalion process, however, was Ponti's doing. He picked her gowns, picked her films, picked her parts. He not only encouraged her to learn languages, he gave her supplementary reading: *Madame Bovary* in French, *Don Quixote* in Spanish (little thinking she would one day co-star in a musical version of it), and Eugene O'Neill's *The Emperor Jones* in English (to which she reacted so strongly that Ponti wasn't at all surprised in 1958 when Sophia more than held her own with co-stars Anthony Perkins and Burl Ives in a screen version of O'Neill's *Desire Under the Elms.*) Always indirectly—by leaving a book on her dressing table, never by forcing his ideas upon her —Ponti reshaped her personality and her tastes. When, after a while, she went to live with him—first in his apartment in the Palazzo Colonna and then in Marino—he was the one who decorated their homes. "I need Carlo at my side," she said. "I am sure of myself only when he is near me."

In spite of themselves, Sophia and Carlo were falling in love. "When we first met, he was just a kind producer who gave me a chance," she said. "But the more we were with each other, all kinds of bonds held us together. He was friend, counselor, lover, father, teacher, everything. Without him, I was never a complete woman."

Though Carlo was more than twenty years older and three-and-a-half inches shorter than Sophia—giving rise to jokes that "he's twice her age and half her size"—this was no real obstacle. Her precocious maturity made her doubly attractive to Ponti. And Sophia, still searching for the father she'd never had, was happiest of all in Carlo's company.

There *was* an obstacle, however, and a serious one: Just like her own father, Carlo Ponti had a wife—plus two children.

CHAPTER 3

The Two Mrs. Pontis

You have shown me the sky, but what good is the sky?—Aldonza

Back in 1946 Carlo Ponti had married Giuliana Fiastri, the daughter of an Italian general. They had two children—a girl, Guendalina and, two years later, a boy, Alex. According to Sophia, "Carlo's marriage had ended before I ever met him"—and indeed, Giuliana Fiastri Ponti was willing to divorce him or seek an annulment, both of which, however, were impossible in Italy of the 1950s. Ponti, himself a lawyer by training, was amazed at the hopeless secular and religious legal labyrinth he entered but ran the gauntlet gamely. He and his wife applied for an annulment from the Vatican's Sacred Rota: the only court honored by Italian law in such matters at the time. Ponti's lawyers argued that he hadn't conscientiously believed in the sacrament of marriage at the time of the ceremony, but because Ponti had been well into his thirties when he married and the union had produced two children, this was a hard line for even his advocates to swallow, let alone espouse. The annulment was denied.

"There *are* cases of annulment for famous people," Ponti insists, "but they are kept quiet. By the time we applied, there was so much publicity that people would have said we got it because we paid someone off."

At that time in Italy, some three million citizens, including Nobel Prize poet Salvatore Quasimodo, Communist Party chief Luigi Longo, and Sophia's favorite director, De Sica, were living with mates who weren't their spouses, but in an openly legal status (with many of the rights and obligations of matrimony) called *established concubinage.* It was akin to common-law relationships in many States. Nobody raised an eyebrow, let alone an uproar. But, even though *established concubinage* might have afforded Sophia the money and power that her union with Ponti promised, this was not all she was after. If ever any woman lusted after respectability and thirsted for conventionality, it was Sofia Scicolone, born of an unwed mother and thwarted in her own quests for, first, normal wedlock and, later, motherhood.

Even Sophia's mother, particularly Sophia's mother, much as she liked Carlo Ponti, warned her daughter not to repeat the past and "end up like me, unmarried, with maybe children?" Sophia, however, was even more determined to improve the future: "All I want to be is Carlo's wife and have his children." Both needs took more than a decade to fulfill.

Once, in a retrospective moment, Sophia told Donald Zec that her need for Carlo "has always been total and uncompromising. It took him a long time before he decided he would marry me. Think of his situation. He had a wife, two children. He was a famous producer. I was just as troubled as he was. If he had sacrificed them to our love so easily, so quickly, then perhaps, I thought, he might one day do the same for me. All I knew was I adored him. He was my man. My only man. I wanted him desperately as a husband and as the father of my children. Finally it had come to the point when I knew that he was not going to make the decision unless I put him on the spot. After all, it's universal, not just Italian, for a husband to try and get the best of both worlds: a nice situation with his family, and just as nice a situation going for him with his mistress. That was not what I had in mind for Carlo and me."

The pressure from Sophia brought the issue to a boil in 1957, when she went to work in America for the first time. "You know how Americans are," she pleaded. "We cannot live together in California unless we are married."

This was an exaggeration even then, although the holier-than-thou Hollywood of the 1950s—reeling from the one-two punch of a Congressional witch-hunt for communist infiltration followed by a repressive blacklist—was indeed a relatively puritanical place. While not yet married, Sophia and Carlo led what was almost an exaggeratedly conventional married life there. They lived in director Charles Vidor's villa in Bel-Air; Sophia called it "a typical Hollywood house with portico, big lawn, swimming pool, and so on." She worked days at the studios and spent her evenings at home with Carlo, watching television. Since, in public interviews, Sophia was making such utterances as: "It's important to feel married when you're not. Some people who are married, you wonder how they are married," the private pressure she put on Ponti must have been tremendous.

"In Mexico," Carlo Ponti had heard, "you can get a divorce by telephone." Not knowing what number to call, he got himself a notary and, in August of 1957, a proxy divorce from Giuliana, with whom he had already made an amicable financial settlement.

Then, on Tuesday, September 17, 1957, in Juarez, Mexico (just across the Rio Grande from El Paso, Texas), Señor Mario Ballesteros married Señor Antonio Lopez Machuca. There was nothing homosexual or illegal about this. Both gentlemen were lawyers. This was a proxy wedding, with Machuca standing in for Carlo Ponti and Ballesteros standing in for Sophia Loren. And the honey-voiced harpie of Hollywood, Louella Parsons, scored an all-time first by being the one to phone the bride to tell her: "You were married an hour ago. You are now Mrs. Ponti."

Sophia's response was joyous: "Carlo is my life! I want seven children!" But this particular "marriage" didn't last.

Within a matter of days, a member of the Sacred Rota wrote an article in which he warned that "concubinage should never be called marriage," and the Italian Men's Catholic Action group called a boycott of all Loren films. And then the inevitable pillar of Italian morality, a Milan housewife named Luisa

Brambilla, arose to denounce the newlyweds in her capacity "as a mother of a family to save the institution of matrimony in Italy." Exercising a right that is available to any citizen, under Italian law, for a few hundred lire, Signora Brambilla filed criminal charges against the Pontis as participants in bigamy.

Although her case dragged on for nearly a decade, Signora Brambilla disappeared before it ever came to trial. She was rumored, by the mid-1960s, to be living in a convent. Sophia told me once, when I asked if there had been any organized opposition behind Signora Brambilla: "Maybe she was a member of some neighborhood Catholic club or association for the protection of the family, but nothing more than that." Nevertheless, in her wake, similar *denuncia* actions against the Pontis were filed by a male hairdresser in Genoa, a lawyer in Chieti, a group of concerned mothers worried about good morals in Italy, and—what hurt the most—some people in Pozzuoli, Sophia's old hometown.

In her account of the legal proceedings ("Bigamy Italian Style"; *Life,* July 23, 1965), Sophia's friend and onetime biographer, Dora Jane Hamblin, noted that the hairdresser, "like most Italians, seems to be madder at Sophia than at Carlo, despite the fact that she couldn't possibly be a bigamist because she was never married before (if she was ever married at all)." A letter-to-the-editor of *Oggi* proposed that Sophia "should be burned in public."

In his face-to-face armchair analysis of Sophia, Alberto Moravia made more of Signora Brambilla than Sophia was willing to. Moravia told Sophia he saw Brambilla as a "symbol of whatever it is that prevents you from achieving a normal life and thereby drives you to prove yourself more and more both as actress and as woman." And he asked her: "Doesn't it seem ironic that of all people you, who have longed all your life for a real family, should be denounced as a bigamist and, in short, be prevented from making a family of your own?"

"Ironic, yes," Sophia replied. "But a better word for it would be rotten."

To avoid going to jail for one to five years, Sophia and Carlo were forced to have his Mexican divorce and remarriage nullified and, for a while, to live and work outside their native Italy. But even after the Mexican annulments, the Italian criminal investigation continued and, every time she set foot in Italy, it was possible that the police would confiscate her passport and perhaps even arrest her.

"I give up!" Sophia exclaimed at one point. "I'm married, I'm not married! I'm this, I'm that! Enough! I *feel* married, and lots of married people don't."

After all the addition and subtraction, however, Sophia could sum it up thusly: "I was still a concubine. I was back to living in sin." As late as 1963, as godmother, when she went to the christening of her newborn niece, Alessandra, in a Catholic church, a prominent Milan theologian rebuked her in the next day's press as a "public citizen" who "should have stayed in the shadows" instead of participating in a religious ceremony. This was followed by a denunciation from the Vicariate of Rome.

It got so that Sophia, for once in her public life, found herself virtually tongue-tied with the press. But even while trying to spit out an uncharacteristic "no comment," she managed to put across a point, as witness this early 1965 utterance: "My husband—that is, my former husband—I mean, my fiancé—well, you know Carlo—he and I won't want to discuss this matter because it only upsets us."

The criminal prosecution for bigamy dragged forward. Sophia and Carlo were ordered to stand trial on July 6, 1965, in Rome, but they were out of the country, in London. Ponti's lawyers appeared in court on their behalf and, after a half-hour hearing, obtained a postponement till autumn.

Something else was afoot. The French Solution is what the Romans call it. To establish residence in France, a Catholic country that already permitted divorce, Carlo Ponti had bought into (to the tune of more than a million dollars) the Residence George V: a posh apartment house opposite the famous Paris hotel of the same name on the avenue of the same name. And since January of 1965, he and Sophia and the first Mrs. Ponti and her son and daughter had all gradually become French citizens. As Carlo Ponti put it when his coup was revealed: "I'd gladly become an Eskimo if I had to, just to stay married to Sophia."

To which Sophia purred: "Of course I'll be an Eskimo, too, if Carlo wants, but I'll always feel Neapolitan."

Four days before Christmas, 1965, a French judge awarded the first Mme Charles Ponti a divorce on the grounds of her husband's adultery. This Yuletide gift from their new motherland was celebrated by all the Pontis, including the one-to-be.

Around that time, Sophia was making *Lady L* under the direction of Peter Ustinov, who told me a decade later in Paris:

"One feels one knows Sophia very well even before one meets her. But—and this is a terrible thing to say!—before she had her children, one wondered whether her whole life with Ponti wasn't an extremely clever kind of complicity: that, in point of fact, she might have been living a kind of business arrangement."

Ustinov had heard all the jokes about him and her: "But as soon as she actually began to have the children she was obviously longing for, it became quite clear that hers was a relationship with a man much older than herself, which was a perfectly genuine one motivated by the strongest and simplest links in the world, and one felt ashamed of ever having considered them suspect. One had been suspicious only because of the extremely exposed position of both of them.

"Until the babies, one could never believe the relationship was as simple as it looked because the public image kept impinging upon the private one, even when you got quite close to them. Even when one saw them behaving rather normally in life, one thought: Aren't they both extremely clever to carry it off so well! Or, can it be that they are really just like that—very much in love? With the erosion of time, they have no need to prove anything to anybody. It's happened by itself."

A couple of days later, when I conveyed Peter's "terrible" confession to Sophia, she exclaimed:

"He's right! He's right! He's not the first to say it, but he's right. You see, I'm no different from who I always was. *They* have changed. *Peter* has changed. At least, his and *their* ideas about me have changed. *They* had trouble believing what they saw, but what they saw was true, and time has told that finally it was a good marriage and it has worked. I know it's very strange, very rare, but it does happen sometimes."

On the even rarer occasions when Carlo Ponti would talk about his relationship with Sophia before they were married, he would talk in terms that were more topographic than graphic:

"She has all the best that is Italian. Neapolitan gaiety and artistic sense, plus a Milanese sense of proportion and balance, which she learned from me." Or, more ironic than boastful: "I am a sober, plodding Milanese. Sophia is a full-blooded, warm-hearted Neapolitan, fundamentally lazy and irrational, with a tendency to overdramatize things. Few can realize the incredible efforts and untiring sacrifices she has made and is still making to overcome these handicaps. I have followed her daily struggle, and I love her for that, too."

Sophia has always adored jazz; Ponti has never even liked it. Nevertheless, on those first visits to America, he would go to jazz concerts and smoky night clubs "because she does." Once they went with De Sica to catch Peggy Lee's act in New York. "At three in the morning, it wasn't finished," Ponti recalls, "and Sophia was still enthusiastic, beating time with her heels. I was tired and cold, so I removed Sophia's fur stole, covered myself with it and went to sleep. I noticed that De Sica, too, although with more decorum, managed to take a nap."

A small-g godfatherly type who, the first time I met him, struck me as one who might welcome a game of *bocce* or a round of *grappa* even more than a bout of business (which goes to show how blandly deceptive appearances are), Carlo Ponti used to wear three-button single-breasted jackets pulled short and tight over a chunky figure that had long ago lost the battle of the bulge. Under Sophia's tutelage, he now dresses much more elegantly and expensively, but the effect is much the same. As late as 1976, Rex Reed was describing Ponti as "short, paunchy, balding in his stuffy suits and purple socks, he looks like an apple vendor on the streets of Milan." But Ponti is happy that way and he has said: "I like living with Sophia because she takes me as I am. I am too busy to bother about the cut of my suits. I have never been a dressy man and I care nothing about choosing my ties. Sophia gives the necessary orders for my clothes, adding her personal touch with a few ties from Dior now and then." There was a time, in fact, when, for all the talk of him as the father she never had, she was mothering him as if he were her own little boy.

What the unflattering descriptions contrasting Ponti's appearance with hers are saying and what the recurrent question of "What does she see in him?" is really asking was once paraphrased crudely but neatly by biographer Zec in these words: "Either Ponti is a stallion in sheep's clothing or this broad's father-fixation has taken her mind off the action."

Sophia told Zec: "What nobody could understand then, and still can't, is the extraordinary power of the man. He generates a tremendous excitement for me. He is a sensitive lover, a cultured friend, the understanding father I never had. Every woman's needs are wrapped up inside that man. Well, all my needs anyway!"

And back in 1965, as her long struggle to become the second Signora Ponti neared fruition, she spoke of Carlo to Israel Shenker as though the wedding had already taken place:

"He is my husband. He means a great deal to me. He is my life. For me a husband means a companion for my life, a father for my children, a guide in my life. I think before [him] I was much more irrational. Now I use a little bit my brain before I answer. . . .

"Carlo is very rational. He has his feet on the ground all the time, and when I try to dramatize things he calms me down. He explains things to me. I like that. I think for an actress it's very important what kind of man she chooses for a husband because life for an actress is very important."

On Saturday, April 9, 1966, "Sophie Scicolone, spinster, also known as Loren" married one "Charles Fortune Pierre Ponti, doctor of law" at the Registrar's Office in the Town Hall of Sèvres, outside Paris. Sophia, in a particularly fine mood, signed the register with a flourish: "Sofia Scicolone, *artiste*." Her sister came up from Rome for the wedding, but mother Romilda stayed behind to babysit the Mussolini children. When the simple civil ceremony was over, Sophia was relieved, but philosophical. "Okay, it's official. Now we have a piece of paper with a rubber stamp on it," she said. "But it's a little like reading a theatre program long after you've seen the show."

The absurdity of the Pontis' well-publicized plight made theirs a key case in the battle that resulted in 1970s liberalization of divorce Italian style—and one of the first to file under the new law was Maria Mussolini, whose marriage to Benito's jazz-musician son, Romano, had ended. Even more ironically, when the Neiman-Marcus department store in Dallas staged an Italian Fortnight a few years later, Italy's Ministry of Foreign Trade sent the Texans "the pride of Italy": a French married couple named Ponti.

Chapter 4

Sophia Sexpot

By the time Sophia had signed in at City Hall of Sèvres as "artiste" in 1966, there was no questioning this particular claim. Perhaps the artistic history of Ponti's protégée begins where their embattled marital history began: on the set of her 1954 *Woman of the River,* when Ponti came to her during the last day of shooting and handed her an engagement ring. Ponti, who had been husbanding her talents toward international stardom for nearly three years by then, gave Sophia her first major role in *Woman of the River,* which was a conscious imitation of *Bitter Rice,* the 1949 movie that had launched Silvana Mangano as a world sexpot. For *Woman of the River,* six writers (including Basilio Franchina, who was to become a recurrent figure in Sophia's career, and the late Pier Paolo Pasolini) came up with a similar story in the same setting—the River Po rice paddies—as an excuse to put Sophia into the tightest, wettest shirt and the hottest 1950s-model hot pants. The results were even more sensational than *Bitter Rice.* Columbia Pictures gobbled up *Woman of the River* and peddled the heroine all over the globe as "Sophia the Sizzler"—who, to almost everybody's surprise, could also act! Carlo didn't tell her until *Woman* was a hit that he had invested his last cent in it. "If he had," Sophia said later, "I wouldn't have had the courage to face the camera."

That same year, Sophia starred as a Neapolitan pizza vendor in one episode of a four-part film, *Gold of Naples,* directed by Vitorrio De Sica, a fellow Neapolitan. Thus began a working relationship that lasted twenty years.

Like Ponti, De Sica rejected the idea of acting school for Sophia. "You're a natural force," he told her. "Whatever you do is natural. Acting schools can't teach that, only inhibit it. You'll do many films and learn as you go along. For you, it's the best way." On the set, he would tell her to "respond with your entire body, not just your face and voice. Every bit of you must count, including the tips of your little fingers."

Sophia took to his teachings like a mermaid to water—as witnessed by any moviegoer who ever watched Sophia stroll through an artificial storm in *Gold of Naples*. Although she developed bronchial pneumonia doing retakes, *Time* Magazine rejoiced in her "long, unforgettable walk in the rain through the streets of the city, drinking the applause of venal eyes." According to the anonymous *Time* critic of the time, "Sophia's self-congratulating look seemed to say 'Look at me, I'm all woman and it will be a long time before you see such a woman again.'"

De Sica told the world: "Ah, Sophia! A young, unbroken filly so full of southern vitality, so unspoiled, so pliant! Her acting ability is not yet so fully developed as her physical presence. If it were, we could announce a new Duse. We must wait for that." But not terribly long. Even before Sophia's filmographer, Tony Crawley, proclaimed in 1974 that "Loren's legend has long since overtaken that of the diva, Duse"—the Italian stage actress who was Sarah Bernhardt's only rival—Charlie Chaplin was telling biographer Donald Zec: "Sophia Loren has a touch of Eleonora Duse."

What Sophia didn't know about *Gold of Naples* was that Ponti's partner De Laurentiis had objected to her being cast in the film— outwardly because he thought the part called for a bigger name such as Lollobrigida, but perhaps also because his wife was starring in another episode and he didn't want Sophia to eat up Mangano the way she had Pampanini. De Sica, however, stuck up for Sophia in his own neo-realistic way: "We've got to take Loren. We don't have anybody else who fits. Besides, she won't want much money." De Laurentiis finally gave in, saying: "Take her then, but you'll regret it"—which nobody ever did. In some ways, however, this dispute marked the beginning of the end of the Ponti–De Laurentiis partnership. Even without knowing about her near-miss-out, Sophia was so nervous on the first day of filming *Gold of Naples* that, for the only time in her life, she drank two Cognacs that morning and almost croaked her opening cry of "*Pizzaiola!*"

De Sica's tutelage of Sophia continued in four consecutive films directed by others, but co-starring him and her. In *Too Bad She's Bad,* based on an Alberto Moravia story, she played con man De Sica's pickpocket daughter who was romanced and reformed by a cabbie. This hero was played by another Neapolitan, Marcello Mastroianni, who was enchanted by Sophia: "She reminds me with great longing for the pleasure of my youth."* In *The Sign of Venus,* a Russian tale by Chekhov that had been Romanized by five Italian writers, De Sica was a seedy poet and Sophia a *femme fatale* impregnated by a fireman (Raf Vallone). In *The Miller's Wife,* Mastroianni and Loren were husband-and-wife in a Naples of 1680, ruled by a lecherous Spanish Governor (De Sica). Then, in *Scandal in Sorrento,* Sophia, as a sharp-tongued fish-seller known as Sofia the Heckler, wore a low-cut fire-engine-red gown to dance a sizzling mambo with De Sica, playing a Carabinieri commandant.

From film to film, Tony Crawley writes, "Sophia *did* improve each time out, and always shone particularly well when De Sica was in the cast. Of acting ability, comedy timing and . . . style, he had plenty to offer and to teach. She also learned humility from him; never once did De Sica criticize or overrule orders of the directors of their films. For these assignments, like Loren, he was simply an actor."

Those four films were made in a time span of less than a year (1954–55). Around that time, Ponti hired a press agent named Mario Natale to promote Sophia. What Natale created was literally blown out of proportion: A Battle of the Bosoms with Gina Lollobrigida. At an Italian Film Festival in London during Oc-

---

*Technically, this was not the first Sophia–Mastroianni–De Sica collaboration, since all three of them had worked in a 1953 film called *Our Times* (in America, *Anatomy of Love*), but in separate episodes of it.

tober of 1954, the two stars snubbed each other and Sophia was quoted as asking wistfully: "It is true that my measurements exceed Gina's, but is that a reason why she should be so furious with me?" In reply to which Gina confided in Hedda Hopper: "Sophia's may be bigger, but not better."

Statistically, both ladies were at home in the same range: Sophia measuring in at 38-24-38 vs. Gina's more petite, yet hourglassier, 36-22-35, but the fine Italian hand of press agent Natale could be discerned in this feud and all that followed. Each actress accused the other of being a pleasant peasant incapable of playing a lady on or off the screen. They competed for leading roles and leading men and not only over the latitude of Los Lollos, but over who made more money, who paid more taxes, and, only lately, who paid less tax. Nevertheless, this women's war was a man-made phenomenon of press agentry and Sophia has said: "I never took the rivalry seriously and I trust she didn't either." Sophia is, in fact, grateful to Gina for at least three roles that the latter declined or discarded: Sofia the Heckler in *Scandal in Sorrento* and the title roles in *Aida* and *Lady L.*

While Loren and Lollobrigida were feudin' and fussin', Ponti was off knocking on doors to sell Sophia to the American and British movie moguls. "An actress has to have starred in American pictures," says Ponti, "in order to acquire an international reputation. Look at Bardot. In spite of her tremendous success, B.B. remains a provincial actress in some ways because she never went to America and, as a result, her films are shown only in specialized cinemas."

Around the time of *Too Bad She's Bad,* Ponti cabled Sophia from America to BRUSH UP YOUR ENGLISH. YOU'LL NEED IT SOON. Sure enough, August 15, 1955's *Newsweek* featured a four-page spread on "Italy's Sophia Loren, a New Star—a Mount Vesuvius" and, a week later, she adorned the cover of *Life.* By then, Sophia was studying English every morning from 5 to 7 A.M. with Sarah Spain, an Irishwoman who made her read T.S. Eliot before breakfast. It still took awhile before Sophia stopped ordering "Scotch on the stones."

Newsweek and other publicity brought Hollywood producer-director Stanley Kramer to Rome. He was looking for a European leading lady for his epic of the Napoleonic wars, *The Pride and the Passion.* Marlon Brando hadn't liked the script, but hinted he might be interested in working with Loren. "It's the damnedest thing," Marlon mumbled about her. "When you see it, you don't believe it. Then you look again and you still don't believe it."*

Seeing was believing. Stanley Kramer looked at Sophia, looked at *Woman of the River,* walked into Ponti's office, and offered him "two hundred thousand dollars for her; take it or leave it." Ponti, who might have been prepared to pay almost that much to land Sophia the job, swallowed hard and accepted without protest.

Brando never materialized for *The Pride and the Passion* (though he and Sophia did get together in 1966's *A Countess from Hong Kong*), but Sophia found herself filming in Spain with Frank Sinatra (Brando's replacement) and Cary Grant, both of whom were reported to have fallen in love with her—as were Peter Sellers and Peter O'Toole, Omar Sharif and Richard Burton later on. . . .

We come now to the area of the *factoid,* perhaps the most memorable of the relatively few words and many inventions in Norman Mailer's 1973 book, *Marilyn: A Biography of Marilyn Monroe,* itself something of a *factoid.* Applied to Sophia's life, at least, a *factoid* is a legend—perhaps untrue, perhaps exaggerated—which is repeated and embellished so much that it takes on a life, or even a subculture, of its own. The whole episode of Daughter Sophia and Mother Romilda confronted at Cinecittà by an enraged Signora Scicolone emerging from the throng of would-be extras for *Quo Vadis?* and the subsequent interview with Director LeRoy have achieved so many variations that it must be hard for even Sophia to remember how it really hap-

*Brando was less explicit than the British journalist who came away from Sophia's first London press conference exclaiming: "She's great, aren't they!"

pened to her, though the versions presented here are ones I verified with her early in our friendship.

Thus, most of the romantic couplings which made headlines ("Sophia Loren: The Superstars Who Fell in Love with Me—Frank Sinatra . . . Cary Grant . . . Paul Newman . . . Omar Sharif . . . Peter Sellers") were *factoids* contrived, more often than not, by the studio publicists for whichever film Sophia was making at the time.

Of Sinatra offscreen, the less said the better. Making *The Pride and the Passion* (based on C.S. Forester's *The Gun*) in "Windmillville,"—Sinatra's politest christening of the searing plain on which rain in Spain mainly didn't fall during filming —he was homesick and lovesick despite regular airlifts of pastrami and dill pickles from the Stage Delicatessen in Manhattan and occasional visits from his estranged wife, Ava Gardner, for whom he still pined.

Sophia came to Spain predisposed to be smitten by Sinatra, whose singing—along with Peggy Lee's, Ella Fitzgerald's, and Tony Bennett's—ranked tops with her. Besides, she and he were both Italians, more and less. Putting it mildly, however, to know Sinatra is not to love him, and there was certainly nothing romantic about his encounters with Sophia. Mimicking a Mafioso all the way, Sinatra kept greeting Sophia with a bantering "You'll get yours," the humor of which never amused her. But when, between takes, he called her "a broad," she denounced him in her early but explicit English as a "mean little son-of-the-bitch" and one hundred onlookers cheered. Taken aback but duly impressed, Sinatra eventually pronounced Sophia "a gasser."

Cary Grant is another story and perhaps the only one of Sophia's "romances" that is not totally factoidal. Barely a year after winding up *The Pride and the Passion* with Grant in Hollywood, where filming shifted from Spain shortly after Sinatra flew home prematurely, Sophia and Cary made *Houseboat,* a domestic comedy, in Hollywood, too. From the outset, Grant charmed her by addressing her with debonair aplomb as "Miss Brigloren," "Miss Lowbrigid," or "Sophia Lollo. . . . I never can remember those Italian names" and she, still new to English pronunciation, called him *Kerrygront.* Born Archie Leach in Bristol, England, in 1904, Cary Grant is almost a decade older than Carlo Ponti: a vital statistic that is just as hard to believe now as it was in 1957–58. And back then when Sophia was legally unmarried on front pages around the world, it seemed much easier for the naked eye to match her up with Cary than with Carlo. Even Grant himself—casting calves' eyes at her on and off the set, across a crowded studio commissary or the tiny tables of a flamenco restaurant with castanets and cameras clicking—couldn't understand this "father fixation" of hers with a man six to nine years his junior. Whenever and wherever they were apart, *Kerrygront* besieged her with bouquets and gave interviews saying she was "so sensuous that most men would long to tear the clothes off her on sight."

Sophia treated Cary's crush lightly, even to the extent of emphasizing that she would prefer "a husband who is ugly. I have a Neapolitan temperament. If I had a husband who is good-looking, he would attract other women and I would get jealous." For all her flippancy, Sophia certainly meant at least some of what she was saying. Cary Grant came up against not just her love for his puny, paunchy rival, but also the immense reassurance Ponti gave her. Later, in a kiss-and-tell women's magazine confession, Sophia said of Grant: "I knew he loved me and that if I chose to, I could marry him." But she added that they were so much alike their insecurities would have preyed upon each other. At the time, Grant was married to Betsy Drake and, instead of Dyan Cannon, who bore him his only child in 1966, Sophia might have been the fourth Mrs. Cary Grant.*

Grant is reported to have proposed to Sophia in her dressing room just before the big love scene of *Houseboat.* And she has been quoted as saying: "I can't marry you, Cary. I think you are a marvelous man, kind and wonderful to me. But I am already

*All four of Grant's marriages have ended in divorce. His first two wives were heiress Barbara Hutton and actress Virginia Cherril.

in love with Carlo Ponti. Soon, when his divorce is through, we will get married. I am sorry, it's just not possible. . . ." If one started to hear the voice of the *factoid* here, it was soon to be hushed by the gush of Louella Parsons bearing the glad, if temporary, tidings of Sophia's proxy marriage to Ponti in Mexico. Cary Grant wished her well and, even when the Sacred Rota and Signora Brambilla rose to undo the knot, he never again tried to reverse her "no, *grazie.*" The moment was past.

"I was really very sorry for him at the time," she said of Cary Grant to Donald Zec more than a decade later. "He had his own problems of insecurity and the mixture with my own would not have made for a lasting marriage. He thought psychoanalysis might help me, but I know as much about myself as any psychiatrist could possibly discover. Anyway, my complexes have been good to me. They help to make people what they are. When you lose them you might also lose yourself."

For a long while, Grant parried queries about whether he still loved Sophia with a bland "Doesn't everybody?" But more recently, whatever torch he may have carried for her has burned with a cold blue flame. In early 1978 Grant was seventy-four, retired from films for a dozen years, and roving the world as a good-will ambassador for the international cosmetics firm Fabergé, on whose board of directors he sat. (At a fund-raising event in Seattle, where he noted that people don't recognize him as quickly as they used to, Grant added that when they do, "they say 'You still look great.' What's going on in their heads is the disappointment in how I do look. Then they immediately wonder to themselves: My Gawd, have *I* changed that much, too?") When Sophia sent an interviewer to him to talk about *her,* what happened next was reported in a "news" item:

> How could anyone say no to Sophia Loren? Cary Grant just did.
> Sophia has been calling up all her famous Hollywood chums,
> asking them to agree to be interviewed. . . . When Sophia called
> Cary, she made the mistake of saying there'd be no hard feelings
> if he declined. He did and she's having hard feelings.

Even while Cary Grant lay siege to her heart during the

making of *Houseboat,* Sophia remained absolutely professional throughout, and she expects the same of anyone else who works with her, onscreen or off. In *Houseboat* child actor Paul Peterson was supposed to cry in a key scene, but he was enjoying himself too much on the set. After several retakes, Sophia suddenly slapped the boy, shook him hard, and said to him: "Listen, Paul! They're giving you a lot of money to do this and if you don't pay attention then they shouldn't pay you. I'm working hard, why don't you, eh?" Stung to tears, the boy hardly had to act and the very next take was convincing. Sophia hugged him and director Melville Shavelson came over to hug them both. In 1978, when one of her co-stars in *Brass Target* didn't know his lines, Sophia gave him a look of contempt usually reserved for the shallow journalist who fights his way onto the set and then pops some question such as "How old are you?" or "How do you spell your name?" that scarcely requires an exclusive interview. (This happens more often in my profession than I like to admit.) Much earlier in her career, at a time when many a movie star might have sold body and soul for a page in *Life,* a *Life* interviewer turned up half an hour late and was greeted with the two worst epithets an Italian can express.

"You are badly educated," were the first words from Sophia's lips.

"But it wasn't my fault!" the Lifer pleaded. "I was stuck in your damn Roman traffic."

"No matter," said Sophia—and then she spoke the second: "You have very bad manners." In retrospect the accused told me: "And she was right. Sophia is never late."

Through the late 1950s and into the early 1960s, Hollywood and the legal need to stay out of Italy during the divorce controversy kept her working away from home. During that time, her face and figure adorned a series of otherwise undistinguished American and British films costarring her with Alan Ladd *(Boy on a Dolphin),* John Wayne *(Legend of the Lost),* Tony Perkins *(Desire Under the Elms),* William Holden *(The Key),* Anthony Quinn *(Black Orchid* and *Heller in Pink Tights),* and Tab Hunter *(That Kind of Woman)* among other names that enhanced her stardom in pictures that didn't. *Time* overstated the case only moderately by complaining that "she was matched with leading men whom she could have swallowed with half a glass of water."

For her to play opposite Ladd, who was two inches shorter than Sophia, a trench had to be dug so they could walk side by side along the beach on the Greek island of Hydra. There was certainly little or no romance in that or in Ladd's unflattering description of working with her: "It's like being bombed by watermelons."

Dolphin's director, Jean Negulesco, a Rumanian-born painter turned film-maker, was so taken with her that he spent more time portraying her on canvas than on screen. This gave rise to rumors of a relationship between artist and model, though Negulesco was thirty-four years Sophia's senior. Negulesco ought to have been flattered. Instead, his denial was much worse than the accusations. When Sophia read it, she erupted in sobs. "She would be a hellish girl to fall in love with," said Negulesco. "There's too much of her. And she never stops loving herself. Always at the mirror." It was rebutting a similar gratuitous insult that led to Sophia's most notable non sequitur: "I have never been to a beauty parlor in my life. When I go there, they ruin me."

Moviemaking proved something of a sauna to Sophia as she rushed from the plain of Spain and potted palms of Hollywood in *The Pride and the Passion* to take what was described as a "delicious drenched-dress dive" into the Aegean for *Boy on a Dolphin* with Ladd and then flew off to Libya to make *Legend of the Lost,* a Sahara Western with Wayne. The Duke pronounced her "a gorgeous hunk of investment" and added that "she makes all us men look like ninnies. She's been bitten by scorpions, marooned in sandstorms, but nothing can stop that gal." As for romance, Sophia put it thusly: "We didn't happen to care about each other because it was so hot. All we cared about was the desert. Libya is no place to make friends or have happy relationships."

William Holden was wary of Sophia when they met in London to make *The Key.* He confessed to Donald Zec: "Beautiful women have always thrown me. I really don't know how to handle them." So he made a rule where actresses were concerned, "to play it absolutely cool, almost cold on the outside." He managed to adhere to this rule even when Sophia "didn't walk in, she swept in. Never saw so much woman coming at me in my entire life." Holden's outward indifference persisted until, one day on the set, he was handed an Italian slime sheet with the notorious ten-year-old topless photo of Sofia Lazzaro brandishing her breasts in *It's Him—Yes! Yes!* Conservative capitalist that he is,* Holden reacted with bitter scorn and Sophia said: "What is it?"

"This," said Holden, handing her the magazine. "Isn't it dreadful?!"

"I don't think they're dreadful," Sophia said. "They look pretty good to me."

Later, Holden told Zec: "I got to thinking about it, and I thought: Goddamit, they *were* beautiful. What the hell was I doing knocking it?! It was just my moral concepts of the time. I realized how chic Sophia had been about it. From then on we began to get through to each other. But it was a long time before we showed any affection"—and that was as far as it went.

From the start, Hollywood was taken aback by Sophia's early-to-bed, no-nonsense workmanship. Stanley Kramer was miffed when she failed to attend his lavish wind-up party once *The Pride and the Passion* was in the can; her job was done and she'd flown home to Rome with a minimum of fanfare in order to bypass the bigamy furor. Anthony Quinn (with whom Sophia had worked briefly in Italy in 1953's early spear-and-scandal *Attila the Hun*) complained that it was no fun working with a leading lady who spent more time with her secretary than with

*Co-owner of the posh Mount Kenya Safari Club and a 1,260-acre game ranch, with many business interests around the world and a base in Switzerland, Holden and his holdings prompted the US Congress to tighten tax loopholes on income earned by Americans residing overseas, and this section of the US Internal Revenue code is still known as The William Holden Law.

him. "I couldn't understand it. On the *Pink Tights* location, she'd just never go out. Always locked away with this girl Ines.* I'd say to her, 'What the hell do you do all day?' But it never made any difference. She was friendly on the set, but when the work was over, it was over. I could never get close to her. If she wants to know you, she sets the ground rules. Otherwise, it's forbidden territory behind a piece of beautiful crystal-clear unbreakable glass." And at a pre-filming *(Desire Under the Elms)* party for Sophia at Romanoff's restaurant, the guest of honor aloofly ignored a challenge from Jayne Mansfield to match mammaries. Having played the same game with Lollobrigida, Sophia knew her other assets were built to outlast the pinup concoctions of the Hollywood dream factory and the Cinecittà *pasta* kitchen.

*Ines' last name is Brusci, a detail she confirmed to me in a 1969 letter after I questioned it. But so many writers have mislabeled her Bruscia that, resigned to *factoid* replacing reality, Ines has accepted her media identity unprotestingly.

CHAPTER 5

Two Women and an Oscar

BY THE TIME SOPHIA LOREN LEFT HOLLYWOOD in 1960, she was an international household word and her stardom went wherever she went. In any language and on any location in the world, the powers and the glory-seekers came to her because, no matter how bad the picture, if it had Sophia, the bottom would never fall out of the box office. She was international insurance and she could name her terms, pick her spots, and place her pets (such as De Sica)—particularly with Ponti right there behind her to wheel and deal on her behalf.

Clark Gable came to Capri to co-star with Sophia and De Sica in *It Started in Naples,* Gable's next-to-last film.* (Although Sophia had grown up on the Bay of Naples, she had never seen its most famous island until Gable drove her around Capri in a horse-drawn carriage.) Sophia's work drew this gruff tribute from Gable: "This girl makes you think—all the wrong thoughts!"

When Sophia went to London to play the title role in a screen version of George Bernard Shaw's *The Millionairess,* the word was that her co-star, Peter Sellers—who portrayed an Indian physician running a clinic in London's East End—had fallen head-over-heels in love with her. Until Sophia, Sellers' sexiest co-star had been sexagenarian Margaret Rutherford, so it came as a shock, on the first day of filming *The Millionairess,* to find

---

*Later that year, Gable suffered two heart attacks, the second of them fatal, after the strenuous filming of Arthur Miller's *The Misfits* with two other doomed co-stars, Marilyn Monroe and Montgomery Clift.

himself giving this beautiful stranger's bared back a massage. And therein lay the rub. Although Sophia reassured Sellers with a facetious: "Of course it's all right. You're a doctor, aren't you?", the factoidal version of this encounter goes on to say:

> Slowly he spread his hands over her back gently kneading it from the nape to the waistline. Sellers does not remember precisely how many retakes there were, for in that simple opening shot he had fallen "very much in love with her."

He had massaged his way into a tricky situation. . . . which was heightened by the presence of the Pontis' friend, scriptwriter Basilio Franchina, who had come along as (in Sellers' words) "a sort of watchdog" and who—as Sellers and Sophia started sharing spaghetti dinners and Chinese cuisine—warned the co-star in his most ominous Sicilian: "When the husband finds out about this there will be trouble."

Although Sellers has described Sophia publicly as "magnificent, fantastic, one hundred percent woman" and said, "I was never in love with any woman as deeply as I was with Sophia" and has even gone so far as to suggest that "if Carlo went tomorrow, God forbid, she'd come to me," there was never any trouble from Ponti. Sellers says that "Carlo and I are good friends. He's always pleased to welcome me." Perhaps because it is easiest to take a clown lightly, Sophia can say: "Yes, I love Peter very much, in my way. Not the way I love Carlo."

In addition to Basilio Franchina as advisor and chaperon, Vittorio De Sica had come along with Sophia to play the part of Joe the baker in *The Millionairess*. Thus was De Sica on hand to comfort her when she experienced the first of her half-million-dollar jewel robberies. Fortunately, Sophia was out when burglars broke into her bedroom in a Hertfordshire country house. (She would not get off that easily the second time around: in New York, a decade later.) Her 1960 robbers made off with diamond, ruby, and emerald necklaces, earrings and brooches. Many of the gems were uninsured and Sophia reacted to her first robbery as though it were a rape, for at that time—still childless, insecure, and not legally married—each stolen jewel had meant "some memory of my life with Carlo while reassuring me that I could never go hungry again." But De Sica told her: "We are both from Naples and God has given us other things."

It was De Sica, too, who counseled both the Pontis that neither Hollywood nor international stardom would do justice to Sophia's potential. Ever the mock cavalier, he began a serious statement about her by saying: "In spite of having the usual womanly defects, she is the only really spiritually honest woman I have ever known. Sophia is a typical result of today's Italian cinema"—by which he meant the expensive extensions of his own neo-realism rather than the bargain basement Hollywood product Ponti and De Laurentiis were making at the time.

"Sophia," De Sica continued, "represents the artistic expression that we look for, the lack of speculation based on effects. The American cinema, with all its mechanism, is no more than an industry. Art doesn't enter into it. Our Italian cinema is more precarious, but our people have individualism." And he preached and pleaded with Ponti that Sophia's next film should be an Italian story made in Italy in Italian.

Thus did De Sica direct 1961's *Two Women,* which was where Sophia forever earned the right to sign herself *"artiste."* She owes a great deal to De Sica, but she probably owes her Oscar to Anna Magnani, who was anything but a personal friend. Magnani—whose scorching 1945 performance in Rossellini's *Open City* had opened America up to Italian films—had crossed the Atlantic a decade later to make the Hollywood screen version of Tennessee Williams' *The Rose Tattoo.* Her towering rendition of a widowed Sicilian-born seamstress named Serafina Delle Rose, buried in her own grief but awakened by a simple-minded truck driver (Burt Lancaster), won Magnani the 1955 Oscar as Best Actress over Susan Hayward, Katharine Hepburn, Jennifer Jones, and Eleanor Parker. It was an impressive breakthrough for *all* foreign actresses but, when called upon for comment, Sophia spoke her mind about Williams' story and Magnani's role: "No Italian woman should depict an Italian woman like that." Magnani, in turn, called Loren "a Neapolitan giraffe."

Box office being box office, however, Magnani and Loren were a potent combination. So De Sica cast them as mother and daughter in *Two Women,* Cesare Zavattini's screen adaptation of Alberto Moravia's 1957 novel, *La Ciociara,* about a widow and her nineteen- or twenty-year-old daughter on the run from the Allied bombardment of Rome. Sophia, at twenty-six, looked forward to being Magnani's daughter; not since *The Gold of Naples* had Sophia felt such total identification with a role, for "I had lived through the real thing with my own mother."

Suddenly, at the last minute, Magnani withdrew. Then fifty-two, she told De Sica: "I'm too young to play Loren's mother. Let her play the part herself."

That is exactly what De Sica did. He had the script rewritten, lowering the daughter's age to fourteen and the mother from fiftyish to "a woman in her thirties." With Eleanora Brown replacing Sophia as the daughter, everything served to make the film's tale of war, rape, and corruption more vivid—but the sudden switch had Sophia "scared to death," she told me. "I had not the experience of being a mother, let alone the mother of a teen-age girl. But De Sica was one expert I trusted totally, so when he said I could do it, I went along with him. Besides, the part of the mother was much more interesting."

For the first week of filming *Two Women,* Sophia was "very tense, but when everything went smoothly, I began to feel at ease. I didn't feel out of place the way you do when something is wrong. When you're insecure, you feel as if you have a hundred things to do all at once. You raise your voice. You laugh too much. Or you just don't understand anything that's going on around you. Me, I felt fine. I was myself the way I like myself best, which is when I'm relaxed."

In *Two Women* she found that, from her own wartime witnessing, her mother's "gestures, language, and attitudes came to me as naturally as breathing." So did the awards and rewards. She won Best Actress honors at film festivals in Cannes and Cork, from the British Film Academy and the New York Film Critics Circle, Belgium's Prix Uilenspigoel, and West Germany's Bambi. And she was nominated for the Academy Award for the best female performance of 1961.

Her four Oscar rivals were formidable: Audrey Hepburn as Holly Golightly in Truman Capote's *Breakfast at Tiffany's*; Geraldine Page's fallen spinster in Tennessee Williams' *Summer and Smoke*; Natalie Wood's nervous breakdown in Elia Kazan's *Splendor in the Grass*; and Piper Laurie's unexpected contribution to the poolroom drama, *The Hustler*. Even Sophia didn't think she had a chance. No Oscar had ever been awarded to a foreign star in a foreign-language film: Magnani, six years earlier, had made *The Rose Tattoo* in English.

Seeing Sophia as the likely winner, however, *Time* Magazine gambled on her for its April 6, 1962 issue, which came out the week before the award ceremonies. The cover story, titled "Much Woman," began by enshrining her with typical *Time*-style bite:

> Her feet are too big. Her nose is too long. Her teeth are uneven. She has the neck, as one of her rivals has put it, of "a Neapolitan giraffe." Her waist seems to begin in the middle of her thighs, and she has big, half-bushed hips. She runs like a fullback. Her hands are huge. Her forehead is low. Her mouth is too large. And *mamma mia,* she is absolutely gorgeous!

and then hedged Henry Luce's bet by warning that "Hollywood prejudice is unlikely to break down all the way in one year. So the odds are that the winner will be one of the other four nominees."

A famous picture of Sophia shows her jumping for joy in Rome upon receiving the news by phone from Cary Grant in California that she had won the Oscar. It was seven o'clock in the morning of Tuesday, April 10 in Italy, but it was still the night before on the West Coast of America. Sophia and her secretary and the photographer had sat up all night waiting for word, but the picture was not posed. "Who wouldn't jump for joy at such a surprise?" Sophia asked me when I recalled that photo. "If I'd felt any chance of winning, I'd have been in Hollywood that night." She hadn't gone there because she was working in Italy and was quite sure Audrey Hepburn would win. Still, she hadn't gone to bed either, for it was the Sophia I know now—then already battling to be the second Mrs. Ponti and just embarking upon the battle to have a baby—who said: "Even though you're pessimistic, you can still hope as long as you're alive."

CHAPTER 6

Sophia Loren, Superstar

THREE YEARS AFTER *Two Women* Sophia was nominated for another Oscar. This time it was for *Marriage, Italian Style,* a De Sica comedy in which she had no trouble playing the mother of a twenty-two-year-old son. But Sophia went to bed early on Oscar night. Up against Julie Andrews as Mary Poppins, she knew who would win.

In between Oscar nominations she made two Samuel Bronston spectaculars, both directed by Anthony Mann: In *El Cid* she fractured her collarbone and later had to go to court to fight for equal billing with Charlton Heston. No love was lost (or to be found) between Sophia and a co-star who—having played three presidents, three saints, and two geniuses on the screen—intimidated even her. And Heston later complained in print (in his published diaries, *An Actor's Life*) that Sophia was "more star than pro" because she refused to age on celluloid. For Sophia, in the Bronston-Mann *Fall of the Roman Empire,* playing the daughter of Alec Guinness (as Marcus Aurelius) for a million-dollar fee was a warmer experience in which she also made a lifelong friend (and while doing so taught Sir Alec to dance the Twist), but it was a less successful epic than *El Cid.*

The frothy French comedy, *Madame Sans-Gêne,* served Sophia well as a vehicle, but a tepid thriller made in Paris with Tony Perkins, *Five Minutes to Midnight,* did not. Director Anatole Litvak echoed Anthony Quinn's earlier complaints about Sophia: "In all the weeks in Paris, she only went out twice. One can't even get her to a night club unless she convinces herself

RIGHT: At seven, first communion: "I was dark and scrawny. I didn't look like much." (The Bettmann Archive, Inc.)

BELOW: Early Sophia Starlet photo. (Globe Photos)

LEFT: Sophia Starlet showed her legs. . . . (The Bettmann Archive, Inc.)
ABOVE: . . . and, in the harem scene of *It's Him—Yes! Yes!,* even more. . . . (Globe Photo by Georg Michalke, P.I.P., Rome)
BELOW: . . . and then much, much more. (Globe Photos)

In *The Gold of Naples,* Sophia played a pizza vendor. (The Bettmann Archive, Inc.)

When Sophia went Hollywood for the first time, as *The Pride and The Passion* shifted from the plain of Spain to the potted palms of California, Sophia sat with co-star Cary Grant and producer-director Stanley Kramer (center). . . . (Globe Photos)

ABOVE: . . . and met Kirk Douglas and Laurence Olivier . . . (Globe Photos)

LEFT: . . . and even found a moment to dance with Anthony Quinn, her three-time leading man (*Attila the Hun, Black Orchid,* and *Heller in Pink Tights*) who later complained that he "could never get close to her." (Globe Photos)

RIGHT: In *Boy on a Dolphin,*
which co-starred Alan Ladd,
Sophia stole the show by taking a
dive—practically a skin dive.
(The Bettmann Archive, Inc.)

BELOW: Wet filming came close
to giving Sophia pneumonia at
least once, but always showed
her to advantage. (Elio Sorci,
P.I.P.)

950.

ABOVE: Director, mentor, confidant, and occasional co-star, the late Vittorio De Sica guided Sophia to her Oscar for *Two Women.* (P.I.P.)

LEFT: Clark Gable's next-to-last film, *It Started in Naples,* was made on the island of Capri with Sophia, of whom Gable said: "This girl makes you think—all the wrong thoughts!" (Georg Michalke, P.I.P.)

ABOVE: Mr. and Mrs. Carlo Ponti meet another mogul, Joseph E. Levine, right. (The Bettmann Archive, Inc.)

LEFT: Pregnant in this famous episode of *Yesterday, Today and Tomorrow*, Sophia miscarried offscreen while filming another segment of the same comedy hit. (Springer/Bettmann Film Archive)

LEFT: In *Arabesque*, Gregory Peck chased Sophia around London, but they came together in Hollywood for an Oscar presentation at which Sophia was just a beautiful bystander. (Globe Photos)

BELOW: Presented to royalty at the Cannes Film Festival. (P.I.P.)

it's a question of public attention. Actually, once she's there she has a great time, but she'll never let herself have fun for fun's sake. A good actress needs human experience of all kinds and must live broadly in order to feel. I kept telling her, 'Sophia, go out and live a little,' but there's nothing doing. Even her rare vacations are a big bore, concentrated on physical recuperation, which is also part of the plan."

Sophia's fiftieth film, *The Condemned of Altona*, by Jean-Paul Sartre and directed by De Sica, was partially filmed in East Berlin with the co-operation of the late Bertolt Brecht's Berliner Ensemble and particularly appreciated by Brecht's widow Helene Weigel, but not by public or critics: even Sophia's admirer, Stanley Kauffmann, found her much "too melony and modern" and miscast.

While De Sica was still warning Sophia that "Hollywood is in danger of fossilization" and she should stay away from there, he was directing her in one episode of *Boccaccio '70* in the early 1960s. (The other two sketches, starring Romy Schneider directed by Visconti and Anita Ekberg by Fellini, were less notable.) And *Time* was quick to report:

> There is no fossilization in *Boccaccio '70,* in which Sophia is . . . playing an illiterate Neapolitan girl who works in a traveling fair and delivers her body each Saturday night to the winner of a raffle. The fair itself is alive with superb detail, from the smallest of watermelon seeds to the largest of the paunchy Italian farmers with hot breath and sausage fingers. In this milieu, Sophia is not a star showing off but a figure that belongs.
>
> In an outgrown red dress, her hair a disheveled beehive dripping fresh honey, she laughs, and smirks, and races the blood of the aged. A big bull gets loose and panics the fairgrounds, thundering and charging through the crowds. The animal stops and takes a long fierce look at Sophia. She slowly removes her blouse. The bull stands glazed a moment, then runs off snorting in inexplicable terror. A man in the crowd speaks for all when he says: "God bless her."

Another episode film, *Yesterday, Today, and Tomorrow* (1963), in which Sophia and Marcello Mastroianni played the leads in all three segments, was the true beginning of glory for the De Sica–Loren–Mastroianni triumvirate. (It was followed by *Marriage, Italian Style* a year later and, less successfully, by *Sunflower* six years thereafter.) Such was the chemistry between the two that, even when interviewed separately about each other, they talked almost in dialogue:

SOPHIA: "Marcello is a man who thinks like a man, talks like a man—is a man. He has so much magnetism, he brings out the very soul in a woman."

MARCELLO: "There is a woman who thinks like a woman, talks like a woman, behaves like a woman—never a star. We communicate with each other by instinct. With her I do not need to labor. It is like a meeting of two souls."

In the Neapolitan episode of *Yesterday, Today, and Tomorrow* one could marvel, as her friend Peter Ustinov did, at how this woman who had not yet borne any children of her own could "walk like a pregnant woman, struggling uphill with a pile of laundry on her head and all sorts of aches and pains in the back and not only overweight in front, but clutching her hip in agony on an uneven surface—all the folklore of a big city frightfully well observed—without her having to be told what to do." But when Ustinov asked her, "Where did you learn that?", Sophia's response was: "Learn? I've seen them in the streets every day for fourteen years of my life!" Ustinov attributed this gift to "the part of her that was born mature, that lived among them without fully belonging to them, which—coupled with a sense of humor—enables her to comment in her performances on the world around her."

Sophia, on the other hand, insists that she is always part of what goes on around her and never part of the audience: "I came from the *popolo*. I lived like them and thought like them. So it's just a question of putting forth that little treasure you've got inside of you at the right moment—in my case, of putting all my strengths on the screen. *My* little treasure was the experience I remember: how people talked, how I talked at the time,

all things I can never forget because I still talk that way sometimes. Even in another language, I find myself making Neapolitan gestures, movements, expressions, taking Neapolitan
attitudes."

Sometime during those three critical years, from *Two Women*
(1961) to *Marriage, Italian Style* (1964), which established Sophia Loren as a universal superstar and not just a globe-gir-
dling golden sexpot, Alberto Moravia asked her to tell him
"what film roles you like best to play."

"Passionate, tragic parts," Sophia replied. "Strong, highly
emotional people."

"And in life," Moravia persisted, "what role would you like
best to play?"

"In life, I'd like to be just the opposite of what I am in art—
cool and collected, with a strong inner life," Sophia told him.

Moravia interpreted this contrast thusly: "So you are looking
for the normal life conceived as one in which parents marry,
there is a family, life is calm and ordered, children grow up and
marry in turn, and one is cool and collected with a strong inner
life. But for one reason or another, this normalcy eludes you.
In fact, you don't manage to be as calm and cool and inner-
directed as you would like because your *joie de vivre,* your vivacity, your whole temperament prevents you. And therefore you
strive to express yourself through your art. And to express
yourself you play the part of abnormal characters or people
toward whom you feel drawn precisely because they are so
different from what you would like to be in real life."

Around that time, Sophia had a recurrent dream, which she
shared with both *Time* and Moravia:

"I dream that I am on a beach, at sunset, and the sea is very
calm and immense and smooth, like an endless piece of blue
satin. The sun is fiery red and it is sinking. Suddenly I start to
run along the beach, and I run and run and run. And then, still
running, I wake up."

Moravia, at least, was eager to run with this one. "Shall we,"
he began with no small harrumph, "interpret this dream—not
in the Freudian or modern way, but as the Chaldean seers

interpret the dreams of Nebuchadnezzar in the Bible?"

"Let's," said Sophia, knowing that wild horses and winged chariots could scarcely stop Moravia from sinking his sensibility into her imagination.

"The sea is the normalcy that you are forever trying to reach. The red, red sun is artistic success. You could stand still to contemplate the quiet sea, but instead you want to run toward the sun of artistic success. Now you know what happens to people who want to reach the sun?"

"What?"

"They travel very far, almost without realizing it, because while the sun is far, far away, it comforts them and lights their way as they journey onward."

Sophia's voyage unto normalcy, however, had a gauntlet to run that not even the novelist Moravia could have mapped.

CHAPTER 7

Mr. Ponti Builds a Dream House

"I AM GOING TO GIVE YOU the most beautiful house in the world," Carlo Ponti told Sophia Loren on September 17, 1957, the day they were married—or thought they were—by proxy in Mexico. By the time they were indeed legally married in France almost nine years later, Carlo had delivered unto Sophia—at a cost exceeding two million dollars—eighteen acres surrounding and including the Villa Sara: a designated historical landmark dating back to the seventh century. In the Alban Hills, a half-hour's drive from Rome just off the Appian Way, it was built for a powerful cardinal thirteen centuries ago, but the present fortresslike edifice goes back to "only" the sixteenth century. (The Pope's summer residence, Castel Gandolfo, is five miles away.) Although the villa in the town of Marino is an Italian National Monument, the Roman Superintendents of Antiquities and Fine Arts did allow Ponti to "improve" it with "plumbing and repairs"—including gold bathroom taps and an ultramodern chicken coop—but not to tamper with it artistically or architecturally, though Sophia and Carlo later changed its name to Villa Ponti.

While specifying that Ponti must never sell the villa without first offering it to the nation, the authorities never said anything against embellishing it. Ponti, who had first laid eyes on the Villa Sara in 1945, right after the war, and acquired it in the early 1950s, now engaged a landscape architect and gardener named Imerio Maffeis, who recalled with wonder: "Things began to arrive from everywhere. They were in Germany for *The*

Condemned of Altona and suddenly there were hundreds of azalea plants sent by Mr. Ponti from Hamburg." And when staff writer Dora Jane Hamblin and photographer Alfred Eisenstaedt produced a ten-page color spread for "LIFE Visits a Dream House in Italy Built with Money and Lots and Lots of Love" (Sept. 18, 1964), Dodie Hamblin reported, rather prophetically in the light of the Pontis' later tax troubles:

> From Spain, during shooting of *El Cid,* Carlo sent a five-foot thirteenth-century granite baptismal font, and a fourteen-foot marble table top which almost outweighed the font. While Sophia was unknowingly winning an Oscar shooting *Two Women* near Naples in 1960, Ponti was knowingly scrounging the entire area for antiquities which he is understandably reluctant to describe in detail—it's technically against the law to buy genuine antiquities in Italy, on the grounds that they are the property of the state. An exquisite sixteenth-century marble fountain from a crumbling villa in Sorrento arrived to decorate the lounge by the swimming pool; a shipment of white birch trees came in from Russia. "I have planted here only trees and shrubs from cooler countries in the north," says Ponti, "and see, they do well!"

Carlo Ponti was, in fact, one of the most innovative amateur gardeners in Italy, according to Dodie Hamblin, who now resides on the other side of Rome, in Trevignano: "I think he and I are the only people in Italy who plant roses under olive trees. He tried it first—in Marino—and it worked, but it doesn't work under cherry trees."

While making the foundation for a poolside guest house, Italian workmen uncovered a pre-Roman cave. Today, a long flight of steep, gray stone steps leads any welcome guest down into antiquity; for less adventurous wanderers, Ponti installed an automatic elevator. Above the cave rose the guest house: a four-story pink *palazzo*—newly built, but with sixteenth-century curves and painted to look old, with cannon balls and a frieze of stone statues offering further protection from the present. Inside it were four modern apartments, one of them (where Richard Burton would stay in 1973 after breaking up with Elizabeth Taylor) having a floor-to-ceiling library formed from choir panels of a seventeenth-century church.

There were also a sauna, a conch-shaped 135-foot swimming pool; a split-level man-made pond with mechanical waterfall and a grassy little island populated by a grinning stone lion and a Greek column that came from one of Carlo's forays into southern Italy; and a tennis court. In 1966, between rounds of researching a biography of Sophia that never materialized in print, Dora Jane Hamblin used to play tennis at the villa with her heroine, who is not particularly agile at sports. "We used to lob a few in a kind of half-assed way," Dodie Hamblin recalls. "I used to perspire like mad and Sophia always called me 'The Fountains of Rome.' "

Sophia herself didn't perspire and one day Dodie said to her: "That's not healthy! It's terrible if you retain all that water."

And Sophia said: "I pee a lot."

The three-story manor house was blushing red outside; rococo inside. Within, eighteenth-century frescoes were painted on pastel walls beneath handsomely carved and painted, sometimes mosaic, wooden ceilings. Its fifty rooms (fifteen of them bathrooms) included six libraries (three of them fashioned from Italian church choirs), a mini-cinema, and an antique bed Ponti had bought after hearing it once belonged to former British Prime Minister Anthony Eden.

In her upstairs bedroom, Sophia would be surrounded by frescoes of the four seasons that were carefully removed from a downstairs room, transferred to light canvas, and reset on her walls. Even though the Pontis had not yet moved in, Sophia donned one of the sheer nightgowns she favors and, posing for Eisenstaedt and his camera, pretended to take a phone call in her carved and painted Louis XVI bed, made in Tuscany. *Life's* caption concluded on a note of irony: "The handsome ceiling is merely eighteenth-century painted wood."

To their vast sunken living room's splendor, the Pontis added modern chairs and sofas custom-made and comfortably upholstered in Rome to flank a stunning marble table cut from an enormous stone found in the villa's catacombs, where early

Christians sought shelter in volcanic rock and which Ponti made into what *Time* described as "the world's weirdest wine cellar." Installed upstairs, the slab of bluish marble was supported by an ornate base of gilded wood from the Louis XVI period. There were also pushbutton Venetian blinds; an armory of silver bowls, vases, and trays; and humidors that played Vivaldi and Mozart whenever you removed their lids.

The better to link the centuries encompassed within their living room, the Pontis—by the time I first visited them in 1969 —had added their own dazzling collection of hallucinated Salvador Dali and Francis Bacon paintings, a couple of soothing Canalettos, a Picasso, a small Renoir, and a Henry Moore sculpture. Lavishly illustrated volumes about each artist were placed strategically near his work and I began to appreciate why, in the publishing trade, they are called furniture books. Elsewhere in the Villa Ponti, Carlo's other Picassos and Renoirs, Modiglianis, Matisses, Magrittes, and Graham Sutherlands had been transferred from his apartment and office in Rome, but not much of his collection of modern Italian art had made the trip. These included many exquisite Giorgio Morandi still lifes, drawings by Giuseppe Guerreschi and Renzo Vespignani, some sixty Sergio Vacchis, and more than a hundred canvases by Enrico Morlotti. According to Israel Shenker, who viewed the collection in Rome in 1965, the Morlottis all looked like each other, though "the older ones look like Picassos" and Ponti once toyed with the notion of "plastering the walls of his Marino country house with drawings by Guerreschi, but was dissuaded by friends who pointed out that the man's work was depressing."

Around that time, Ponti took Shenker for a drive out to the villa in Marino, which was still unpopulated by anyone but caretakers and watchdogs. And Ponti confessed: "I'm ashamed to admit it, but I haven't slept here a single night. Ask me why I bought it."

Shenker obliged: "Why did you buy it?"

"Madness, sheer madness. I like to know it exists, that there's a place I can stay one day and do things the whole day. It's ready to move into. We could come here today and live here.

The beds are all ready, everything's in place. Even the guest house for our friends is ready. But I need two weeks to see that the final things are done, and I never seem to get the two weeks."

"What about during vacation?" Shenker asked.

"We don't go on vacation," Ponti answered. "I don't know what people do on vacation. I suppose we do, day to day, what others do when they're on vacation. That's the drama of our life."

Soon thereafter, however, Ponti found the fortnight and he and Sophia moved into their villa in Marino well before a French license made them man-and-wife a year later. Sophia told Dodie Hamblin that she was still getting acquainted with her dream house, for "a house is like a person; you must be together for a while to be comfortable." Often, she would think back to her grubby childhood in Pozzuoli and then just looking around her living room in Marino would make her "feel important. It makes me feel that I have done something in life and that I have achieved big things and that I have been very fortunate—and it makes me feel well. . . . Most people have two homes in their lives: one they grow up in and one they move to when they marry. I never really had the first as a child, and now the villa gives me safety and a kind of tradition." And Ponti, who had let the Villa Sara stand empty for so many years, soon came to realize why he had bought it in the first place: "I guess I didn't really know why I wanted it until I married Sophia."

Despite the safety and tradition in which she was now enveloped, if not insulated, Sophia confessed early to a stranger visiting the Villa Ponti: "Even now, with all this, I never feel totally secure. Everything one has, one can lose." A little more than a decade later, those words—and the Italian tax authorities—would come back to haunt her, but in the meantime, something else was missing from the Pontis' multimillion-dollar dream-come-true: a child to share it with.

CHAPTER 8

To Be a Mother

IN THE MOST FAMOUS EPISODE of *Yesterday, Today, and Tomorrow,* Sophia Loren played a Neapolitan slattern who stayed out of jail by having babies whenever her sentence was due to be enforced. But Sophia's own pregnancy ended earlier in the filming—during another episode shot in Carlo Ponti's native Milan area. One grim day in 1963, Sophia was rushed from the set to a Milan hospital with what was officially described as a toothache. But the stabbing pain was somewhere else—and, though she prayed that, granted motherhood, she would ask no more out of life—she felt as if "hands were reaching out to take the baby from me." And the press soon learned that Sophia had been in her fourth month, but wasn't anymore.

In 1969, recalling her miscarriages, Sophia told me: "I blame the Italian doctors. They neglected one or two simple things and I lost my babies. I just would have needed to take care of a couple of tiny details that any woman copes with if she knows she has a baby coming. But they never told me about any of this."

I asked about the nature of these tiny details.

" '*ormones,*" Sophia replied in her fluent, by then otherwise flawless, English. (Since the letter *H* 'ardly exists in Italian, her English did have this one cockney twist.) "Just a lack of 'ormones, it turned out, was why I was losing my children. All I really needed was two pills a day and plenty of rest."

She went back to work soon thereafter and, eventually, it came time to film the pregnancies episode in Naples. A man who was working on location with the movie recalled that "the real drama was Sophia's face between takes. She was always looking at the extras. Many of them were grubby, pregnant Neapolitan women with big bellies and three or four dirty little kids pulling at their skirts. Their husbands had hired them out to help support the family. And here was the star of the world —the woman who had everything—watching them with the most envious look I've ever seen. It really hit me. It's the only time I've ever seen envy in Sophia's face."

When I asked Sophia about this, she said her old friend was wrong:

"Envy is not something I know. I would get sad for myself whenever I saw a mother holding her child. I was happy for the mother, but I was sad for me that I couldn't have this happiness. Still, I was sure that one day I could have a baby of my own because I *knew* I could have children.

"If you want something very badly and know that with a great effort you can get what you want, then of course you make the effort. If it's not all just words and sounds, but something you can actually do, then of course you do it. And if there had been just one chance in a million for me to have a child, I would have taken that one chance.

"You have to be ready for sacrifices. But if they're *all* that stands between you and what you want, then you can be successful. . . .

"The second time around, I stayed in bed for three-and-a-half months and lost the baby anyway. So it wasn't just rest I needed. I needed medicines, too, but they weren't given to me."

Her second miscarriage came early in 1967. From the end of *Marriage, Italian Style* (1964) onward, however, Sophia's filmmaking played second feature to her successful quest to marry Ponti (consummated in 1966) and her failures to bear his children. Of her relationship with Ponti at that time, Sophia was quoted as saying:

"I was afraid he would leave me to go back to his wife. I knew he loved family life and that he suffered by staying away from his children. So, in order to keep him, it was absolutely necessary for us to have a baby. But the months sped past, then the years, and nothing happened."

Years later when I asked her about this, Sophia denied the quote. She emphasized to me that Ponti's marriage was truly over, Alex and Guendalina nearly grown up, and she and Ponti would simply have settled for the status quo if nothing more legally binding could have been arranged.

Between miscarriages Sophia went to England to lend redeeming visual impact to *Operation Crossbow,* a leaden war saga, and *Arabesque,* a fast-moving, trendy chase-thriller with Gregory Peck, directed by Stanley Donen. And she flew to Israel to film "the only part I ever had that I could never once believe in": the title role in *Judith.* Sophia played the Jewish wife (working for the underground Haganah) of a Nazi war criminal training Arab commandos in Damascus.

"What do you do with a part like that?" I asked Sophia.

"When you have a role that has nothing to say," she replied, "you don't know where to look or what to do, so you have to build something out of nothing, with or without the help of the director. That's when you can get into trouble, though. But I looked inside of me for the things that weren't there. You have to draw upon other experiences in your life rather than the character's." She wouldn't say which experience she drew upon for *Judith,* but I could guess that the grief and determination with which she confronted childlessness helped her through the turmoil of an unlikely role as a mother whose husband may or may not have killed their son.

In that cinematic interim Sophia did make a couple of flawed but noteworthy films. One was *Lady L* (1965), an ambitious failure based on Romain Gary's novel, with Sophia bearing babies sired by her anarchist chauffeur Armand (Paul Newman) while married to the impotent Lord Lendale (David Niven). Carlo Ponti had genuinely admired director Peter Ustinov's three-hour version and wanted to "roadshow" it (reserved seats only). What emerged from various conferences and cutting rooms, meetings and messages, however, was a mangled two-hour movie which bothered more than it intrigued. For the powers-that-be—in *Lady L's* case, MGM and Ponti—had de-cided that the costly, overblown Elizabeth Taylor–Richard Bur-ton *Cleopatra* had killed off roadshow epics, so Ustinov's work of art paid the price.

The other high point was the critically underrated comedy, co-starring Marlon Brando, *A Countess from Hong Kong* (1966), which Charlie Chaplin wrote and directed, embellished with his own music, graced with a cameo appearance as a steward, and defended to his death: "I loved Sophia Loren in the part and I loved my picture. . . . It had beauty and good human qualities. What do people want these days?" Sophia has always agreed with Chaplin and points with pleasure to recent well-received reruns on TV and at film societies, a decade's distance from the overheated critical expectations and cosmic consciousness of the Swinging Sixties. Perhaps she takes particular pride be-cause the idea of teaming Brando, Chaplin, and Loren origin-ated with Carlo Ponti. And a dinner meeting of Sophia with Chaplin at his home in Vevey, Switzerland, during the filming of *Lady L* had inspired the master to dust off and update a twenty-five-year-old script of his that actually was inspired by "a visit I made to Shanghai in 1931 where I came across a number of titled aristocrats who had escaped the Russian Revolution. They were destitute and without a country; their status was of the lowest grade. The men ran rickshaws and the women worked in ten-cent dance halls."

As Natascha, a titled but impoverished White Russian stowa-way in diplomat Brando's cabin aboard a luxury liner, Sophia was splendid: "I put all the love I could into that film—not for Brando, but for that incredible man Chaplin who invented our profession, our whole business." And, in fact, the film's major failure was Brando, shambling and mumbling through a com-edy he never seemed fully to comprehend. Perhaps Brando's most animated moment on the set came when he playfully pat-ted Sophia's backside. It is known that Sophia's response was anger, but factoidal historians differ as to whether she slapped Brando's face or merely grabbed his arm and said: "Don't ever do that again. I am not the sort of woman who is flattered by it."

Early in 1967 the headlines and news flashes tolled the sad news:

SOPHIA LOREN HAS LOST HER BABY

There were rumors that she had been in danger of losing her life during the course of an operation. Carlo Ponti, who had stayed in the clinic all night, wept. After Sophia Loren suffered acute pain and hemorrhage, the decision was taken—in consultation among the doctors, Ponti, and the patient herself—to operate. The surgery was performed by Professor Pietro Marziale assisted by Professor Atlante and a team of emergency personnel. Blood and urine samples were taken while Sophia Loren was still in a drugged condition after the anesthetic, but no results of the tests have been issued. Telegrams of sympathy have arrived from all over the world, including messages from Princess Grace of Monaco, Marlon Brando, Jean-Paul Belmondo, Juliette Greco, Peter Sellers, Audrey Hepburn, the film director Gillo Pontecorvo, and Charles Chaplin, who has telephoned several times for news of the actress's health.

—from the Rome newspaper *Paese Sera,* Saturday, January 12, 1967.

Sophia's younger sister, Maria, recalled those bad times for me:

"Each time Sophia lost the baby, she was down, really down. When I saw such sadness, I couldn't stand to look at her. The second time, I went to see her in the clinic and they had put her in the maternity section! Everyone I saw and every sound I heard from the hall was gay and happy. The private rooms have pink ribbons or flowers on some doors, blue on the others. All except one room, which had nothing on the door—and then I went right to it because I knew it had to be Sophia's.

"She was all alone with her sadness. I used to tremble for her. She would tell me: 'I am an actress. I am famous. I have a beautiful home and a wonderful husband. I travel everywhere. But you, Maria, *you* have your daughters.'

"You could only hope that a woman like Sophia would have a child. She's a fantastic wife and you could tell she'd make a fantastic mother. She's such a—I don't know the American word, but it means somebody who doesn't want to go out much."

"*Recluse?*" I suggested.

"Definitely not," said Maria, still pondering. After a minute, she went on: "The word for Sophia, believe it or not, is *homebody*. And if Sophia hadn't had her child or if she'd had just one more awful experience, I think it would have been very bad for her. Maybe, because of her husband's love, she would have overcome her feelings. But that sadness would always have been somewhere near her."

Sophia's recollections were more matter-of-fact:

"You feel bad about it, yes. Bad?! It becomes an obsession. From the very start of the second pregnancy, I knew I wasn't being taken care of properly. I could feel that something was missing. I knew inside of myself that I was going to lose this one and yet I also knew that since I was able to have children, this must not be the right way that I was being treated.

"Carlo was terribly upset. When you sense that these things are happening for some very silly reason, you get hopping mad about it. Carlo kept telling me, 'Enough is enough. Next time you go to the right doctor.' And Carlo was correct."

CHAPTER 9

Dr. Right

A FRIEND "WHO HAD LOST TWO BABIES with the Italian doctors and then had two babies with a Swiss doctor" put Sophia in touch with the right person: Dr. Hubert de Watteville, Switzerland's most famous and expensive obstetrician specializing in "problem pregnancies." Dr. de Watteville, then sixty-one, and his wife Elsa, who works in hormone research, made it no secret that despite their best efforts they themselves were childless.

Physician, heal thyself? Sophia had to admit that despite Dr. de Watteville's reputation as a miracle worker this was the first and only question of confidence she confronted when she went to see him:

"You can go two ways on this. Either you don't trust him because he has no children or else you trust him completely for the same reason. From the way he talked about the subject—so naturally, so simply—you could only guess that he and his wife must have gone through hell to have a child. He's a very straight, very limpid man; when he looks, he looks *at* you, not *through* you. He gave me so much confidence that I found myself believing in anything he said—and I don't believe very easily. But I could certainly believe him when he told me that if science knew as much then as it did now, he and his wife would have had children."

Dr. de Watteville began treating Sophia early in the Spring of 1967, barely two months after the miscarriage and a full year before her next pregnancy. First, he gave her an injection of Pentothal and, when she fell asleep, a full internal examination.

When Sophia awoke, he told her: "I'm sorry. I don't know why you lose your babies. Frankly, there is no reason why you shouldn't enjoy a normal pregnancy. You are perfect."

Nevertheless, he sent her from lab to lab, where various tests eliminated diabetes, thyroid deficiency, infections, internal deformities, and tumors as possible causes of miscarriage. Then he prescribed a diet with a proper balance of vitamins and minerals. And as a routine precaution of *his* practice, he gave her a variety of female hormones—particularly estrogens and progesterone, which helps prepare the lining of the uterus to hold the fertilized ovum during its development.

In 1967, the year of her second miscarriage, Sophia Loren released only two pictures, both misnomers seeking to cash in on the riches amassed by the earlier *Marriage, Italian Style* (1964) and Mastroianni's still earlier *Divorce, Italian Style* (1961), which, along with the Pontis' celebrated conflict with the Vatican, was Cinecittà's principal contribution to the eventual 1970 divorce reform in Italy. Both of Sophia's 1967 releases, *Cinderella, Italian Style* and *Ghosts, Italian Style* were set in Naples: the former a period comedy co-starring Omar Sharif, who had proclaimed while filming *The Fall of the Roman Empire* with her that he was in love with Sophia Loren (but so had leading men Stephen Boyd and Anthony Quayle and producer Sam Bronston during the same film). . . . the latter a spooky farce co-starring Vittorio Gassman but distinguished only by a sight-gag cameo appearance by Mastroianni as a guest ghost.

Revisiting her roots in southern Italy for moviemaking, Sophia seemed remarkably serene for a woman who had lost two babies. On the set in Naples, she took a moment between takes to tell the visiting novelist John Cheever: "What do I like? I like thunderstorms. I like thunder and lightning. Waterfalls depress me. I like the smell of the sea and I like Patou's *Joy* (perfume) and I love the smell of stables. I like the smell of stables, I think, because it reminds me of the milk my mother got for me during the war. It kept me alive. I like bright colors. . . . I think of names as colors. Loren is orange. Ponti is blue."

By the time she'd returned home to Rome, Sophia knew the good news and told me, a little over a year later, what happened next:

"Once I was pregnant, Dr. de Watteville came to Italy and spent the night at our house. He told Carlo that if I wanted this child I would have to live more like a woman and less like an actress from this moment on. He told me that I needed to be relaxed and very optimistic—and to stay in bed for the next four or five months. And if anything wrong started to happen, then I'd have to stay in bed for all the rest of the nine months.

"The next morning, the doctor and I left for Geneva."

The normalization of Sophia Loren's confinement took some doing. It cost $120 a day in rent alone.* With great secrecy, Dr. de Watteville checked her into Geneva's Hotel Intercontinental and ordered her to stay in bed at least twenty hours a day. He says he gave her "sedatives liberally because emotional stress can lead to uterine movement and bring on miscarriage. Where there have been repeated miscarriages, there is always such stress in the form of anxiety. Thus we must give sedatives and confidence to break the vicious circle, assuring women that all will be well and this time they will succeed. That was part of Miss Loren's treatment. And because of her star status, I brought her to Geneva for the tranquility she needed. She had to stop all professional activities—not just making movies, but meeting journalists."

Rome not being Rome at that time without Sophia Loren, it soon became clear that she had disappeared. The press could guess why—but not where. Her mother and sister, living in the capital, were carefully watched, but they afforded no clues. In fact, Sophia's mother, Romilda Villani, didn't visit her in Geneva until late in the pregnancy and Maria didn't go there until Sophia entered the hospital to have the baby.

"Sophia told us quite bluntly that to see us would be a stress,"

---

*With the depreciation of the dollar against the Swiss franc and the appreciation of hotel rates since 1968, that same hotel suite would now rent for more than $500 a day.

her sister explained to me, "because by now her having a baby was enormous to the public and particularly to her family. She knew she'd feel our apprehension for her if we visited. So we did it her way."

Nor had Sophia confided her whereabouts to her friends. "Even if she had tried to tell me," said one true friend, "I would have refused to listen. As it was, I was bombarded by phone calls from America, Japan, Sweden, even from Switzerland. 'Is she or isn't she?' they wanted to know. 'And where?' If you don't know, nobody can blame you for not telling."

The press was hamstrung for awhile because Sophia had no more than a handful of close friends. "I've always been like that," she told me. "I never need to be among people to have fun. The friends I have—if I call them, they come right over. If they can't come today, they come over the next day. After all, how many good friends can you have in life? Four or five. The rest are just acquaintances you meet at a party."

When Sophia's mother's maid sold the secret to an Italian journal, the press swarmed to Geneva. The *paparazzi* zeroed in on the four-room, eighteenth-floor hotel suite where Sophia was secluded with her trusted secretary, Ines Brusci, and the baby growing within: "I was just twelve weeks pregnant when I heard the heart of the baby with a very sensitive device. It was quite a feeling. For once, I knew that something was there. It wasn't a dream. It was there. . . ."

The press haunted the lobby, the elevators, and even the hallway. Reporters tried to hire on with Room Service. All was in vain. "We did our own cooking," said Sophia. "Very plain and low in salt or fat. Spaghetti every once in awhile but not in a rich sauce. Sometimes I had a little craving for ice cream and Ines would get some—but no pickles with it! My husband used to come on the weekends. During the week I'd have long phone conversations with my mother and my sister. I'd watch television—four channels—and do a lot of thinking. . . . About what? About myself, I admit, and about my husband and my family and about people I knew and people I hardly knew and people who wrote to me—and yes, about the baby, but I tried not to think too much about that. . . . No, I didn't take *War and Peace* to bed with me but I did read collections of stories by Chekhov. I'd liked his plays and suspected that his prose might be just as quiet and restful and reflective."

After the fifth month had passed without incident, Dr. de Watteville placed her under less rigid surveillance but maintained strict hormonal control. Sophia says she "sat up a little, but I didn't really move around the suite for another two months. After the seventh month I could be a little more relaxed about it. I knew that even if something happened to me, the baby would still be alive.

"Each day that passed with nothing happening made me happy."

She had referred to "going through hell to have a child" and the press was full of "Sophia Loren's ordeal." But when I tried to commiserate, Sophia informed me:

"As a matter of fact, I think about that period I spent in Geneva with some *melancholy*—no, make it *nostalgia*. It was more than nice; it was one of the most beautiful times of my life —a beautiful experience. For me, there was a new feeling, a new adventure, a new joy every single day—several times a day. Now, when I think that I spent eight months in a room without ever going out just because I was one month pregnant, I cannot believe it."

Through the spring, summer, and autumn of 1968, Sophia Loren lived suspended in the sky above Geneva, a voluntary prisoner atop a luxury hotel overlooking Lake Léman and Mont Blanc. Outside in the real world, the Vietnam war was raging in the wake of Tet. Lyndon Johnson abdicated the Presidency of the United States, Senator Robert Francis Kennedy and the Rev. Martin Luther King were assassinated, and Richard Nixon and Spiro Agnew were staggering to a narrow election victory over Hubert Humphrey and Edmund Muskie. Closer to home, Alexander Dubcek's Prague Spring of freedom blossomed in Czechoslovakia only to be throttled and quelled by a Soviet-led invasion . . . while, across the border, the youth of France rose in violent revolution against the autocratic

Charles de Gaulle: an upheaval which served to entrench Gaullism as well as de Gaulle. Sophia read about these events and watched them on television, but they seemed remote from an insulated "universe where nobody lived but me."

Puttering around her Intercontinental kitchen, she catalogued her own recipes and experimented with others. And "when I finally grew a little bored, I had a brilliant idea to start answering my fan mail. But the more I answered, the more mail I got back. Still, I was grateful for all the medals and madonnas and crucifixes and images of saints that poured in. And the advice! Take Vitamin E. Avoid certain kinds of food. I realized how much people were affected by my struggle to have a child and I was very moved by what they wrote. It gave me great strength to go on.

"Eight months without going out once! If you haven't got a kind of richness inside you and if you really didn't want what you thought you wanted, you'd never go through with it. Believe me, those letters helped me along. It was a nice realization —that people who didn't know me, except through my films, were treating me like their own sister."

I asked Sophia why the public became so involved in her baby.

"I don't know why," she began, thinking aloud. "Maybe it's because an actor or actress nowadays is no longer a myth. He or she is part of the family. Television is in the houses and everyone has a cinema in his own home. So I become a member of the family."

To support Sophia's observation, I cited a couple of studies showing that the deaths of Marilyn Monroe and John Fitzgerald Kennedy had affected many Americans more than deaths in their own families. Sophia said this was interesting, but she didn't think it would be the case in Italy, where families remain more tightly knit than elsewhere. And she went on to say:

"It may also be that because I'd been portraying human and natural characters—peasants, mothers—the contradiction that I wasn't able to have children of my own made people very upset. They knew me as something else. More than that, they could read between the lines of the gossip columns and news stories to know that this yearning of mine was sincere. That must be why they followed me all the way through with such affection and love."*

Sophia described her mood toward the end of her confinement as "optimistic inside of myself, though I was showing pessimism. I rarely talked about the baby I was going to have. If I ever had to speak of him, it was in a very abstract way. I wouldn't even discuss the matter of interviewing a nurse for him until I was eight months along, and we didn't hire anybody until after he was born."

Over a total of more than ten hours spent with Sophia Loren in 1969, I noticed that unlike other beautiful actresses and contrary to Jean Negulesco's unchivalrous imputation of narcissism,—she never fussed with her makeup or even checked herself when she passed a mirror.† She always started our day together looking perfectly, carefully casual—in a series of light blue shifts—and that was that for the rest of the day. But when she talked about her fears during her pregnancy, her hands did play nervously in the air just below those lips whose loveliness photographer Irving Penn attributes to "serenity and early sorrow." And whenever she noticed that I'd noticed this mannerism, she would cross her legs and clasp both hands beneath them.

---

*"From just following the papers, I knew more about Sophia's Fallopian tubes than I know about my own," a young American woman living in Rome told Redbook, editor Sam Blum, who went on to theorize (in the May 1969 issue) that Sophia's miscarriages "had been taken by many Italian women as a personal loss; and her consequent all-out struggle to successfully bear a child engrossed both Italian readers and Italian press as have few other human dramas of our time."

†Neither does Ingrid Bergman, but she never makes up to begin with.

Chapter 10

A Son Is Born

DURING THE LAST WEEK of 1968, Dr. de Watteville decided that Sophia's childbirth should be by Caesarean section. This was because the baby was appearing in a breech position—feet first, rather than head—and there was the danger that the umbilical cord might be pinched when the head emerged. Sophia's history of miscarriages helped dictate the operation.

On Saturday the 28th of December, Sophia Loren finally emerged from her hotel for the short auto ride to Geneva's Cantonal Hospital. The best room in the maternity clinic had been reserved for her. Already, there was a bassinet near the bed. "But when I saw it," Sophia recalled, clasping her hands, "I sent it away. I knew I was having the baby the very next day, but I wasn't taking any chances."

Sophia was still running scared even while she was being wheeled into the operating room on Sunday the 29th: "A nurse saw how nervous I was. So just to keep me busy, she asked me what name I'd give the baby. I said very sharply, 'I don't know,' even though I knew very well. I wouldn't let myself believe until I actually saw the baby."

The operation lasted one hour. Sophia's first words were to Dr. de Watteville: "Thank you, professor, for my baby."

"You have a boy," the doctor said.

Carlo Ponti, Sr., had stayed behind at the hotel rather than risk an emotional farewell when his wife would be rolled away for surgery. As soon as the doctor called, Ponti hurried to the hospital, gazed at his son—all seven pounds three ounces of him—and proclaimed wryly: "This boy has a great sense of humor."

Sophia's sister Maria had "come crying all the way from Rome to Geneva because I hadn't seen Sophia for eight months. That afternoon, when I saw her with the baby, I cried all the more and so did Sophia. She was still sick from the operation, but she managed to speak before I could. She said, 'I am so happy!' " Recalling this five months later, Maria told me: "And that's how she's begun every conversation we've had since then: 'I am so happy!' "

So grateful were Sophia and her spouse that Carlo Ponti, Jr.'s full baptismal name is Hubert Leoni Carlo Ponti—the first for the doctor who brought him into the world; the second for his paternal grandfather. Dr. de Watteville is also the boy's godfather. The christening took place in Geneva when the baby was forty days old, for mother and son remained in the hospital that long to avoid an epidemic of the Hong Kong flu which was flourishing that winter. During that time, the Pontis chose a young Swiss from the many applicants for the job of baby nurse: Ruth Bapst—prim, pretty, and as starchy as her uniform —survived the elimination and is still with the Pontis almost a decade later.

"Ruth was young then, but always with a firm hand," Sophia recalled recently. "And to this day, whenever my son feels that hand, he behaves. From the beginning, when she said eat, he ate. Otherwise, he would have tyrannized us. She would never let anybody but Carlo and me touch the baby. She would say: 'If he gets sick or hurt, it doesn't matter who does it to him because you will hold me responsible.' And I imagine she was right."

Carlo Ponti, Jr., was introduced to the world when he was a week old—at a press conference in the Geneva hospital's hermetically sealed and sterile amphitheatre. One hundred twenty photographers jockeyed for pictures and almost twice as many reporters pressed the doting parents for provocative quotes, but there weren't any—except for the three dots in Carlo Ponti's pronouncement: "We are extremely happy . . . and at this moment I thank the professors who attended Sophia with extreme patience and almost paternal care. I thank them for having given to my wife and me the joy of this magnificent day." In between his fourth and fifth word, Carlo Ponti, Sr., had choked on a sob and his eyes had glistened with uncharacteristic tears.

Inevitably, the question came: "Will Sophia Loren breast feed the baby herself?"

The answer came from Dr. Hans Bramatter, a Geneva pediatrician: "Signora Ponti wishes to do so herself and we, too, will do our best to give her the possibility of feeding her son personally."

Seemingly the most solid news to emerge from this convocation ("as though God were being interviewed on the Creation," one correspondent wrote) was that an eternally thankful Carlo Ponti, Sr., would be endowing—to the tune of some three million dollars—a private maternity clinic in the center of centrally located Geneva. It would have offered women from all over the world with pregnancy problems a chance at the same expensive medical care Sophia Loren received. "The rich will pay. The poor will not," said Carlo Ponti. "There doesn't exist in the whole world something like this. We need it—especially in Europe."

To which Dr. de Watteville added: "It's a marvelously generous offer. It will be primarily for women coming from abroad with special problems—women who don't need or can't afford long hospital stays and might find hotels impractical or prohibitive. But it will also be for men"—and treatment of sterility and infertility problems.

"It will be a *complete* checkup clinic," Sophia told me. "The emphasis will be on completeness. I know from experience that in Switzerland you have to go from one lab to another. There is no one place where you can find everything you need for a woman expecting a baby or wanting a baby. Now it will all be in one clinic. Women would even have their babies at our clinic, not in the hospital."

Her husband had already bought the five-story row houses at numbers 2 and 4 rue Charles Bonnet next door to Dr. de Watteville's home and private offices at number 6. "But in those buildings," Sophia said cautiously, "there are still living some people. And they have to go before we can start building the clinic—so we must wait a few years." As it so often turns out in show business, a short delay may mean forever.

According to the man who—aside from Carlo Ponti, Sr.—would be spending the most time with the baby, "the boy's main problem" was that "he has a jealous mother."

The speaker was Tazio Secchiaroli, who has been Sophia's still photographer since *Marriage, Italian Style* in 1964 and the Ponti children's official photographer ever since little Carlo's christening. There was a time—which continued well into the 1970s, in fact—when Sophia wouldn't sign a contract that didn't provide for her double, hairdresser, language coach, and Ines and Tazio to come with her.

"At the christening," Tazio complained cheerfully to me in the spring of 1969, "when the sister, Maria, had to hold the baby, I discovered two hands underneath Maria's. They weren't supposed to be in my picture. They were Sophia's, of course. And it's been that way ever since. She always clutches the baby to her. When she says she never allows anyone to touch him except the nurse, she isn't kidding—not her secretary, not even the grandmother, seldom even the father. I have spent many hours with that baby for four or five months now, but I have never even touched him!"

Tazio Secchiaroli looks a little like an unkinky Marcello Mastroianni, and it is perhaps fitting and revealing that Sophia and Tazio began their long collaboration on the set of a Mastroianni-Loren vehicle—and certainly surprising to disclose that Sophia Loren's official photographer was, by origin, a *paparazzo*.

The word *paparazzo*—particularly in the plural form, *paparazzi*—is in the vocabulary of every Italian celebrity and among the first words that any VIP visitor to Rome must know before his or her plane touches down. Although its most prevalent meaning is recent, *paparazzi*, unlike *factoid*, is not a newly coined word, but a good old one, meaning "noxious insects," especially cockroaches. In Sophia's time *paparazzi* have come to mean a particularly ferocious Italian breed of freelancing, free-wheeling hustlers who maraud with cameras. The modern meaning derives not from nature, however, but from the name of an actor. Giuseppe Paparazzo, who portrayed such a photographer in Federico Fellini's film, *La Dolce Vita* (1960), in which Mastroianni played a gossip journalist, and Tazio served offscreen as a technical adviser.

According to Tazio's agent, Luciana Schwarz, "In *Dolce Vita,* Guiseppe Paparazzo played Tazio," whose most famous offscreen adventure had happened within a discus throw of the Colosseum back when light comedian Walter Chiari was romancing Ava Gardner. Tazio and a sidekick, Elio Sorci, came upon Ava's auto parked in a dark alley near the Roman arena. Knowing that the elusive pair would scarcely hold still for pictures, they let the air out of the car's tires. Hours later, enraged when unable to make a fast getaway, actor Chiari started punching the two *paparazzi*. Each time he attacked one, the other would flex his Rolleiflex—and all of Italy soon saw an unamused, but highly amusing, Chiari fighting his way free of an Ava Gardner who was restraining him from killing Tazio.

Teaching Paparazzo to play a *paparazzo* brought Tazio into cinema's front door and, four years later, he was dispatched to the set of *Marriage, Italian Style* as executive producer Joseph E. Levine's emissary to an uncharacteristically complaining Sophia. She hadn't liked the still photos of her and, sharing her distress, Tazio offered to try his own hand at the job.

"Sophia always wants to see every picture that's taken of her," Tazio told me. "She even checks every contact and every print of the stills that are made on the set or on location. Well, she was fed up with stagey stills that made her look like a statue posing. It's not that easy on the film set to capture motion with a still camera. But instead of just glorifying a beautiful actress— beauty for beauty's sake—I felt something more going on and I found myself groping for the real woman with my camera."

It was a Friday. When the filming stopped, Tazio Secchiaroli stayed up all night, developing and printing his photos to his satisfaction. Then, rather than entrust them to the Italian mails or let them sit around the studio all weekend, he delivered them personally to the gatehouse of the Villa Sara toward dawn on Saturday and then drove home. He had slept barely two hours when his wife woke him and handed him the telephone, saying: "It's Sophia Loren."

Tazio grunted into the mouthpiece and a voice purred: "Your pictures are marvelous." Still half asleep and thinking he was dreaming, Tazio guessed it was "one of my colleagues pulling my leg or one of a thousand starlets imitating Sophia's voice," which then went on to say: "Why, they are more moving than most moving pictures."

"Sure, sure," Tazio snarled. "Now let's call off this joke so I can go back to sleep."

The laugh at the other end brought him wide awake: "It isn't a joke. It's me. You don't believe me, but I'm really Sophia."

They have believed in each other ever since. And as the father of an older daughter, Lucilla, and a newborn son, David, Tazio found himself pressed into service in 1969 as an auxiliary Dr. Spock. "She's always checking with me: 'When did *your* doctor put your daughter on solid food? When did *your* son start teething?' She won't allow canned baby foods. It must all be hand-ground. The liver for the baby must be fresh. And, oh, is she a terrible worrier! I was there one day when Carlo's crying grew a little faint. Sophia was afraid he was losing his voice. The Swiss nurse explained that she'd given orange juice to the baby and the vitamin C's acid makes the voice go down. Well, Sophia was still so frantic that I think she was ready to phone Geneva. But I told her: 'Yes, it's happened with mine, particularly when the juice is cold. It lasts about two hours.' Sophia looked at me as if I'd saved her life."

Like every really good photographer, Tazio didn't tell me about the work he'd done—*that* one can see!—but of the one that got away:

"The best and worst moment Sophia has given me came when we were going from room to room to take pictures. The nurse carried the baby. When we opened one door, there was a bit of a draft. Immediately, Sophia stood in the doorway spreading her dress so that the baby wouldn't get the draft. It was so staggeringly beautiful and I was so taken aback by the sight of it that I completely forgot I had a camera in my hand."

CHAPTER 11

First Visit to Sophia

TOWARD THREE O'CLOCK on the Monday morning in June of 1969 when I first met Sophia Loren, a maid had roused her from a deep sleep to report: "The baby is screaming and screaming, *Signora!* I don't know what's the matter with him." Sophia sat up in bed, listened briefly to five-month-old Carlo Ponti, Jr., and then said, smiling the eternal smile of the wise mother who knows her own child: "Why, he was just practicing his screams. But I think I'll go look at him—and maybe I'll tape-record him."

She stayed up a couple of hours. Nevertheless, when I came to lunch toward noon, Sophia looked as fresh and perfect as the strawberries she had just picked for our dessert. She was strikingly tall (five feet eight-and-a-half inches) with the whitest teeth that ever smiled at me. But the eyes were and are what you see first when you see Sophia Loren. Honey-colored and startlingly made-up to resemble winged leaves, they—like the rest of her—were still glowing from her middle-of-the-night encounter with her infant son:

"He should be sleeping through the night by now, I suppose. But he's just discovered the sound of his own voice and he screams because he wants to listen to all the noises he can make. He's so happy with them that you know nothing's the matter. He's busy discovering his own reactions and the day just isn't long enough. He's begun to know what he wants and he's working on letting *us* know what he wants. Every day he shows character and starts to be somebody. It's a wonderful time of life for a little boy and his mother.

"Later, after you've met him, I must play you our tape of him. You'll hear what a difference there is between now and his cries two months ago. I think between us my husband and I tape-record every single thing he can say. And every end of the month, we bring in a cameraman from Rome and make a film. After one year, we will put it all together for ourselves. . . .

"Yes, we keep a scrapbook, too. It's natural when you have a child. And when you have one you've wanted as long as we have, the taping and filming are natural, too, don't you think?"

We went for a walk. Sophia said:

"The photographers with the long lenses—they hide in the hills and sneak pictures of me wheeling the baby in the garden. It's ridiculous! Once you've taken one such picture, there's no sense doing it again and again. But the funniest thing is those captions. They say I've secluded myself here, that I'm a recluse, that I'm obsessed with the baby. Well, of course I'm mad about the boy! Who wants to deny it?"

Later, over a cup of coffee, Sophia said:

"People say the first word a child learns is *no*—from all the things he's told not to touch and not to do. But I have news for you, this one's first word will be *mamma*. The other day, I was saying *mam-ma* to him and he made a face like he wanted to cry. (Here, Sophia flashed a babylike pout you've never seen her make on the screen.) I wondered what was the matter and then I realized he wasn't unhappy at all. He was straining to imitate either my sound or my face when I say it. He can't say the word because he's too little. But, oh, he wants to!"

This was the way the beautiful lady was talking when I first met her. "Sophia's day," one of her friends told me then, "is really one long conversation with the baby or else about him: how much he ate, how much he grew, how many teeth." It *was* obsessive. It *was* euphoric. And quite beautiful to listen to and behold—for here, after several tragic and unnecessary miscarriages plus eight months of seclusion in a Geneva hotel, was "the screen's favorite earth mother" at last fulfilling a destiny that nature promises to every woman in this world.

No woman in the public eye had ever made so much of

wanting to have a baby. But neither marriage nor motherhood came "just like that, like eating" to Sofia Scicolone, born out of wedlock almost thirty-five years before the Monday we met and forever determined "never to bring a child into the world the way I was."

Sophia told me: "I'm a little bit accustomed to hard work just to get the easiest thing. Everything I ever wanted from life, I really had to sweat up. But the things that you work for, you really appreciate the most. That's why I think I'm so much luckier than someone to whom things come easy. And I'm grateful.

"There must be a destiny. . . . A woman was born to have children. If you feel like a woman one hundred percent, you want to have children, why not? And if you have to go through hell to have a child, you go through hell to have a child."

Not yet half a year old at the time, Carlo Ponti, Jr., was a black-haired, wise and mature-looking chap with the olive skin of his mother, the perfect proportions of a Mexican sun god in a museum, and the benignly crafted face of his father. The baby was sleeping when I first came upon him and his wary, young Swiss-German nurse, Ruth Bapst, during a stroll with Sophia.

"Well, what do you think?" Sophia asked me, almost anxiously, after barely a minute.

"Even if I didn't know who he was," I said, "I'd know he was of Italian origin, that he had a good head of hair, and—from the way he's sleeping—a clear conscience."

"He'll like you, too," Sophia assured me. "You wear glasses and so does my husband. He's starting to miss his father."

Carlo Ponti, Sr., whom I'd met in Manhattan a couple of years earlier, was in New York again throughout what proved to be my weeklong first visit to his family, in-laws, and friends in Italy. But he phoned home every day I was there and, while I heard only Sophia's end of it, each dialogue was punctuated by fervent *"Si, amore!"* and climaxed by a heartrending *"Ciao, amore!"*

On my stroll with Sophia, it was easy to see that she not only owned the property, but loved it. Pointing out roses entwined around olive trees and calling my attention to a modern Italian sculptured torso called *Maternity,* she spoke as though discovering them for the first time. But she knew where every tree and bush was. "Anything I didn't know before, I learned from being out here with little Carlo," she told me. "That's why I hardly ever leave. Everything I want is right here."

"When you were a child," I asked, "could you ever have believed you'd have such a place as this?"

"Even now," Sophia said with a sigh, "I can't believe it."

During my next day's visit, Sophia picked up this thread of conversation: "This place was bought and designed with the feeling that one day we would have a child growing up here. We didn't know when, but there was going to be a child. I always saw it like this. Otherwise, we might as well have lived in a hotel."

When the baby was just six weeks old, her husband remarked: "Until now, this beautiful home was completely useless because we had it for what? Now that we have the baby, everything works."

Outdoors, *everything* did indeed work, including the family zoo containing fawns (one named Bambi, of course), pheasants, rabbits, ducks, and no fewer than two ibises. One of these gigantic storklike birds did little else but stand around on one spindly leg like a streetcorner loafer. The other did nothing else but bow and bow and bow like a fatuous Roman headwaiter.

And then there were *paparazzi.* As Sophia had warned me, they had staked out nests in the Alban hills to sneak candid photos of the Pontis and any visitor who went near the baby. Once, Sophia apologized in advance in case my photo should turn up in *ABC,* the rag of the day, or the more respectable *Gente* and *Oggi,* perhaps even linking us romantically in the caption. Unhappily, this misfortune never befell me, but I did get an earful of Sophia letting off steam at the invisible, yet omnipresent, *paparazzi:* "They take pictures of me wheeling the baby in the garden and, if I'm in old clothes with my hair not combed, the caption says that people criticize me for this. What *people*?!"

She looked at me for an answer, so I said: "Their editors?"

"You call them *people*?!" she exclaimed dubiously.

"I don't even call them editors," I replied.

Despite all its awesome grandeur inside, the Villa Ponti looked more "lived in" than one might have expected from an international movie producer and his actress wife and much more so than many of the canyon dwellings and ranch houses of their California counterparts. Even that immense living room became almost cozy somehow (and this *somehow* was, I suppose, the star's magic) when my hostess stood in one corner, mixing Bloody Marys and, while doling out the Tabasco and Worcestershire without missing a beat of conversation, talked about her son:

"I took Carlo off nursing at three months. He no longer needed it. Even after just a month, a mother has given her child all the antibodies he needs. The food and milk preparations they have nowadays are certainly as good as anything a mother can give a baby."

Sophia at first struck me as an outspoken opinionated mother: "In Italy we have the Montessori method.* They try not to say no to a child and he can do anything he pleases. But this isn't always good for a child. Because, when he goes on to a school, the teacher will say no to him and it will come as shock and discouragement. And in any situation, so much depends upon *who* is saying yes or no to a child."

The baby was already enrolled at Eton, the British preparatory school, because his mother wanted "him to grow up with English manners and fluent use of the language." Meanwhile, an American magazine had made much of how "she will raise her child with the aid of the work of Dr. Benjamin Spock, as does almost all the Western world." Sophia made less of it.

---

*A system wherein the initiative of preschool children is developed through training that emphasizes freedom of action.

"Spock is the bible here, too, I suppose," she said. "And I do have one copy in Italian, one in French, and one in English. But I don't read it much. The success of this book is because it's so simple, so obvious, that what you do naturally is what it tells you to do. By the time I look up colds or bad weather, I find I've already done what Dr. Spock said. Still, it must be a very useful book for someone who's bringing up a baby by herself—without a professional nurse. A mother gets much more confidence if she's able to read what she's supposed to do."

After talking about children with Sophia at some length, I came to realize that her opinions were not snap judgments or pet theories. She had been watching and listening to children for so long—and thinking, always thinking, about them—that these were considered verdicts that she was now ready to put into practice. Even so, they were invariably tempered by her awareness that every child is a unique individual. When we talked about permissiveness in general, she said: "I believe a baby should *think* he does whatever he wants to do. But actually the parent should be supervising." And when I asked her whether she would ever send little Carlo for Montessori training, she replied: "I don't know. I'll have to see what my child needs."

Later, Sophia observed: "I'm very open to anyone who gives me good advice. But this applies to everything—not just to children. I'm never a prisoner of my own thoughts or my own laws. There are so many people in this world who know more than I do. I like to be surrounded by them—people who have ideas. I mean, not just people who know everything. If any of their ideas apply to my way of living, then I'll use them. Isn't that what ideas are for?

"My own relatives: None of them approves of the way I'm bringing up the baby. Nobody ever does. And everybody forgets. My mother used to take care of my sister's children. One of them didn't sleep at night. The other was a bad eater. But now, if I tell my mother that Carlo wakes up at night, she says, 'That's terrible! Almost six months old and he wakes up at night! What are you going to do about it? Maybe you should make him stay up later at night and keep him outdoors as long as possible. Both of Maria's babies slept through the night right away, y'know.' But if I keep Carlo outdoors until eight-thirty on a summer night, which is early in Italy, one of my relatives will say: 'Poor boy. He stays out all night and never sleeps.'

"To all of them, I just say, 'Yes, yes, you're completely right, thank you.' It's much easier to please people by agreeing with them—and then doing whatever you want to do."

She was as nervous as any new mother though quick to tell me that "the baby must be surrounded by serenity and calm. He has to start having habits, a routine that he likes. He needs a lot of love. Children are so sensitive. From the day they're born, they know whether the atmosphere is right or wrong.

"Over Carlo's crib hangs a mechanical mobile of birds. They fly when you wind them up with a key. The other day, I was turning the key, but I put too much weight on the birds and the whole thing fell. I tried to keep the birds from falling on Carlo's head, but when I did, the part with the key landed right on his face. If it had gone just a little the other way, he'd have lost an eye.

"Naturally, I snatched him up right away. And he cried so much that for awhile he couldn't breathe. It hadn't hurt him much or done him any harm, but I'm sure he reacted because he could feel my own terror."

Sophia told me: "You can spend so much time with children! I don't do anything all day except be with the baby—see what he wants, watch him learn and discover himself, nothing very strenuous for me. And yet I'm so tired at night! It's like I'm coming from thirty hours of steady work. But it's a *nice* kind of fatigue."

The longest she had been away from the baby was twenty-four hours, when she flew to a charity ball in Monte Carlo and "worried about him every minute I was there, but we had promised Ranieri and Grace we would attend."

Not long after my visit with her, however, Sophia was due to start work on a film, *Sunflower,* that would require her to spend three weeks in the Soviet Union. Clinging to her maternity leave, Sophia "tried desperately not to go or else postpone shooting, but Vittorio [director De Sica] absolutely needed a Russian field full of sunflowers for filming and there are only three or four weeks of the year when Russia can guarantee sunflowers."

I asked her what she thought she would miss the most about her son for three weeks.*

"His caress," she said. "Now he starts to caress me. If I go very close to him, he puts both his hands in my face. And oh how I'll miss just being with him! Ever since I have the baby, I don't like to travel and I hate to fly. I don't want to die—now in particular. I have fears now that I never had before.

"When we're at home, I seldom go out. But one night my husband and I went to Rome to see a play. Halfway through the first act, I began to wonder what I was doing in a theatre when I had a child at home who was all I was thinking about. Even an interesting play isn't so interesting as the baby. I wanted to leave after the first act, but I had to stay. Everyone knew I was there and, if I didn't come back, it would have become The Play She Walked Out On."

When little Carlo's famous first teeth appeared, a friend reminded Sophia that "it's a custom in southern Italy for the husband to give the wife a present. Carlo may not know about it" because he is from the North. Sophia gave the baby a hug and the friend a look, both of which combined to say more eloquently than words: *Carlo's given me gift enough.*

That Carlo Ponti, Jr., was already gifted enough, too, was confirmed by a tour of his nursery, which sat atop a spiral stone staircase in the Villa. The most photographed present of those staircase in the Villa. The host photographed present of those size toy giraffe sent by a family friend in America. But there were also, from unknown admirers in Czechoslovakia, hand-

---

*Carlo Ponti, Jr., may have missed out on the trip to Russia, but he wasn't missing from the movie, for he played Sophia's infant son in a part of *Sunflower* that was filmed in Italy.

painted eggs, dolls, and straw figures of mother and child. From French Minister of Culture André Malraux, a print: *The Birth of a Dauphin, 1782.* From Marcello Mastroianni, a collection of silver rattles. From the Union of Hebrew Congregations in America, a certificate announcing that a tree "in honor of Sophia Loren's baby" had been planted in the John F. Kennedy Memorial Grove as a gift from one Sharon Friedman. There were messages of congratulations from Presidents Saragat of Italy and Pompidou of France; a warm note from astronaut Frank Borman, who had just come back from the moon a couple of days before Carlo was born; and one of the stiffest form letters ever perpetrated above the signature of Richard M. Nixon.

The day after the 1968 US Presidential election, as soon as the close result was known, the Pontis had cabled their congratulations to the winner. (When in Rome, Sophia used to be almost as conservative, politically, as her husband, despite their feud with the Vatican over his remarrying.) On the fourteenth day of 1969, a week before taking office, President-elect Nixon "wrote" back thanking them thusly:

> As I undertake the great responsibility of providing new leadership in America, the messages I have received by the thousands from all over the world will be a constant source of strength and inspiration in the years ahead.
>
> Mrs. Nixon joins me in extending our very best wishes to you for the New Year.

Below the signature was typed this further personal greeting at a time when Sophia was still in the Geneva hospital:

> P.S. Mrs. Nixon joins me in extending congratulations on the birth of your son.

And Sophia, who can be sentimental about most anything, had them all framed and displayed with equal prominence: Saragat's, Pompidou's, Borman's, Nixon's, and Sharon Friedman's.

Hanging on the nursery door was a long inspirational scroll that came from America. Sophia took a liking to it. Attributed to Dorothy Law Nolte, it began: "If a child lives with criticism, he learns to condemn." It ended: "If a child lives with acceptance and friendship, he learns to find love in the world."

I could already guess which one of these routes would be little Carlo's early path through life. But I wondered what Sophia thought her son's reaction might be when he grew old enough to read his scrapbooks and realize what fanfare attended his birth.

"I hope he will take it like a joke," Sophia said. "I hope he can have a sense of humor about it. It would be terrible if he took it seriously and had complexes." She gazed at her sleeping son for a moment before going on: "But he's such a natural being that I think he'll take it well." Then, after another pause to admire him: "That's why I want to have another baby soon—to take some of the pressure off him."

If the story of how he happened is presented to him in the right way, I suspect, young Carlo—unlike so many other children in this world—will never wonder whether he was wanted. And that can be a very healthy feeling.

When I tried out this theory on Sophia's sister, however, Maria said: "His reaction will depend entirely upon his own character. He might be upset. He might not care. Maybe he will smile like his father. Or maybe he will feel pain. But I'm sure he will work it out. . . ."

Then Maria told me one last story involving Aunt Sophia and Maria's sensitive little daughter Alessandra. It had happened the year before.

Maria's last name is Mussolini. At the time I visited her in her Rome apartment, she was still married to Romano Mussolini, son of the dictator who founded Fascism. But Benito Mussolini was a man, too, and there are people who still love him. One of them is his granddaughter Alessandra, who was born eighteen years after he was executed in 1945.

To Alessandra Mussolini—whose paternal grandmother, Donna Rachele, shared many memories with her—Benito Mussolini was "a man who would have taken me to pick lima beans if he were still here." But, watching television, Alessandra couldn't be entirely shielded from occasional derogatory references to her grandfather and even, once or twice, the famous photo of the corpses of Mussolini and his mistress, Clara Petacci, hanging in the public square in Milan. When Alessandra was five, this began to upset her terribly. At first, she would ask: "Why did they kill my poor grandfather?" Later, it was simply: "Why do they talk this way about *me?*"

It was hard to explain history to a five-year-old, though Alessandra's parents tried. Alessandra was brought around—or rather, brought herself around—to the point where she could cope by shrugging bravely and saying, half-convincedly: "If they say my name on TV, I must be important."

One day, her Aunt Sophia took her for a drive. At the foot of Rome's Spanish Steps, the Ponti car was recognized and surrounded by a mob of admirers. As the crowd peered in, knocking on the windows and throwing kisses, Alessandra turned to her aunt and said grandly: "Do you see what happens when you come out with me?"

"Oh!" said Sophia Loren. "I didn't know I was out with a celebrity."

The name Mussolini wasn't mentioned, but Alessandra's "Mussolini problem" hadn't arisen again more than a year later. And knowing the resourceful, sensitive, and subtle mother to whom Carlo Ponti, Jr., was born, well, I found myself thinking that if he'll be anywhere near as ingenious as his first cousin, he won't need to fear his fame.*

*The Mussolini mystique in Sophia's life has not been a happy one. Her sister's marriage is now over, but it began with turbulence and tragedy. First, the bride fainted. Then the groom's mother led the wedding procession to *Il Duce's* tomb and gave the Fascist salute. Finally, on Sophia's way out of that town of Predappio, where Benito Mussolini was born, her chauffeur-driven Rolls-Royce struck a motorscooter, killing the twenty-four-year-old schoolteacher who was riding it. Sophia, even more than her chauffeur, was questioned by police for two hours in a local grocery shop while flashbulbs popped.

An only slightly less macabre episode is related by Peter Ustinov, who visited Rome in the mid-1960s and caught up with Sophia at Maria's apartment. While the three adults were chatting, baby Alessandra crawled out onto the terrace. Alarmed, Peter called the sisters' attention to this. They assured him that the terrace was perfectly safe. "I'm not worried about her!" Peter exclaimed "But that's just how her grandfather got started, going out onto balconies."

CHAPTER 12

The Pope's Urologist and the Priest's Wife

I WILL NEVER FORGET ONE INCIDENT of that first visit with Sophia. My wife and two little daughters and I were staying at l'Helio Cabala, a Roman orgiastic-looking, but quite sedate, resort complex high on a hill above the Villa Ponti and the town of Marino. With sauna, masseur, boutique, fully equipped bungalows, tiny hotel rooms with antique furnishings and rustic ceilings on which to hit your head, narrow moss-grown staircases, nightly dancing and day-and-night swimming on an immense terrace overlooking Alban hills and Frascati vineyards (and the Villa Ponti, which may be why Sophia's husband had bought into the inn: to keep out *paparazzi*), Helio Cabala—the name is a Greek and Roman co-production which could be translated as "secret cult of the sun"—reminded me somehow of a Club Méditeraneé built for Peter Ustinov as the Emperor Nero in *Quo Vadis?* Be that as it may, Helio Cabala catered to the family trade, and its English-language brochure spelled this out in no uncertain terms, though perhaps a little imprecision in translation:

> If it is rest and entertainment you seek, you will find them here, for this village is both a hotel and a "holiday-village" (without noise, overcrowding and promiscuity).

Two double rooms, with Continental breakfasts, in those pre-devaluation-of-the-dollar days, had cost us a total of just under twenty-five dollars a night. Sophia had made our reservations for us and, though there was no discount for friends of the co-owners, she had eased my financial burden and spiced our visit by inviting my family to lunch at her Villa a couple of times during our week at Helio Cabala.

Friends in Prague, Czechoslovakia, where we lived then, had asked my three ladies—only half jokingly—if they were coming along to chaperone me. Actually, however, our four-year-old had, just that May, undergone delicate urological surgery by the most noted doctor with the only suitable instrument (made in America) in all of Czechoslovakia. After two weeks in the hospital, she was recuperating nicely. But meteorologically as well as politically, Prague was such a gloomy place in that post-Dubček Spring of 1969 that when our eminent surgeon heard where I was going, he promptly prescribed "a week in sunny Italy" for all four of us—and asked for an autographed picture of our hostess. Just in case anything went wrong on the trip and we needed medical attention for our daughter, her great and devoted doctor, who had been educated in the West, dropped a note to a former classmate of his, now in Rome, describing our child's case history.

One noon, while the four of us were down the hill at Sophia's, a call came for me from Castel Gandolfo, the Pope's nearby residence. Suitably impressed, Helio Cabala immediately referred Sophia's unlisted number: a cardinal sin under most circumstances, but not when you think it's Paul VI calling.

Sophia took the call herself and, with utter awe, told me: "It's —it's Castel Gandolfo—for you."

"My God! The Pope?" I whispered.

"No," she said, putting her hand over the mouthpiece as she passed the receiver to me. "But I happen to know the name. He's the Pope's personal physician." For that was what had become of our sugeon's urological classmate, who was just calling to greet us and make sure all was well. When I hung up, Sophia was still regarding me with her mouth open.

"It's not every day one gets a call from Castel Gandolfo?" I hazarded a guess.

"No," she said ruefully, "and for me from that doctor, never.

But there was a time when I would have given anything for that call."

When Sophia had been having miscarriages, she had been told at one point that this was the one man in Italy who could help her. But he wouldn't give her an appointment because her trouble with the Vatican over her husband's divorce from his first wife might have compromised the doctor had he taken her as a patient. Not in Sophia's matter-of-fact account of this, but in the way she reacted to his name (as though she wanted my autograph because I was somehow connected to him), did I perceive a little of what those frustrating years of concubinage and childlessness must have meant to that tenacious woman.

Sophia now calls herself a casual Catholic: "Yes, Carlo and I are still Catholics, even though I don't go to church, don't go to Mass, don't take communion, don't confess myself. But I was raised a Catholic, I believe in God, and pray when I need help." She bears, in fact, no hard feelings toward the Vatican for the difficulties it put in her way toward becoming Mrs. Ponti. "After all," she says, "the church has a very good side. Many people don't know anywhere to take their problems, except to the priest. Otherwise, they'd dope themselves with drinks or drugs, or do something worse to themselves or others. A priest is the only means of support in many people's lives and I'm all for this."

The Church has never been that kind to Sophia. Even under the relatively brief but benign Papacy of John XXIII, there was trouble when no Italian government official would present Sophia with her Oscar for *Two Women* because of Vatican pressure. Small wonder, then, that Ponti—a man who, like many of us, takes slights to one he loves even more bitterly than the victim does—has been engaged in a running feud with the Vatican for years. Pius XII's niece, an Italian countess, sued Ponti, Mastroianni, and Richard Burton for the way their film, *Death in Rome*, depicted her uncle's conduct in World War II. And when Ponti announced in the mid-1960s that Sophia would play Mother Cabrini, and when he described America's first saint as "a nun [who's] in love with God" and went on to suggest that between sisters and Saviour "the love affair has lasted two thousand years," he was asking for trouble. The Mother Superior of Cabrini College in Radnor, Pennsylvania, denounced Sophia as "the worst possible choice to portray a holy woman"—and there were so many other protests and boycott threats that the film never was made.

The ultimate outrage (and under the circumstances it is something of a miracle that the Pontis have not been excommunicated) came in early 1970 when, just as soon as De Sica's droopy *Sunflower* was in the can ("A fiasco in three acts," said Stefan Kanfer in *Time*), Ponti put Mastroianni and Loren to work for director Dino Risi making *The Priest's Wife*—and, to spice the provocation further, hired Pope Paul VI's former cook, Armando Carzanita, to play a chef in the film.

The Priest's Wife made middling fun, but much controversy. It was a domestic comedy about a miniskirted pop singer named Valeria (Sophia) who is saved from suicide by Don Mario (Marcello), a priest with a bedside manner who winds up fathering her child, winning a promotion to study within the Vatican itself and, acting upon higher ecclesiastical counsel, persuading his expectant fiancée that, while he is already married to the Church, she can live happily ever after as his mistress.

Filming this story in Catholic Italy with Vatican opposition ran more risks than any American layman could imagine. One day, a couple of priests forced their way onto the set by invoking their right to check out the authenticity of any scene which had a church building in the background. As it happened, that was the day when Sophia, in miniskirt, and Marcello, in priest's robes, were supposed to play a love scene, which she and he and director Risi knew would raise the clerics' hackles. So they set up a church sequence they had planned to film later in the day, assembled some extras who were already in costume and, always asking the priests' advice about details, filmed Father Mastroianni celebrating Mass and leaving the church in only slightly unseemly haste. This take was filmed six times, with the two visitors watching impassively but unprotestingly—little knowing that each time Marcello made his exit he jogged to the next set, where Sophia and a second camera unit were waiting. Greeting her with a hug and a lover's kiss, made more soulful by arriving out of breath, Marcello and Sophia made their hurried embrace into one of the more effective and economical scenes in *The Priest's Wife*. The solution, Mastroianni and Risi insisted, came from Sophia, who admits only that "it was the devil in all of us."

One of the few journalists allowed on the set of *The Priest's Wife* was Nino Lo Bello, whose 1969 best-seller, *The Vatican Empire,* had detailed the Roman Catholic Church's immense wealth and real-estate holdings, including (through the Vatican-owned Società Generale Immobiliare) a controlling interest in Washington's Watergate complex. Lo Bello asked Sophia how she reconciled her Catholic faith with her disobedience to Vatican teachings.

"The conflict is painful," she admitted. "But I must act according to my conscience. And we are not making a picture against the church. We are posing a problem that you know and I know is common these days; we read about it every week. And it's a problem the church will have to face and solve like all the others: if not in the next ten years, then maybe twenty, maybe fifty.

"Personally, I always like to think of a priest as a human being. And he should experience all the problems every human being has. That's why, for me at least, I think a priest should get married and have a family. Only by being married, having the wife and the children to care for every day, can he begin to understand other people's problems much, much better. He should really suffer as we all do—practically, not theoretically."

Her husband—as is usual where the church is concerned—spoke bluntly and more abrasively. "When Italian priests say they want to get married," Ponti told Lo Bello, "it is not for sexual reasons, I'm sure, because many have girlfriends on the side."

Despite sporadic bans, many denunciations, and mixed notices, *The Priest's Wife* flourished at box offices around the world and was even shown in Italy with only two scenes deleted. A few months later, however, Sophia went to work making *White Sister,* a tender Italian love story of a nursing nun and a convalescent communist, played by pop singer Adriano Celentano and directed by Alberto Lattuada, Fellini's onetime co-director *(Variety Lights).*

Though blessed with an utterly convincing and ingratiating performance by Sophia in the title role, the gently irresistible *White Sister* took two years to cross the Atlantic and encountered resistance at the ticket windows from a public that could accept Sophia as a priest's wife, but not as a nun and perhaps never as Mother Cabrini.

CHAPTER 13

Holdup at the Hampshire House

A LIZARD SLITHERED OFF THE DOORBELL to allow me to announce our arrival for afternoon tea at the Villa Ponti in November of 1970. Through the locked glass door, I saw Sophia herself appear and wave but, to my surprise, she didn't come to let us in. Instead, after a minute or two, a yellow-liveried servant arrived but he, too, passed by the door and moved on into the next room. He reappeared seconds later, clutching a key he'd gone to fetch. Kneeling, he unlocked a large tanklike floor-to-door padlock which any New Yorker could envy. Unbolting the door, he admitted me and there, right behind him, was Sophia again.

"Excuse the security," she said, extending both of her long, bony hands with double-jointed fingers that even a concert pianist might gaze upon with awe, "but after our troubles in New York last month . . ."

On Sunday, October 11, 1970, at 7:15 in the morning, five men had entered the lobby of the Hampshire House in Manhattan, pointed guns at the residential hotel's weekend staff and handcuffed the employees, cut the switchboard, posted one man in the lobby, and forced the porter to take them up to Mr. and Mrs. Carlo Ponti's twenty-second floor apartment and let them in.

The Hampshire House is one of the landmarks of that imposing three-block stretch of West Fifty-ninth Street which is

called Central Park South: an austere concentration of aristoc-
racy, tradition, power and wealth which also incorporates the
Essex House, Hotel Plaza, Rumpelmayer's ice cream parlor
(where unescorted women, even in pairs, are not welcome), the
St. Moritz, the New York Athletic Club, and a row of young
gingko trees. Carlo Ponti took four rooms in the Hampshire
House on a permanent basis because he liked its "Palladian
style," which is not a reference to Pallas Athena, the Greek
goddess of wisdom, but to Andrea Palladio, the sixteenth-century Italian Renaissance architect whose villas, *palazzi,* and
churches in the Vicenza-Venice region Ponti admired. Distinguished by arched windows, temple facades, and absolute sym-
metry where possible, Palladio's grandeur was imported into
seventeenth-century Engand by Inigo Jones, taken up by Sir
Christopher Wren and others and, in the eighteenth century,
by Lord Burlington, the High Treasurer of Ireland and patron
of the Neo-Palladian movement. The Palladian influence in the
United States can be perceived in the manor houses of Southern plantations, such as Thomas Jefferson's Monticello which is
classic Palladian, while the more vertical Hampshire House is
classified as Irish Palladian. A base in New York became necessary for Ponti in the 1960s, when he found himself spending a
hundred nights or more of every year in Manhattan—and after
some trial-and-error with the Sherry-Netherland around the
corner on Fifth Avenue, he selected the Hampshire House.

If Ponti cherished the Hampshire House for its style, Sophia
used to relish its uncomplicated, but international and elegant,
catering. In particular she enjoyed unwinding from transatlantic jet lag in its cozy insulation. Upon her arrival at Kennedy
Airport, a limousine would be waiting and, as it entered Manhattan, the chauffeur would radio ahead to the Hampshire
House. When Sophia would enter her suite, a steaming hot
bath would have just been drawn. An hour or two later, a light
meal would arrive—without coffee. All incoming phone calls
would be intercepted by the hotel switchboard and her secretary Ines. In bed, watching television, Sophia would push a
buzzer and, five minutes later, a nightcap of hot milk and

honey would be brought to her bedside. Ten hours later, well-rested, she would be ready to face Manhattan at full strength.

She also used to trust in the Hampshire House's small, inhospitable lobby (absolutely unconducive to celebrity-stalking), its discreet staff and switchboard (to fend off unwanted callers, while those Sophia wanted to hear from could dial her direct line), and the privacy and security the hotel afforded her—until the second Sunday in October of 1970.

Sophia was in New York for the premiere of *Sunflower* and the obligatory television interview with David Frost preceding it. For the occasion, jewelers Van Cleef and Arpels had, as they often did for visiting film stars, lent Sophia a diamond ring and other jewelry to adorn her and advertise them. The objective of all this fanfare and glitter had been to reach millions—and among the millions were at least a handful of jewel thieves.

On Saturday night Carlo Ponti had flown unexpectedly to Milan, where his father had died. On Sunday morning, Ines Brusci, Sophia's secretary, was already up making coffee when the men entered. They told her they were repairmen who'd come to fix a gas leak. Alarmed, yet suspicious, Ines started to ask questions—until one of them hit her over the head with the butt of his pistol, whereupon Ines started screaming.

The commotion awoke Sophia, but she thought it came from another suite. Then, however, there was a knock on her bedroom door and a bearded young man strode right in. In the darkened room he seemed to be holding a stethoscope in one hand, so Sophia decided he was a doctor. Her first thoughts went to her son—at that time, twenty-one-and-a-half-months-old and sharing another room of the apartment with his nurse. But then Sophia saw that the "stethoscope" was a large ring of passkeys—and what he held in his other hand was a gun.

"Get up and get out of bed!" he snarled at her.

Sophia told me she still remembers two distinct feelings from that moment. One was "*pudore*—the modesty you might think an actress wouldn't keep for long. But I was wearing my Baby Dolls and when he made me get out of bed, I was ashamed." The other was a certainty the man was going to shoot: "I swear

RIGHT: Peter Ustinov directed Sophia in *Lady L* .... (P.I.P.)

BELOW: ... in which Sophia's then-unfulfilled mothering instinct manifested itself during filming of this scene with David Niven and nine-month-old Andrew Gillis. Two-thirds through the scene, which employed sixty extras, Baby Andrew let out a yell that could have ruined everything. Whereupon Sophia whipped out a baby bottle filled with orange juice to save the day. She had concealed the bottle under her coat. "I thought this might happen," she explained, "so I came prepared." (P.I.P.)

LEFT: Alone, pensive, and childless amidst all her great wealth and luxuries, Sophia longed for one thing: motherhood. (Globe Photos)

BELOW: With director Charles Chaplin, Sophia toasted their bubbling comedy, *A Countess From Hong Kong.* (Globe Photos)

LEFT: Mother and son after the birth of Carlo Ponti, Jr., at the end of 1968. . . . (Globe Photos)

BELOW: . . . joined by the proud father. . . . (Globe Photos)

. . . and, in early 1969, by the world press for a conference in Geneva Cantonal Hospital's hermetically sealed and sterile amphitheatre. (P.I.P.)

RIGHT: Sophia and baby Cipi with Sophia's "kid" sister, Maria Mussolini, who was soon to separate from the dictator's jazz musician son, Romano. (Globe Photos)

OPPOSITE PAGE: When he was just a few months old, Carlo Ponti, Jr., made his debut in his mother's movie *Sunflower*. (Photo by Tazio Secchiaroli, Globe Photos).

BELOW: Not long after the birth of their first son, Sophia and Carlo Ponti flew to a charity ball in Monte Carlo. Sophia said: "I worried about the baby every minute I was away from him" (barely twenty-four hours), but they had promised Prince Rainier and Princess Grace (nee Kelly) they would attend, so they did. (Globe Photos)

LEFT: A team for our times: Sophia Loren and Marcello Mastroianni. (P.I.P. photo by Elio Sorci)

BELOW: Celebrating completion of *Marriage, Italian Style:* Marcello Mastroianni, the Pontis, and director Vittorio De Sica. (Photo by Araldo Crollalanza, P.I.P.)

By the time she finished *Man of La Mancha,* Sophia knew she was pregnant. . . . (Tazio Secchiaroli, Globe Photos)

. . . and Edoardo Ponti was born on the first Saturday of 1973.

ABOVE: On a winter vacation in the Alps, Carlo Ponti Senior and Junior (as well as a good fire) keep Sophia warm while baby Edoardo slumbers off-camera. (Tazio Secchiaroli/Sygma)

LEFT: In Austria, 1978, Sophia sucks the finger that has just been bloodied by the "Silver Razor of Seewirt." (Photo by Peter Cermak)

I saw Robert Kennedy and Martin Luther King in that room with me even while I was praying he'd aim a little lower than my heart."

"Where's the light?" the man barked. Sophia switched on her bedlamp and the man, still pointing the gun at her, began rummaging in her dressing table. "This is junk, junk!" he complained. "I want the real stuff."

Sophia handed him a ruby ring, but even that didn't satisfy him. He helped himself to some Van Cleef treasures that were lying around. "These are junk, too. Where's the big ring?"

That was the one she'd flashed on TV. "It's not my ring," Sophia told him in English. "I borrowed it from Van Cleef, but I gave it back the same night. I beg you to believe me."

He came closer, peering at her through dark glasses. "Where —is—that—ring?" he asked slowly, ominously, and then he added at machine-gun tempo: "Yabettagetit!" With that, he grabbed Sophia by the hair and pulled it until she was kneeling on the floor—still begging him to believe her. The other men had entered the room. They emptied her wallet and took other cash amounting to two thousand dollars.

"Hurry up," one of the men said. "Let's get outta here." But then the man who was holding Sophia by the hair had an afterthought—and asked her a question that changed her life: "*Where's the baby?* Just tell me where the kid is."

Either he or the other man added: "You don't give us enough jewels, we take the kid, too."

Terrified, Sophia pulled loose and ran right past them to a table outside her bedroom. One of the men grabbed her, but she reached for a bag of jewelry from the table and said: "Take this!"

He did—and fled. So did his partners in crime. They were gone none too soon. The baby's nurse, Ruth, had locked him and herself in their room and then had used a direct phone to dial the police—who nonetheless took twenty minutes to respond. Of "New York's finest," Sophia said to me: "The police! They're afraid, too."

The bandits' haul was valued at half-a-million dollars, virtually the same yield as her British break-in a decade earlier. But the second time around, the lesson she learned was never to tempt fate with gems.

"I swear to you," she told Donald Zec in a more reflective mood than the one we caught her in, "from the moment I held my son in my arms again and saw he was safe, I have deleted the word 'jewelry' from my vocabulary. To own something which could make other people resort to murder and kidnapping is a threat, not a possession."

Nowadays, whenever Sophia wears jewelry, which is not too often, it is fake and/or cheap. And Carlo Ponti stopped giving her a gem as a gift every time she finished a film.

Even before we'd been greeted by Sophia on our balmy autumn afternoon out from Rome in 1970, we had noticed a change in the way of life on the grounds of the Villa Ponti. Instead of the friendly gardener and his wife who had waved us in a year earlier, the gatehouse was now manned by an armed guard who'd phoned the main house before we were allowed to proceed. As we strolled toward the house, we encountered a couple of guards being dragged around by German shepherd dogs. When we reached the house, a man with a walkie-talkie had popped out of the bushes behind us, looked us over and, as I put my finger to the front doorbell, he'd rung a side bell twice and retreated into the shrubbery.

While we lingered over "tea," which turned out to be coffee and cake for the adults and milk and cookies for the kids, our daughters started clamoring to go out and play with little Cipi. (*Ci* and *Pi* are the Italian initials, phonetically, for *Ca*rlo *Po*nti, Jr.) A brand-new playground (slides, two swings, and a small merry-go-round) had just been installed a few steps from the Villa; when I spotted the security man in the bushes behind it, he gave me a nod and vanished again.

Later that day, my daughters asked to go see "Big Bird," as they called the bowing ibis in the Pontis' private zoo—a quarter-of-a-mile away, though still on the property. "You can go there if you want," Sophia told us, "but we don't anymore. It's not safe to walk that far from the house." When our girls decided to go anyway, the security man slipped out of the bushes to accompany them.

Meanwhile, back at the Villa, my seventy-seven-year-old mother, who'd been visiting and traveling with us in Europe, began telling her own first-person horror tales of Manhattan. As she told of walking in upon *her* burglars while they were removing her TV wrapped in her bedspread, her story was punctuated by Sophia's fervent expressions of genuine concern:

"Have some more coffee. Your hand is shaking—no, my hand is shaking. . . . You are lucky to be alive, Mrs. Levy, because you saw your burglars. I was told my biggest mistake was to look my bandits in the face. They get scared you can identify them. . . . Mine would have knocked you down. At least! And at your age, who knows? . . . Please don't go back to New York, Mrs. Levy. It's worse there than it ever was here—even during the war. You should stay in Europe with Alan and his family."

There was nothing presumptuous about our hostess seeking to inflict a beloved mother-in-law upon my wife's household in Soviet-occupied Prague, for Sophia and we had become fast friends during our 1969 visit. From then on, whenever any or all of us were in Italy, Switzerland, or France and Sophia happened to be nearby, we would ring up and she would invite us over—for business or for pleasure, but always as friends with whom she could talk about living and child-rearing: the differences between sons and daughters, pleasures and troubles, shared or unshared, school or scandal, people and attitudes, movies and poetry. Over the years, my wife and I would come to know a woman two years our junior and we three would watch ourselves and our children grow older and, perhaps, wiser. In both our families, Carlo Ponti perhaps excluded, Sophia seemed the most mature: a worldly philosopher whose views on everything that mattered—from tonsillectomies to tuna fish, property and violence, taking snapshots and teaching children art, mating, motherhood, brothers, sisters, family—were worth hearing.

In the wake of her adventure in Manhattan, Sophia had become a trifle reclusive, though she'd welcomed us warmly and invited us immediately when I'd rung up from Rome. "But I've canceled some filming and postponed some dubbing," she told me that afternoon. "It was a terrible shock to me. Always, long before last month, I've dreaded waking up in a room so dark I won't know where I am. That can be horrible—like being dead without knowing you've died. When I sleep with Carlo, the lights are out, but *he's* there. When Carlo's away, like now, I keep a night light on.

"Ever since the 'ampshire 'ouse, if I'm asleep and somebody walks into my room without my knowing, like Ines or Ruth or Cipi, my heart goes to my throat right away. I'm in a terrible state when this happens because that's how the bandits came into my hotel room—while I was asleep in the almost-dark."

Though lively enough, it was a slightly morbid, if not melancholy, afternoon at the Villa Ponti—perhaps a sneak preview of the way the rich and powerful would soon be living in kidnap-prone Italy. With my mother and our hostess regaling each other with misadventures, I might have been watching a movie called *Cassandra Circle.* I have never again seen Sophia this way —not even when, the next time I saw her, a little more than a couple of years later, there had been a recent episode right on the grounds of the Villa Ponti.

An ex-constable and railway worker named Sinibaldo Appolloni, a "harmless crank" with a history of mental disorder, had first entered Sophia's life in 1967 when he showed up at the Villa with a bouquet of flowers for the woman he claimed as his "mother-in-law": Romilda Villani, Sophia's unwed mother. Two-and-a-half years later, he had reappeared, claiming paternity of the newborn Cipi. The proof he gave police was a mass-produced autographed photo of Sophia. But in September of 1972, when Sophia was five months pregnant with her second child, Appolloni sheared his way through the Marino estate's barbed-wire fencing and then, brandishing an ax, stood outside the main house demanding that "you give me my son because he's mine."

"Cipi was napping and I was inside the house," Sophia told me later, "so we just locked ourselves in while one of the servants went out to talk with this man. I knew him as a nuisance, but I wasn't prepared for what he did. He waved his ax at anybody who tried to get near him and, when the police came, he actually fought them. Now he's under treatment again—at a mental hospital—but we will always keep one eye on what he's up to."

On a couple of 1973 visits to Marino, the security seemed more intense than ever. Highly sophisticated electronic scanners had been installed, but the cheerful Italian couple had been restored to the gatehouse—freeing yet another security man for undercover duty in the underbrush, I presumed. No, said Sophia, the Sinibaldo Appolloni episode had served to show that even watchdogs, human and canine, were fallible. Besides, she added, the woman in the gatehouse, Clothilde, always was and will be the estate's ablest guardian.

It was then that we picked up the thread of our 1970 conversation about terror with a little perspective in time—which is why I'm telling this out of sequence.

"Time heals any kind of wound," Sophia began in 1973, "even though, if you have that kind of moment I had in the 'ampshire 'ouse, you will never forget. When I go back to America, that apartment doesn't give me good memories."

"So you stay somewhere else?" I guessed.

"Oh, no! We own that apartment, so we keep it. It's too good a value—and, besides, Carlo's children* use it, too, when they're in New York."

"But how you can face staying there?"

"Because if you want to overcome a fear, sometimes you just insist on living in the same place, doing the same things, carrying on normally. You think that you're going to forget what happened there to you—as much as you can. But if it's something that really shocked you, then you will never forget it,

---

*Ponti's children from his first marriage, Guendalina and Alex, were twenty-six and twenty-four respectively in 1973.

never forget it! You'll live it every day, as soon as something similar happens: when the dark comes, when you turn on the light, when you hear a stranger's voice. Even today, when I hear my secretary raising her voice the slightest bit, I remember how she was screaming when those men hit her over the head."

I was moved to express my admiration for the determination with which Sophia, like the most diehard New Yorker, stayed put because she had what she wanted and wouldn't let fear destroy her.

"Why not?" she responded. "All my career, all my life, I've had to fight back hard—particularly in my private life. Each time, I won, but from the beginning, I had to fight just for food and shelter, so the roof over my head is sacred to me—and who am I to scorn the Hampshire House?"

By George, she said it! And I marveled at this invincibility that wouldn't allow her to let go of anything she's achieved or to stop fighting to achieve what she wanted—even if it was just to retrieve a couple of dropped *aitches*. And this determination— to work for and work at everything that's supposed to come naturally—has always been one of Sophia's inner sources of strength.

CHAPTER 14

Dulcinea

"WITH THE MICROPHONES TODAY and the reverberations you can get with mechanical things, you just have to talk and it sounds like you're singing," Sophia marveled not long after she sang *The Secrets of Rome* for a TV special on "Sophia Loren in Rome." She and Peter Sellers also recorded an album of nonsense songs when they were making *The Millionairess;* according to Sophia, "it sold three hundred thousand copies in England."

Nevertheless, when she was signed to play the tricky musical lead in *Man of La Mancha* as Aldonza, the kitchen slut Don Quixote mistakes for his "sweet lady and fair virgin" Dulcinea, Sophia took nearly two months of lessons and coaching just to learn her four songs: *Aldonza, Dulcinea, It's All the Same ("One pair of arms is like another")* and, of course, *The Impossible Dream.* Meanwhile, writers were being hired and fired, director Peter Glenville was replaced by Arthur Hiller, there were tantrums and tie-ups by the Italian technicians, and Sophia and her co-star, Peter O'Toole, were thrown onto their own resources during the chaotic filming in Rome.

Sophia's approach was to rise above herself, treating her vehicle as though it were a screen test or audition upon which everything depended: "This is a challenge. I have never appeared in such a musical before. I sing a little, but I don't even know yet whether they will use my voice. . . . I hope I can do it, as it's very personal to me: to tell something by singing, to portray emotions in a song, this is a very beautiful thing."

O'Toole, on the other hand, gave up early. He pronounced his own lyrics "miserable" and some of Sophia's "true tripe," sleepwalked through his dual role of Miguel de Cervantes and Don Quixote de la Mancha "hoping for the best," and concentrated upon carousing without and conversing with his co-star. He called her "Scicolone" and told the world "I love that cow!", which somehow didn't offend her half as much as Sinatra's calling her a "broad." In a more reflective interview O'Toole informed Donald Zec: "My first impression was of a well-turned-out, extremely skillful piece of machinery. It was much later, when we began to work together, that I could see her for what she was. No crap, no artifice—just an extraordinary, sexually attractive lady."

When asked how Sophia's sex appeal worked on him, O'Toole replied: "Listen, there's so much of it there, who could ignore it? But it was not that bloody cliché of my falling in love with her. Just a straightforward, enormous sexual attraction."

Man of La Mancha was the most violent screen musical since *West Side Story.* In a crucial scene Quixote and Sancho Panza rescue Aldonza from a band of lusty muleteers and then the Don insists nobility demands that he go to his enemies to "raise them up and minister to their wounds." Touched by his idealism and declaring that they were her enemies, too, Aldonza refuses to let the old man wash their wounds but goes to tend them herself. While she is doing so, one of her patients clamps his arms and legs about her, precipitating a gang rape with whipping.

Sophia refused to let a stunt woman take her lumps for her and she defended herself so ably that, according to O'Toole, "she punched and kicked everybody at least once, and I can tell you she kneed more than one of those bums in the orchestras."*

That particular scene had another consequence later, that Sophia hadn't anticipated. At the age of three, her son Cipi had

*Orchestra seats are called *stalls* in Britain and, in this case, *orchestras* is rhyming slang for balls.

begun to notice that his mother was different from all other mothers and was asking "how" as well as "why." As part of his education, Sophia took him into the Villa Ponti's posh little cinema and screened the slow-moving, seemingly tame *Sunflower* for him "because he was in it when he was six months old and I wanted him to see himself, too. Just after the scene he was in, though, came a very powerful scene on a train where I screamed and threw myself on the floor." Cipi sat rigid, said nothing, and had nightmares for many a moon. Sophia vowed "no more of my movies for my son until he's older and can understand it's only make-believe," but, in the first flush of enthusiasm for *La Mancha*—already thinking of it as a musical version of a classic children like, and forgetting its many scary moments—she made "the big mistake" of inviting Cipi to watch it with her. After the rape scenes, Cipi went rigid again and had a bad night's sleep.

The next morning, however, the first thing Cipi said to Sophia was: "How is Jimmy Coco?"

As Sancho Panza, the rotund Jimmy Coco took a beating or two himself in La Mancha. But Cipi was making the effort—a hard one even for a child twice his age—to dissociate performers from their roles. A little later in the day, Cipi told his mother: "Those men who knocked you down; I saw what happened to them! They're all skeletons and you're fine. You're yourself."

No critic could have said more to please Sophia Loren. Having looked at something that disturbed him, her son had found a way to fight back or get over it and get on with life.

Telling me this, Sophia then summed up the *La Mancha* experience thusly: "It was a long, difficult, tiring film to make. Some people still aren't quite sure how the movie ended. But I can tell you it had a very happy ending for me. The day after filming was finished, I found out I was pregnant again."

CHAPTER 15

Meet Cute in Geneva

AFTER CIPI HAD BEEN FULFILLING HER MATERNAL NEEDS for some time, I once asked Sophia if motherhood had affected her acting in any way.

She took a minute to think that one over and then replied:

"Well, now that I'm one myself, I'd add a little to each mother I've played. The look you give to a child if you've got one, well, you have to have experienced it yourself. Otherwise, you can't be truthful when you're acting it. It's a special look that you give your own child: you just have another face. I never can repeat myself, anyway, but if I had *Two Women* to do over again, I'd do it differently—and maybe not get an Oscar."

In late Spring of 1972, almost as soon as she knew she was expecting another baby, Sophia Loren broke the news to her three-year-old son, Cipi. "I couldn't be as I was before," she explained to me later, "walking and jumping and running around with him. When he started asking why, I didn't want him to worry that I was ill."

The project was presented to Carlo Ponti, Jr., as a journey. "Cipi adores travel," Sophia said, "so just the idea of taking a plane to a place where he'd never been—except to be born— was enough to delight him. He started looking forward to it. So did I."

Anxiety was lower this time around. "After all, Cipi was right there. He was a reality to me," Sophia said. "It wasn't like when I was waiting for him and hoping and hoping because I had no child yet. Still, I had to follow the same routine as before: staying in bed most of the time, being very careful, taking the same kind of hormone treatments I'd had before. But the big difference was Cipi—and the time went by much more nicely and comfortably."

Even Sinibaldo Appolloni's ax-wielding attack on the Villa Ponti in September of 1972 had failed to faze Sophia. A few days thereafter, hewing to schedule in her sixth month, she had flown to Geneva with husband, son, and entourage of secretary, baby, nurse, and cook. The Pontis now owned an apartment in the building that housed Dr. de Watteville's offices on the Rue Charles Bonnet, so her regimen was less Spartan and she and her doctor could see each other often. (According to press reports, Carlo Ponti sat by Sophia's bedside and read her the verse of Giacomo Leopardi, Italy's outstanding poet of the nineteenth century.) Dr. de Watteville told her early that the delivery would be Caesarean. "Actually," Sophia told me, "we could have waited for a normal birth. But if you wait around until the last moment and then you have to do a Caesarean anyway, it's very bad and there can be complications that are better to avoid. So we decided to do it right away."

On the sixth morning of 1973, a Saturday, Sophia had a seven-pound-four-ounce son at Geneva Cantonal Hospital— and, shortly after 8:30 A.M., the anesthetized mother was informed "it's a boy." She told me later: "That moment is something that, even though you're mostly asleep, you remember each time. It just stays in your mind."

But she didn't like what happened next—for even when you're Sophia Loren, you must be subservient to hospital routine. Sleeping off her surgery, she woke toward 1 P.M. "and I really wanted to see the baby then and there. It happens to every mother. I wanted to know if he was okay, if he had everything. 'Why don't you bring me the baby?' I said. And I kept on asking why and they kept reassuring me, but they didn't bring me the baby. I became very suspicious. I stopped asking and started ordering: 'Don't tell me! Show me! Bring me my baby!' Instead, what did they bring me? A Polaroid picture of him taken a half-hour after he was born! It was beautiful, but I was mad. 'A mother wants her baby, not a picture of him!' I told them. After two hours, they brought him in—and everything was okay. I held him and I thought: 'This is a really pretty baby.'"

It took a few days before the Pontis gave their new son a name. "We called him Edoardo because it is a beautiful name, an old Neapolitan name," Sophia explained. "But it is also the first name of the author of *Marriage, Italian Style*."* The reason for the delay in naming the baby turned out to be that the Pontis had been expecting a girl and were going to name her after her mother just the way Cipi had been named after his father. They hadn't planned for the other contingency at all. "If you have a boy, you want to have a girl next," Sophia told me with a characteristic shrug. But she not only adjusted to fate, she enjoyed it and made a blessing of it: "Now that I have another boy, it'll be much better for Cipi because they can be better company for each other. They can really be friends. I like that! I like the idea of having two boys. No, I'm not at all sad. I wanted a girl, but when they told me it was a boy, I thought 'how marvelous!' So forget about Little Sophia. I'm sure I can only have boys now!"

This was the way Sophia was talking in early February, 1973, when Edoardo Ponti was just four weeks old—which is when my family and I flew from Vienna, where we had been living for a couple of years, to Geneva, where the Pontis were staying the winter.

My family was doing a little shopping before the stores closed, so I was the first to arrive and, after going up to Dr. De Watteville's reception room by mistake, I was directed to the Pontis' apartment half-a-flight downstairs.

"*Psssst!*" On the steps, I heard a hiss—and there was Sophia crouched beneath the stairwell and beckoning me to join her. I

---

*Eduardo de Filippo spells his first name with a *u*, however. The beloved Neapolitan actor-playwright is one of the only three natives known all over Italy by first name only. The other two are Sophia and Gina.

did so, wondering what plot was afoot. It certainly was a "meet cute" right out of one of De Sica's Neapolitan comedies.

Two women came out of Dr. de Watteville's offices and Sophia shushed me. We listened to them talking in French. Later, inside her spacious apartment, Sophia, who was wearing a green silk Dragon Lady tunic and black slacks and didn't yet have her figure back, admitted:

"Yes, I eavesdrop. Why? Because I envy them. They go up those stairs so full of hope, so anxious to conceive, and most of them do. If they have just the smallest chance, he sees to it that they have the babies—just as he saw to it that I had mine. And when these women come down, I like to listen to them talking on the steps. Then I'm doubly jealous, because it's no secret that I'm really in love with Dr. de Watteville. Just hearing them, I want attention from him, too."

The living room in which we were sitting still resembled the doctor's consulting room it had once been. A stiff leather chair stood behind an imposing glass desk. Enormous silver lamps made one feel as if any moment the command would come to "open your mouth and say *ahhhhh*"—an effect that was not at all neutralized by a shimmering silver sculpture hung behind a temporary-looking bar. To anybody who had ever visited the Villa Ponti in Marino, it was clear that their Geneva apartment had not been furnished by Sophia or Carlo or by any interior decorator they would ever hire. Its most imposing features were the double doors between rooms—insuring the privacy of the doctor-patient relationship—and Cipi, in fact, had discovered that with a pair of those doors shut, the dark and tiny vestibule formed between them was a wonderful playroom for racing matchbox autos, playing hide-and-seek, and crouching to pop up like a jack-in-the-box and frighten unwary adults. He called each of these areas "my little house in Geneva."

The Pontis' plans for a centralized de Watteville Fertility Clinic were already a dream of the past, Sophia told me with genuine sorrow:

"There were problems here and problems there, so unfortunately, we had to forget about the whole thing. It just couldn't be done. We couldn't get permits to put laboratories and technical facilities all in one place. Carlo spent so much time for nothing and so did Dr. de Watteville. It went on for two years. It was maddening. The authorities and some Swiss doctors, too, they just didn't like the idea of us having something that wasn't here before and that they didn't have. The details I don't know; only the disappointments after my husband spent so much time with the architects, the drawings, the plans, the doctor, everything! But at the moment we were ready to do it, we couldn't."

Sophia sighed, but then she said: "Many of those women I see on the staircase are Italian. And I comfort myself that, even though Dr. de Watteville was already well-known, the publicity about how I had my first baby brought them here."

My family arrived, and Sophia took us up to see the new prince, who was sleeping. Fairer-skinned and rounder than Cipi had been as a baby, Edoardo (soon to be called "Dodo" by all but Cipi, who didn't believe in baby talk the way his elders did) had less hair than his brother ever had, but what he had was reddish. Since we couldn't see him in action just yet, we had to take Sophia's word that "he has blue eyes at the moment. Of course, all babies do, but he may keep them like Cipi did. Yes, I think this baby is going to grow up with light hair, very fair complexion, and blue-gray eyes. You'll see! When he cries, it's a high-pitched cry: not like a girl, but like a lamb. Yes, he has a lamb cry. Otherwise, he has a nice deep voice. How does he look to you?"

What can one say of a four-week-old baby one has just glimpsed sleeping? All I could reply was: "He looks like a very businesslike baby to me."

"Businesslike?" Sophia repeated, her eyes narrowing.

"Yes," I said quickly. "All his motions, even while sleeping, are businesslike. He's busy being a baby, busy doing all his baby things, busy making the most of his role as the baby of the family."

I was drawing upon our experience with our younger daughter, but this satisfied Sophia: "Ah, they're nice. I think it's the best thing that's happened in my life—having children. It's

great. It's really the only thing that counts—the only thing." By
now she was purring, but just from this wary exchange, I held
my breath as I thought of what an unhappy woman this might
have been if she hadn't found the right doctor in the nick of
time. After all, she was thirty-eight when Edoardo was born.

Tiptoeing out, however, I asked Sophia if sibling rivalry had
asserted itself yet with Cipi.

"We did have a little problem when I came out of the hospital," Sophia said. "Cipi speaks Italian and English with Carlo
and me, but he speaks German with his nurse Ruth or when he
is angry. He finds German the best language to get angry in.
Well, when I came home here from the hospital, the first thing
he said to me was *'Geh weg!'* [German for "Go away!"] Even
while his eyes were filling with tears of relief to see me again, he
kept on saying *'Geh weg! Geh weg!'*

"What a nice greeting!" Sophia had exclaimed, taking it in
stride. But nurse Ruth was not amused. And when Cipi—who'd
always been a good eater—refused to have dinner that night
and had to be fed, little by little, like an infant rather than a lad
who had just turned four, Ruth told his mother: "This is very
strange. When you were away, he was just fine."

"That's impossible!" Sophia had snapped back. "What are
you talking about, 'he was just fine'? I was away for two weeks
and now that I'm back, he's showing me he resents me and also
that he thinks he wants the same babying Edoardo's getting.
That's perfectly healthy."

Now, she reported, Cipi's sibling problem was already under
control: "We got him out of it just by not paying too much
attention to the way he was acting. We gave him what he
wanted to eat when he wanted it and didn't force him to eat
when he didn't. Appetite, it always comes back! He was going to
cry and make a big scene about not eating, but this was ridiculous and we never gave him the chance to think we'd take it
seriously. We just went on with it and now he's back to normal
again. You have to *play* with a child. Otherwise, his every *little*
problem becomes a real problem."

The conversation turned back to Edoardo. "Already, he

starts to see and he follows my image," Sophia reported. "I don't know what he sees, but he sees something—because he really looks at me when he's awake. And he starts to make little sounds already: not just crying, but tiny sounds. He starts to live! As soon as he hears the door, if he's crying, he stops crying. Then, if nothing happens, he starts to cry again. He already knows the meaning of the door. When the light goes on, he waits—and then, if you don't pick him up or touch him, he goes back to crying. One month old! Habits, habits, he starts with the habits already! We are all obsessed with habits."

Sophia 1973 was vehemently opposed to habits, while Sophia 1969 had told me how Cipi needed to be "surrounded by serenity and calm. He has to start having habits—a routine that he likes." But she had learned from experience that "if Cipi ate always with the same person, then he couldn't eat with anyone else. If he went to bed with me or Ruth in his room, then he couldn't sleep without one of us. Or, if he was not surrounded by the same people, he was a problem. He wanted to be only with his mother or his nurse, not with anybody else—and that's bad, very bad. He became very dependent—and oh boy, was it ever a tragedy when I had to go to work or just from Marino into Rome for a day!

"Habits are terrible things. They're bad for grownups, too. I remember how we were entertaining Alec Guinness in Marino and I asked him: 'What would you like to have in the morning?' And he said: 'Breakfast? Well, Sophia, I don't always eat in the morning. Sometimes I do and sometimes I don't. When I do, I'll have tea one morning and coffee another morning and a light Continental breakfast one day and a big English breakfast another day. I just don't want to wake up one morning and find I've come down with a bad case of habit. *That* would scare me.'

"What Alec said seemed strange to me at the time—but now I think I understand."

CHAPTER 16

The Gift of a Naïf

WHILE WE WERE THERE MEETING BABY EDOARDO, his four-year-old brother Cipi had been having a tantrum. From time to time, we could hear him proclaiming in his four languages—German, Italian, English, and French—that "I want my *Naïf*."

It turned out that Cipi was referring to a sentimental work of Yugoslav religious art in a Geneva store window. Four years earlier, he had been sent a couple of these primitive works for being born—one of Rumanian origin; the other Slavic—and since then they had become a motif, if not a mania. Sophia told me there were now eleven in Cipi's room in Marino.

He had spotted this particular Naïve painting two weeks earlier, fallen in love with it at first sight, and pressured his parents for it from then on. This morning, his father, who was leaving for New York, had gone out to make a change in his plane reservation. But Cipi had guessed that Carlo Ponti, Sr., was about to surprise Carlo Ponti, Jr., with the coveted Naïve. Just before I'd arrived, however, Carlo, Sr., had come home empty-handed, and Cipi had erupted in the howls we were hearing.

Now, on his way out to Cointrin Airport, Carlo Ponti, Sr., wearing tan topcoat and blue beret, had concluded hastily that the only way to console his son was to "buy it for him! What are they asking for it?"

Sophia named a sum in Swiss francs that came to a little more than $850 at the time.

"They're robbers!" Ponti exclaimed. "Buy it if you can get it for half." Then, with a quick round of introductions and handshakes (and curtsies by my daughters), he was gone, and secretary Ines Brusci was dispatched to the antique shop.

"Do they have Show-and-Tell at Cipi's nursery school?" I asked Sophia. "Can you image him producing a $400 Naïve on Monday?"

"No," said Sophia. "It wouldn't happen. Because Cipi isn't a collector and he doesn't think of the *Naïf* as a painting. He's grown up surrounded by art. His father and I talk a lot about art. A *Naïf* painting is something he likes to look at—for his own pleasure, not to feel important, not to spread it around that this is his."

Half an hour later, Ines returned, bearing only her umbrella. Cipi had joined us by then, but now tears the size of raindrops began rolling down his cheeks and he ran from the room.

"It wasn't in the window when I got there," Ines explained, "so I went inside and the robbers told me they didn't know where it was or whether it had been sold or not. But I know what they're doing! They know the Ponti child wants it, so they'll hide it a little to drive the price up, not down."

"Then they're not clever robbers," Sophia said firmly, "because now they'll get nothing for nothing." With that, she excused herself and went to comfort Cipi.

"Of course he's inconsolable," she said when she returned ten minutes later. "But, at times like this, I'm glad I have two boys. My sister has two girls and I've watched them closely. A boy will forget a setback like this."

We were taking an eight-day ski week holiday in Caux, high above the palm trees of Montreux on Lake Geneva, and Sophia invited us to stop in again on our way home. In between, one weekday afternoon, I came down the mountain for a visit to Villeneuve, where the painter Oskar Kokoschka wanted to tell me, with slightly grudging admiration, "how Carlo Ponti smelled a rat and saved his son" from a fate worse than fame.

Oskar Kokoschka? OS-kar Ko-KOSCH-ka! The name rings out like a hammer on an anvil or, said a few times in rapid succession, it sounds like some sort of Slavic sneeze. But Oskar

Kokoschka, now ninety-two and still painting, is nobody to be sneezed at, for he is one of the towering talents of the twentieth century: painter, playwright, storyteller, teacher, poet and philosopher, genius and colossus. The name Kokoschka—sometimes just the initials "O.K."—is a household word in Central Europe, though less well-known elsewhere in the West (except to museums, connoisseurs, and dealers, who pay up to $150,-000 for one of his paintings*). Spanning all the major artistic movements of three or four generations, Mr. O.K. influenced and even sired a remarkable number of ideas whose times have come and, in some cases, gone. Born in Austria, he was the father of German Expressionist drama and author of an autobiography, *My Life,* containing some of the finest German prose written in this century. He was a friend of Rilke and Thomas Mann as well as the embittered lover of the late Alma Mahler, the composer Gustav's widow who went on to marry the architect Walter Gropius (founder of Bauhaus), and the novelist Franz Werfel *(Song of Bernadette).*

In February of 1973, a few weeks before his eighty-seventh birthday, Mr. O.K. was painting like some angry, inspired demon—slashing away at a nearly ceiling-high Crucifixion scene inside his tidy little green-and-white house not far from the lakeside castle at Chillon of whose prisoners Lord Byron sang: "Look at this!" Kokoschkca commanded, pointing to an apple-cheeked Roman soldier who was prodding that Christ on the Cross in His ribs. "The soldier's job is just to see that Christ dies slowly, but he's bored and so he has to poke Him. . . . I call this *Ecce Homineus,* 'such are men,' not *Ecce Homo,* 'such is man.' Men are beasts and all that thousands of years of civilization have added is only a little varnish, a little clothing, on the beast." Then, having drawn his moral, the compact, jut-jawed Kokoschka asked his Czech wife Olda to serve tea while they both told me how a combination of circumstances had brought

*Five of his works are in Chicago's Art Institute, three in Washington's Phillips Collection, and five are in New York: four at the Museum of Modern Art and one at the Guggenheim.

them into contact with Sophia Loren and, for awhile, into combat alongside Carlo Ponti, Sr.

Once upon a time, a decade-and-a-half ago, there was a West German powdered-milk mogul with creatively commercial—or perhaps commercially creative—pretensions. He nursed a vision of commissioning Pablo Picasso to paint a portrait of the child that Jacqueline Kennedy, then the First Lady of the United States, was expecting at the time. But Picasso ignored the millionaire milkman and the baby died before the mogul could even approach the Kennedys. Soon thereafter, John Kennedy was no more and Jackie was no longer First Lady, so the German milk mogul had to put his own artistic vision on the shelf—until Cipi Ponti was born at the end of 1968.

This time around, the milkman took a devious route. Acting as his intermediary, the Marlborough Gallery in London approached Kokoschka with the "news" that Mr. and Mrs. Carlo Ponti wanted him to paint their son. Marlborough then contacted the Pontis and told them Kokoschka wanted to paint a portrait of Cipi. Everybody was enthusiastic all around and several sittings were arranged. Cipi quickly took to "the big boy who teaches me to paint," while Sophia was delighted and amused to be in the company of an octogenarian rake who always looked her over with a young man's eye.

Sophia's and Cipi's reports on their sessions with Mr. O.K. were so glowing that Carlo Ponti, Sr., decided he wanted to surprise them by presenting them with the finished portrait. He called London, ready to bargain, and asked Marlborough to name a price. He was told curtly that the work was not for sale. Mystified and frustrated, Ponti phoned Kokoschka—and found the artist a trifle perplexed, too, for he'd just had a call from London, out of the blue, telling him he could not sell the portrait to Ponti. Artist and producer compared notes about who had sought out whom in the first place. Then Ponti, with a few well-placed phone calls to his worldwide network of contacts, quickly ascertained who was behind the masquerade and why he wanted a Cipi-by-Kokoschka.

"Cipi on milk labels?!" Sophia moaned when she heard.*

"Kokoschka on a million cans of milk!" Mr. O.K. exclaimed, with a trace of artist's ambivalence.

Ponti called in his lawyers. After many threats, claims, and counterclaims, a settlement was reached: Kokoschka finished the portrait of Cipi, which the German milk mogul paid handsomely for, but donated directly to a museum in Munich with a stipulation that commercial reproduction was *verboten*. And the Pontis wound up with a couple of Kokoschka's preliminary drawings of Cipi, which they cherish even more than their Canalettos.

From every experience, Sophia is able to draw a positive lesson—and from this episode, it was Mr. O.K.'s currently unfashionable, but visually unerring, philosophy of art. "All children are born geniuses," Kokoschka told Sophia more than once, "but life teaches them to lose their genius."

"But how?" Sophia asked.

"It begins with parents," Kokoschka replied, "and goes on with teachers."

When we revisited Sophia-and-sons in Geneva on our way back to Vienna the following weekend, I asked her how she was applying the wisdom of Kokoschka.

"Whenever Cipi has wanted to paint," she answered, "I have always encouraged, never disparaged—and once I have him in a room where he can't harm anything important, I never supervise or criticize. And I never force him to paint when he doesn't want to.

*In 1978, however, Sophia Loren was not averse to taking a seven-figure sum (to be donated to charity) to make a TV commercial for Filter Fresh purifiers of drinking water, a rival of Teledyne Water Pik's Instapure product. Asked "Why Sophia?" an official of the Ted Bates advertising agency replied: "We want the visibility. And she's highly credible, speaks very well, has done cookbooks and is known as a housewife and a mother as well as an actress."

I asked Cipi if he had any paintings he wanted to show us. He hung his head shyly and blushed a little. "Don't worry," Sophia assured us, "when you come to Marino this spring, I'll show you his little museum." Now Cipi ran from the room and came back a minute later proudly clutching a gold frame containing the slickest Naïve painting I've ever seen.

"Did YOU paint that?" I asked him incredulously.

Cipi giggled. This time, it was Sophia's turn to blush. "I bought it from the robbers," she admitted.

"For how much?" I asked.

She named a figure that came to five hundred dollars and added: "I don't know what Carlo will say when he finds out."

CHAPTER 17

Photos by Sophia Loren

IN THE SPRING OF 1973, when the American family Levy trooped into the art museum that was the Villa Ponti's downstairs living room, shortly before noon, I admired two new, but very old, Picassos that had appeared on the wall since we were there last, two-and-a-half years earlier. A barefoot Sophia poured from a decanter her own white wine: "We make several barrels a year: a simple wine, but what tastes better than wine you've seen growing before your own eyes?"

Enter Cipi, almost on cue—followed by his efficient Swiss nurse, Ruth, who reported that Edoardo was still sleeping and our lunch would have to be timed to end at 2 P.M., when the three-month-old baby's next feeding was due. Ruth also repeated a dialogue she'd just had in the garden with Cipi, who, ever since Edoardo's arrival, had been brooding about how people and plants grow. Ruth had mentioned that "if you put a potato under the earth, more potatoes grow."

After a couple of minutes, Cipi had said: "Why don't we put *Ed-do-ard-do* under the earth?"

A trifle shocked and ever on the alert for latent hostility, Ruth had asked: "Why?"

"Because if we plant *Ed-do-ard-do*," Cipi had responded, "maybe we get many *Ed-do-ard-dos*."

We all laughed with delight. "He wanted to plant Edoardo!" Sophia exclaimed. Cipi, blushing, buried his face in the lap of his mother's elegant purple slacks as she turned to us and said: "So much for sibling rivalry!"

Actually, she added when Ruth left, there had been a recent sign of it. Cipi had complained that when he'd walked in on Ruth addressing Edoardo in sweet Italian baby talk, she had turned to Cipi with a sharp Germanic *"Was willst du?"* ("What do you want?") And Cipi had asked his mother: "Why does Ruth talk to me this way when I haven't done anything wrong?"

Ruth would never do it again, we were assured. But Sophia recognized, too, that she must prepare her older son for the differences between how adults talk to children and how they talk to infants. So she and Cipi had taken turns playing all the roles in an improvised playlet whose only lines were *"Ciao, Edoardino!"*, *"Was willst du?"*, and *"Goo-goo!"*

To Geneva two months earlier, we had brought Cipi some leather shorts from Austria—and now, for our visit to Marino, he was wearing them. This time, we had brought a pair of embroidered knee socks to go with his Lederhosen. But knowing that small boys don't always adore clothing as a gift and having learned from playing with him in Geneva that Cipi collected matchbox autos, we'd also brought him a small, inexpensive matchbox bulldozer with a tiny plastic man in the driver's seat.

"I—don't—have—one!" Cipi exclaimed in English—and we could have hoped for no more fervent thanks from The Boy Who Had Everything, including a dozen Naïve paintings in his upstairs bedroom. Cipi was clearly delighted with the toy bulldozer as he ran it around his mother's lap and the furry pouf she was perched on, then along a priceless marble tabletop and across the brown wall-to-wall carpeting. "It—goes—faster!" Cipi squealed. "I—wanted—this!"

"Isn't the little plastic man small?" my wife remarked.

"No," said Cipi. "I'm a giant." And I was delighted to see for myself that, unlike so many carefully guarded children of celebrities and statesmen, this little boy knew how to play! (A few years earlier, as a young father in Manhattan, I'd encountered John F. Kennedy, Jr., in a Central Park playground and, after watching little John-John's hesitant overtures with a pink rubber ball toward other children and even such an adult stranger as myself, I'd realized with dismay that the boy didn't know how to play.)*

Making whirring and grinding and smashing noises beneath us, Cipi went on toying with the bulldozer while his mother spoke about "spoiling my children. It's a question of nature. Is it spoiling to give your child anything he asks for if they're things he can have? I don't think so. See how much he appreciates the little toy you gave him! To me, this is proof that children with good natures *cannot* be spoiled if they are spoiled the right way. I could never spoil my baby against his nature; I could only spoil him in the right way because I know *him* and I know his character. Both my little boys live in very normal and natural surroundings."

I started to cast an ironic gaze around the Renaissance sumptuousness in which the Pontis dwelled, but my eyes were drawn to little Cipi running his matchbox bulldozer through all this splendor. And I saw what Sophia saw: a small boy, growing up nicely, if comfortably, within a childhood that was, externally, just as unrealistic as his mother's childhood was all too realistic. Sophia was ahead of me; she had thought it all through:

"You can never spoil a child with too much love. Some parents *think* they're spoiling their children by wanting them to have the little things they didn't have during their childhood."

"Yes," I agreed. "For me as a boy, going to a movie was a treat. For my daughters, it's not."

"But you're talking about more than thirty years ago!" Sophia said. "Now they have movies in their own home—television!—and, anyway, these are other times. Their childhood and your childhood are two different levels of existence. Look at me! Sometimes, when Cipi is naughty, I feel like saying to him:

*Nevertheless, a 1978 *Forum* Magazine poll listing "The World's Ten Most Admired Mothers" ranked Sophia Loren seven notches behind Jacqueline Kennedy Onassis. The list: 1. First Lady Rosalynn Carter. 2. her mother-in-law, "Miz" Lillian Carter. 3. Jackie. 4. Ex-First Lady Betty Ford. 5. singer Cher Bono Allman. 6. tennis star Evonne Goolagong Cawley. 7. Beatlefrau Linda Eastman McCartney. 8. singing actress Shirley Jones Cassidy. 9. singing actress Diana Ross Silberstein. 10. Sophia.

'If I'd done *that* to *my* mother, she'd have thrown a bucketful of water in my face.' I feel like saying it, but I don't. I'm more patient with my children than my mother was. For a while, she had me taking piano lessons when I was a kid. If I'd continued, I'd probably still be black-and-blue today, because whenever I made a mistake, my mother would hit me on the head.

"Not that my mother wasn't patient, but she was living in a different atmosphere what with the war and so many problems that I just don't have now: money and where are we going to find something to eat—big problems that I was hardly allowed to be aware of. So if I used to do something bad to my sister— and we were terrible children; we fought all the time!—it was cold water in the face for me and I'd learn my lesson.

"But I also learned that there were other ways to drive my mother crazy. She'd scold me and I wouldn't speak to her, wouldn't answer her for a whole day, just stay silent and look at her. Only now do I recognize how terrible I was and how hard she worked to be good to Maria and me. I re-live it when my own child does something a little like what I did and I know how bad it makes me feel and then I know, for the first time, how bad I must have made my mother feel."

"Lunch is served!" a servant named Marcello announced. Sophia led Cipi and us into an ornate dining room with pan-eled, flowered ceiling and grand-opera chandelier. The meal— served by a waiter in white gloves—was green noodles in a tomato sauce as the *pasta* course; a veal roulade stuffed with eggs and ham; tiny roasted potatoes, green peas, fresh country bread, a green salad, and a hazelnut napoleon. Cipi sat to So-phia's right. Sometimes she fed him while he was busy maneu-vering his new bulldozer up and down the dining table. Such was Sophia's intensity that all six of us shared a sense of triumph when Cipi finished everything on his plate.

That was the meal at which Sophia defined starvation for me (*"when your stomach is empty . . . you feel like fainting . . . you'd like to eat . . . the empty table"*) and remarked: "Even now, food has a great importance to me. When I can sit at a table and eat dishes I like with nice friends—for me it's a holiday."

"Do you ever have a weight problem?" I wondered.

"No, if I ever have to lose a couple of pounds, I simply skip dinner. Or, when my husband is here, I prepare something he likes that I don't—like steaks and salads. Me, I've always loved *pasta* and eaten it by the ton. When I first came to Rome, I couldn't leave anything on the plate—no matter how much I didn't want it—because, after a few years of starvation in the war, it was still a sin to throw food away. Besides, for awhile, I needed more weight and spaghetti was cheap."

Sophia's 1968 confinement to the Geneva Intercontinental had resulted not only in Cipi, but also—with the ubiquitous screenwriter Basilio Franchina and a gourmet colleague, Vincenzo Buonassisi, acting as literary midwives—in a handsome 1972 cookbook called *In the Kitchen with Love,* by Sophia Loren, a compilation of her favorite recipes and her family's. In its pages Sophia admits that she prefers fried pizzas to oven-baked and that her sister fries them better; she also advocates eating pizza with one's hands and insists, too, that chicken wings, French fries, and fruit have more flavor when taken by finger rather than fork. When the book was published (by Rizzoli in Milan and Doubleday in New York, among others), Sophia gave a copy of the Italian edition to her cook Livia, who never consulted it beyond the photos and the autograph page. "Why should I?" said Livia. "I already know how to cook." And Sophia knows how to keep her help. When I raved about the homemade dessert, which was not from her cookbook, Sophia immediately told Marcello to convey my compliments to Livia.

Most of the table talk at lunch was not about food, however, but about photography and freaks. Not that Sophia was a "photography freak" like Gina Lollobrigida (who has published a couple of collections of her work), but she said there were "periods when I like to shoot pictures. I use my secretary's Canon, which I find especially good for close-ups. I like to get people's faces, capture a movement or an expression. I'm not interested in backgrounds or taking pictures of rooms and buildings. Maybe it's because I'm an actress."

Right after saying this, Sophia excused herself from the table for a minute. She came back with some thirty black-and-white photos of her children playing together or crying or bathing— with only an occasional adult intruding in the picture. "I know these are not special pictures," she said, almost but not quite apologetically, "but they're mine and, for me, they're special."

They were much more than that. Those photos by Sophia Loren were all sharp, loving, and more candid than Tazio Secchiaroli's or Alfred Eisenstaedt's or any I'd ever seen of the Ponti family. "If she could only photograph herself," I found myself musing, for if these pictures had one common flaw, it was that none of them showed *Mrs.* Ponti, who went on to say:

"I like to take pictures of babies. I like children because they're so honest and they don't know I'm shooting pictures of them especially when they're newborn, so they really are themselves. When they've reached the age of three or four, they already know. They make faces. It's fun, too, but not as honest anymore. So I keep a camera close by and try to get the natural moments.

"My husband is another matter. He doesn't know how to pose before a camera and he detests it. He does things that he never does normally and naturally. He poses badly. If I see I can make a good picture of Carlo, I just shoot it without asking."

We talked about women photographers. I mentioned that I used to collaborate with Diane Arbus, best known for her intimate renditions of freaks. Sophia wanted to know everything about her and how "Deeyann," at forty-six, had slashed her wrists and died in her Greenwich Village bathtub less than two years earlier. "July was always the worst month of the year for Deeyann," was all I could tell Sophia, "and July of 1971 was worse than any other."

In a rare public outburst, Carlo Ponti once wrote of Sophia and himself:

We are freaks. Our world is different and we have to lead a different life. We are the makers of dreams for those other, normal people who may look askance at our way of life. Actually, our one great ambition is to be like them, undistinguishable. But how difficult for the well-known to achieve that state of blissful anonymity! Our privacy as a couple is always threatened, and consequently we move from country to country or across the ocean, from house to flat and back again, in the effort to safeguard it. We don't hold others responsible for this lack of privacy. The fault, if any, lies in ourselves, or rather in our chosen professions. An actress and a producer are nothing but freaks. Not by choice, but by implication. That is what people want us to be.*

In that day's newspaper was an Associated Press newsphoto of Mihaly Mezaros, now known as Michu, the smallest man in the world (thirty-three inches, twenty-two pounds), arriving from Budapest at Kennedy Airport in New York to join the Ringling Brothers Circus. My younger daughter had clipped it and now she showed it first to Cipi, then to Sophia.

There was nothing pious about Sophia's reaction. First she giggled. Then she exclaimed: "Why, he's even smaller than Cipi!" And she added: "It's a fascinating life—the world of the circus."

"It must be dreadful," my wife said, "to realize that everyone's growing bigger and you're not."

But Sophia said: "It's just something you have to learn to live with—like anything else."

Sophia had surprised me. I reminded her: "The Italian doctors told you that you couldn't have babies, but you didn't try to live with *that.*"

"Because, even though I'd lost three of them," † she replied,

---

*From "At Home with Sophia," an article by Carlo Ponti in the September 1962 issue of Huntington Hartford's handsome, but now defunct, *Show* Magazine.

† When pinned down, Sophia will refer to "only" two miscarriages, but she has, several times, alluded to three in conversations with me. Most, though not all, New York *Times* and Time-Life library clippings cite three miscar-

"it didn't seem natural for me not to have babies. I *knew,* I didn't know why, but I knew I could. No, you're right that I don't accept expert advice blindly. And I try to make things work if I can. I accept Nature—but only after everything Human has been tried. If I put all of myself into something and I don't succeed, then it's impossible for me and I won't fight fate."

Hearing this, I recognized that whatever Sophia's fate might have been she would have made the best and the most of it.

Immediately after lunch, Sophia went upstairs to feed Edoardo and we had the privilege of eavesdropping (with permission) on an intercom that Sophia kept in the living room to monitor the baby's needs whenever nobody was with him.

Edoardo's feeding, however, was only background music as I browsed through Sophia's lovingly kept archives of *Our Baby's First Seven Years,* two handsome scrapbooks categorized and issued by Chicago Lying-In Hospital. "A fan sent me the first one," Sophia had told me, "so of course we had to buy the second for Edoardo." It is from these books that Sophia can always document such casual assertions as "Edoardo smiled his first smile at five weeks; with Cipi, it took two-and-one-half months." My own favorite entry, in both volumes, was on the page reserved for "Newspaper Headlines on Date of Birth." There, Sophia had scrawled: "See separate scrapbooks."

The pictures in both volumes showed scenes any parent would want to remember: christenings, birthdays, trips, and outings as well as the everyday doings that are a mother's delight. But the photos weren't just by Sophia Loren, but by Lord Snowdon (Anthony Armstrong-Jones, ex-husband of Britain's Princess Margaret), Peter Sellers (an excellent photographer, too, who once filmed Sophia for *Vogue),* Otto Storch, Eisenstaedt, and of course, Tazio. And the beaming grown-ups in

---

riages (1963, 1965, and 1967 are the dates when given) and the New York *Post,* which has always tended toward excess, cited four on its "Woman in the News" page of January 4, 1969, as did *Newsweek* (January 27, 1969) and the 1973 edition of Earl Blackwell's *Celebrity Register.*

the photos included Dr. Christiaan Barnard, Marcello Mastroianni, and Marshall Tito of Yugoslavia, on whose Adriatic island of Brioni the Pontis have vacationed for as long as a month at a time. Over the intercom I asked Sophia what she was doing in one of the Tito photos and she replied: "I'm slicing a pear for Cipi after cooking for the Titos. A sweet man! Tito adores *pasta,* but the first time I cooked for him I didn't know what kind of spaghetti sauce he likes, so I made four different kinds and he ate all four of them. Then I cooked some eggplants for him. He helped me in the kitchen, tasting all the way, and then, as if I hadn't made enough food, he cooked a wonderful big fish for us! After that meal, only Cipi was hungry!"

A color picture of Cipi and his mother with the Titos was signed by the Yugoslav dictator and his wife (now estranged) Jovanka Brod. "I asked my secretary to take this picture and the Titos to autograph it," Sophia explained, "because it will be very nice for Cipi to have as a souvenir when he grows up. Some day Marshal Tito will have to give Edoardo equal time."

Now the new prince was brought down to greet us, with a satisfied burp. Edoardo wore an oversized white-and-blue gown suitable for a christening. "He won't have his christening till June," Sophia informed us, "but we decided to let him wear this while it fits." Indeed, Edoardo had doubled in size since we'd seen him in Geneva months earlier. "He's more of a person, too," I noted aloud to Sophia, whose arm was cradling the back of Edoardo's head while she petted it. As though discovering it for the first time, Sophia showed us "how perfectly formed his head is in back—like a drawing."

When Edoardo had been handed over to the nurse and our kids had gone off to hunt the ibis, we talked a little more about photography and Sophia suddenly offered to take my picture. Without further ado, she led me over to a living-room window seat, above which a Canon lay casually on the ledge. "This is Ines' camera," Sophia said, "but she and I use it. We're both alike in not knowing the first thing about how to take a picture, but we shoot so many that one of them is bound to come out.

Besides, cameras nowadays are so perfect that you can make all kinds of mistakes. That's why I prefer black-and-white to color; there's more contrast and Tazio Seccharoli can do more in his lab to fix up our mistakes."

Then Sophia invited me to take off my shoes and socks, sit down sideways on the window seat, and stretch my legs along it, while she, barefoot from the beginning of our day together, did the same from the opposite end. When the two of us were facing each other and my feet touched hers, she picked up the camera, aimed it at my face, checked the distance but hardly focused it, and clicked off half-a-dozen close-ups. I knew right away that the emotions on my face would be unique—as would those of any man sitting foot-to-foot with Sophia Loren.

After I'd had a few solo rounds of posing, Sophia invited my wife to squeeze in beside me. Weeks later, after Tazio had developed and printed them, Sophia sent us a set of prints— and they've appeared with her credit line on various editions of my books, in *McCall's* Magazine, the Viennese newspaper *Die Gemeinde,* and elsewhere. Each time, Sophia's fee has been a contribution sent directly by the publisher to the United Nations Children's Fund (UNICEF) in her name. A few of my readers have complained about one or another "Photo by Sophia Loren" accompanying my work. The gist of their criticism is: "That's a nice picture of you by Sophia, but I'd much rather look at a photo of Sophia by you."

Back in Geneva, Sophia had promised to show us "Cipi's museum" when we came to Marino. When the girls rejoined us, Sophia marched us up the secret spiral staircase that is right before one's eyes in that dazzling living room but, like Poe's purloined letter, tends to escape the eye. Past an upstairs living room, through a couple of bedrooms, down a hall, turn right, and we came upon Cipi with his playmate David Secchiaroli (Tazio's son) watching *Rumpelstiltskin* on TV.

We watched with them for awhile and then went down the hall to look in on Edoardo sleeping in splendor under a gold-and-silver Russian icon in a room also adorned by no fewer than forty-seven Cipis: water colors and finger paintings, all framed, all certifying to definite artistic talent.

Sophia was proudest of "Cipi's Blue Period—particularly this one here, which is all blue, but in the middle there's this hand, just a print of Cipi's hand, *do you see it?,* and it looks so nice! When you see these things that children do, you really see what Naïve painting is. They are so beautiful, so innocent, which their *Naïfs* are not anymore." As a case in point, she cited the Yugoslav Naïve bought from the gnomes of Geneva and now installed in Cipi's bedroom.

It was nearly time to go. Sophia would soon rejoin Cipi, feed Edoardo again, take supper with Cipi, and go to bed: "Yes, to bed. We lead such a quiet life, even when Carlo is here. Neither of us has time for *la dolce vita.* We don't do strange things and we don't give strange parties for strange people.

"I've been back from Geneva for a month now and I've gone into Rome just once—to have lunch with my sister. I'm more active when I'm working: I like to talk a lot and I like to play cards. But when I'm not working, I like to be by myself. Before we had Cipi, I used to stay in bed and watch TV. But I don't anymore. Cipi is an early riser; he wakes up at five-thirty and plays his little carillon. Yes, it wakes me, but I don't mind because I start feeding Edoardo at six o'clock and it's such a nice sound to awaken to. Even when the baby goes over to the bottle, which will be soon, I'll keep much the same hours until I start work." She was scheduled to start in late spring on *The Journey,* with Richard Burton.

"What do you do with the day when you don't have visitors?" I asked her.

"Oh, I have to follow what happens with the children and take part in it. Even with help, I'm on hand a good eighty percent of the time. And then, in a big old house like this, there is a lot to do. Every day, something breaks. It's easier for us to get repairmen than it might be for others; they all want to come out and see the place, see me, see the children. They do their work, but then they like to hang around or leave something a little unfinished or a little wrong so they can come back a hundred times. So it's better for me to stay with them all the time they're working and be nice to them, but see that they do the job right once and for all.

"Working or not working, by eight o'clock in the evening, I'm dead. I'm in bed at eight. I could go to bed before then, but I'm ashamed to. If people call up at eight-thirty in the evening and they're told 'Sophia's gone to bed,' what will they think? So I answer letters in bed and take calls until nine."

Knowing that in Italy, where kids stay up to midnight, TV's prime-time is only beginning when Sophia goes to sleep, my wife asked Sophia if she ever stayed up later to watch a special program.

"No," Sophia told Valerie. "I don't look at TV much any more because, as soon as I turn it on, I fall asleep. But I think that's any tired mother's reflex, don't you?"

CHAPTER 18

The Summer of 1973

DEATH AND DECAY HUNG LIKE A FUNERAL PALL over what proved to be Vittorio De Sica's final film, *The Journey*. It started with the story, based on a Pirandello novel, of a turgid love affair between an ailing Sicilian widow (Sophia) who loves, but cannot marry, her brother-in-law (Richard Burton). Sophia has seldom looked lovelier than she does in this slow-moving Eastman-color voyage from village to Palermo to Naples to an inevitable death in Venice on the eve of World War I, but the viewer may never have spent a longer ninety-five minutes in a movie house. Still, that particular ordeal is a picnic compared to the marital breakup and medical tragedy that were visited upon the Villa Ponti even before filming ever started. They were not Sophia's, admittedly, but distressingly close to home.

Sophia was preparing to go on location in Sicily and my family and I were packing to fly to Japan for the summer of 1973 when I phoned her in late June to exchange *bon voyages*. Even then, a conversation otherwise gleaming with anticipation took a slightly morbid turn when Sophia warned me not to eat any raw fish in Japan.

Being a devotee of *sushi* and *sashimi*, I couldn't promise that, but thought I would handle it diplomatically by saying: "Well, if I'm coming back through Rome in October, I'll take you out for mussels."

"Don't you dare!" Sophia said.

"Why not?" I asked. "Did I say something wrong?"

"I'd tell you why not," Sophia replied cryptically, "but it would ruin your trip."

Nevertheless, when I did see her in October, I reminded her of our chat but, by this time, I didn't need any warning. A fierce epidemic of cholera in Naples had been attributed, in part, to contaminated mussels.

"I wasn't surprised," Sophia told me over tea in Marino. "I grew up on the Bay of Naples and I used to see where the mussels grew up. It was terrible!"

"Where did they grow?" I asked.

"Always near the sewers. I ate them then, but only when I was starving; never now. And I always knew I was right. The other day, on TV, they showed an experiment. They put a mussel into a glass of filthy water. After two hours, the water was perfectly clear. All the filth had gone into the mussel. Now who wants to eat that? They absorb everything. Everything!

"Don't ever eat mussels—or oysters.* You can get hepatitis from both of them. I love fish, but I never even serve the children fresh fish at home: only frozen fish, *always* frozen fish. Especially at the seaside because there they sell you something they call fresh fish, but it's not fresh at all. I don't even give the children tuna in cans. There's a high percentage of mercury in it."

Sophia was running scared after a summer like no other. It had begun when Richard Burton flew into Rome, ready to make *The Journey* right after he and his wife, Elizabeth Taylor, had separated in New York because "maybe we have loved each other too much." Then Sophia told me what had happened next at her end:

"I'd already invited Richard and Liz to stay with us, because in a hotel they would be surrounded and maybe even harmed by *paparazzi*. It is not a nice feeling to be in such a mob scene; it is dangerous. Here in Marino, they could live in our guest house by the swimming pool. They could stay in, go out, bathe,

---

*In Sophia's cookbook, there is only one recipe for each: rice *tiella* with potatoes and mussels, and skewered oysters.

do whatever they wanted, and we would leave them alone. Yes, the *paparazzi* would be hiding in the hills with their long lenses, but at least they wouldn't be close.

"Well, first, just Richard came, right after the separation was announced. But when we heard that Elizabeth would be coming soon—to make a movie in Italy and maybe to reconcile with Richard—we had to take every precaution."

Elizabeth Taylor landed at Leonardo Da Vinci Airport on Friday, July 20, 1973, with squadrons of police deployed on the tarmac to defend her against an even greater number of photographers. With bodyguards propelling her by both arms, she was hustled over to a Rolls-Royce in an airport parking lot without any Customs or immigration formalities. Inside the Rolls were fur seats, color TV, a bar, and Richard Burton. After a long embrace that should have been enough to satisfy the pokiest *paparazzo,* but wasn't, the Burtons took off in their chauffeured Rolls-Royce with a police escort plus a motorcade of recklessly driving wheeler-dealer photographers in hot pursuit.

Repelled at the gate of the Villa Ponti, the *paparazzi* besieged the Hotel Helio Cabala and occupied the surrounding hills with telephoto lenses. For the next week, even as far away as Japan, I could never escape aerial views of a chubby Elizabeth Taylor in a nightgown, a bikini, flowing robe, or blue jeans—but only later did Sophia's narrative fill in the gaps for me:

"I didn't want to interfere with their relationship down there, so I dropped in as little as possible. So I knew even less than you were reading in the paper. After ten days though, Richard told me their marriage was over. I felt very sorry for both of them. After twelve years of living together, it's always very sad. Well, of course, maybe they had their reasons to separate. Maybe they were— They were— I don't know, maybe it didn't work any more. I never ask because I just don't. I mean, if they want to talk, they talk without your asking. Otherwise not."

"Isn't it hard to be around such a situation?" I asked Sophia.

"Well, it's hard for anyone who's sensible and sensitive. Yes, I think I knew more or less what kind of feelings were going through them at that point. You feel sad for someone you like and admire. In fact, you feel sad when two people you don't know at all break up. And it's really sad when you happen to like both of them so much."

I pointed out: "You say you could tell what sort of feelings were going through them. How do you know? Just empathy? I mean, you and I have never been through it."

"You can just tell," said Sophia. "If you're sensitive enough, you can tell from a look or a gesture or just a word here or there. Still, if you're not inside of the couple, how can you tell whether they're right or wrong to do what they're doing? Maybe they're wrong. Maybe they're right. Who knows? I never like to criticize anybody's attitude or deeds or resolution of a problem because, first of all, before one can judge anything, you really need to know the truth. And what is the truth in these kind of circumstances? It's impossible to find out. Even the two people it's happening to don't know what is truth. One day, they know one thing; next day, they know another. So I am lucky if I can only speak for myself. Who knows what other people are doing with their own life?"

"Did you feel a slight sense of guilt about having a happy marriage in the midst of this one that was coming apart?" I asked Sophia.

"Not really," she said, thoughtfully. "It's hard to remember my own emotions because I found myself so involved in theirs, even at the distance I made myself keep. If I think about it now, I was always more agitated, more anxious than I usually am as a hostess. It's just not nice to have guests who look upset, who are upset. You want to help, but you are pretty much unable to because it just doesn't concern you. You have to be very careful about helping sometimes. It isn't help when you can't help."

Meanwhile, Elizabeth Taylor started making her film, but Sophia and Burton didn't. Sophia went on with her recollection of a summer to remember:

"Movies are such a big business nowadays that before you can start a film it has to be insured. Everybody has to have a checkup from the insurance doctor. We all had it and thought it was okay. They had done X-rays, too. But two days before we were to leave for Palermo, they discovered something wrong on De Sica's chest X-ray. So the company said: 'We are very sorry. We can't insure the film because the director seems seriously ill.'

"This really came as a bad blow to us because we all love Vittorio, so it struck us worse than any other postponement. There was talk elsewhere about finding another director, but my husband was concerned only about De Sica because he really adores him. Carlo took Vittorio to Geneva, where there's a professor who once operated on Carlo."

"I read in Japan that De Sica had a heart attack," I told Sophia.

"No, no, lungs," she said. "He had a big growth. He smokes too much. The doctor said it looked very bad and, after a week of tests, he operated on Vittorio, who is seventy-two. The operation lasted about four hours; that's how serious it was. Then we had to wait for the analysis, where they look at what they've taken out. It's very rare that anything which looks so bad on an X-ray is *not* malignant, but the tests showed it wasn't. Some people found it hard to believe and thought maybe the doctors were fooling De Sica and us. But when the picture got insured, that was a very good feeling. We are supposed to start October fifteenth."

For two months of this unexpected hiatus, after Elizabeth Taylor moved out to the Grand Hotel in Rome, Richard Burton stayed in Marino. Whenever Burton tired of rattling around the guest house, however, he was always welcome up at the main house.

"The conversation with Richard was always wonderful," Sophia told me, "because he's such an interesting man. Besides, he adores children. He spent a lot of his time with Cipi and taught him many things from Shakespeare. If you say the word Hamlet to Cipi, what do you think he'll say back to you?"

"To be or not to be?" I guessed.

"No," she said, "he'll give you the end of *Hamlet*—you know: 'The rest is silence.' Because Richard told him the whole story from beginning to end. He not only likes children, he really likes to play with them and knows how to play, how to treat them as equals. Cipi always says to me: 'When is Richard Burton coming back?' "

"Was he always around?" I asked her.

"Always on the grounds," she replied. "He never went out, never went anywhere. Just sauna, swimming pool, playing with Cipi, and walking around the property—a very healthy life. I hope he can keep it up."

The Burtons subsequently divorced, remarried each other, redivorced, and married others. De Sica died in Paris on November 13, 1974, the day after *The Journey* premiered there. The film failed to impress the critics and was a weak sister, by Sophia standards, at the box office; she said this was because "it is not the kind of film they do nowadays. It goes really against the pornographic or sex films of today and I think it was worth making the attempt. . . . Erotic films and those with mindless violence aren't the real movie industry. The real movie industry turns out films like *Two Women* and *Dr. Zhivago*. The others are what I call fad films. They'll have to end eventually. After all, what is there left to show?"

Eventually, too, Elizabeth Taylor described Sophia Loren as "a miraculous woman, an Earth Mother," and Sophia has said of Elizabeth: "More people should be like her." But it was Richard Burton who wrote in the March, 1974, *Ladies' Home Journal* that Sophia "would be an outstanding woman in any age. She is as beautiful as an erotic dream" with "a mouth wide and generous, like an invitation to rape. Tall and extremely large bosomed. Tremendously long legs. They go up to her shoulders, practically. Beautiful brown eyes, set in a marvelously vulpine, almost satanic face." Pronouncing her "sane as bootlaces," Burton called Sophia "a great *cwtcher* (Welsh for *comforter*) . . . great mother . . . great cook, too. And great crook—cheats you at cards any time."

"I'm lucky at poker," Sophia once told me. "I play with nothing and I have a flush. I play a lot of poker while waiting around on the set during filming. I once won two hundred dollars while making one film, but I limit my losings to one hundred dollars a film or I'd cry a river and ruin the movie."

Sophia admits that, after her family and acting, her third great passion is playing cards: "For one thing only will I abandon my pleasant solitude: poker. It is a very beautiful game: exciting, unpredictable, courageous"—which is a pretty fair description of Sophia, too.

While evidence of her cheating at cards is hard to come by, she is a "bad bluffer," according to Nino Lo Bello, who played cards with her on the set of *The Priest's Wife.* "After she bluffs someone out of a pot," says Lo Bello, "she likes to show the cards in her hand and make a big thing out of having hoodwinked her opponent—who, next time, is not bluffed again. That's how I won fourteen dollars from her."

Lo Bello also witnessed one of Sophia's better bluffs, when he and press agent Hunton Downs and photographer Tazio Secchiaroli were playing poker. In one deal, the showdown for the pot came between Tazio, who had a pair of kings, and Sophia, who held only a pair of jacks. After betting and raising and betting some more, Tazio called her bluff and showed his kings. Sophia threw down her two jacks and blandly announced she had "two *pair*."

As she was raking in the money, Tazio protested: "Just a minute, Signora. What do you mean, two pair? I see only a pair of jacks. What's the other pair?"

Sophia replied: "A pair of aces!"—and stuck her chest way, way out.

With Richard Burton's tributes to Sophia ricocheting around the globe, there were, inevitably, rumors of a romance. These somehow gained impetus when Elizabeth Taylor showed up on the set of *The Journey,* hoisted a glass of champagne and, with blithe spirit, toasted the marriage of Sophia and Carlo Ponti.

Sophia, however, was more than convincing with her "just good friends" denial after *The Journey* was over.

"Richard and I were good friends when we made the film, we're good friends now, and we'll always be good friends, I think. He is very attractive, very brilliant. When he likes someone, and he knows he can trust that someone, he can really sparkle. But he must feel relaxed—and that's how Carlo and I made him feel in Marino."

The important consideration to Sophia was that "on the screen, I must say Richard and I look very well together. It is very believable that we are in love. I am very pleased with our teaming because it is often very difficult to find the right partner for me." And so it was that the following summer would find the two-shot team of Loren and Burton playing together in London and the British village of Brockenhurst's railway station. They would be filming a television version of Noel Coward's thirty-year-old movie classic, *Brief Encounter** for NBC's Hallmark Hall of Fame. Their interpretation of a drab middle-aged suburban housewife's discreet romance with an equally married family doctor would never come close to eclipsing memories of Celia Johnson and Trevor Howard. But for Sophia Loren, at least, this *Brief Encounter* would pave the way for, not quite three years later, *A Special Day.*

Brief Encounter, in turn, was based on a ten-years-older one-act play, *Still Life,* which Coward wrote for himself and Gertrude Lawrence in *Tonight at Eight-Thirty.*

CHAPTER 19

Sophia Faces Forty

I VISITED SOPHIA THRICE IN 1973—in Geneva in February; in Marino in April; and again in Marino early that October on my way home from Asia. We spent a rainy, melancholy, autumnal Saturday together sipping champagne and exchanging recollections of the summer. Sophia had a bad cold and I had one coming on. I remember that our day began with a paper hunt —for Kleenex. Ines was away and nobody could find anything in the Villa Ponti. After a while, Cipi and his nurse Ruth turned up a box of tissues from Edoardo's lair, and it was even more welcome than the champagne.

"Do you want to have any more children, Sophia?" I asked toward the end of my visit.

In a tired, almost melancholy, certainly toneless voice, Sophia said: "I don't think so. I'd be afraid of a third Caesarean. Two, I guess, is okay. But a third Caesarean, that's really painful—and scary. Psychologically, it's awful to go all alone into that room without being asleep. They prepare you for surgery without giving you anything before—for the sake of the baby—and then they put you to sleep just when the doctor says he's ready to cut. It's a terrible experience. Normal birth I don't think is so awful. It's something natural. But not a Ceasarean!"

Just then, we heard Edoardo crying. Sophia started to go up to him. Then she remembered her cold and stopped on the spiral stairs until she could hear Ruth coping. As the cries subsided, Sophia said: "Have you ever heard anything so sweet as a baby's cry? I'd like to have a million of them."

"A million?"

"Not really. Not even seven, but I'd have liked three or four. Because I think parents should be able to stay with their children—with all of them, with each of them. If you have too many children, how can you raise them properly? How can you stay with them all the time? Only by living just for your children, but then you can't do anything else. Already with two, I have my hands full—and I have people to help me!"

We started to say goodbye and Sophia's parting banter began: "I'll see you on my next child—"

"Congratulations!" I responded in kind. "Are you trying to tell me some news?"

"No, no," said Sophia, laughing. "I'm thirty-nine now and I retired from motherhood with Edoardo; unfortunately, I retired."

"So this was just a cryptic clue?"

"Yeh, yeh, sure."

(A week later, TV and newspapers and wire services *all* had Sophia pregnant again—complete with bulletins from Geneva that the baby was due six months later, in April of 1974, and quotes that Sophia was determined to have a girl this time. When I reached Sophia by phone from Vienna, she said it wasn't so. Her sister, Maria, was having a gynecological operation from Dr. de Watteville and Sophia had flown to Geneva to visit her. "Somebody saw me returning to that address," she said, "so they put one-plus-one together to make three.")

Standing on the doorstep of the Villa Ponti, Sophia had an afterthought.

"So I'm going to be forty next year?" She said with an eloquent shrug. "When I was thirty-nine a fortnight ago, Cipi painted a dinosaur for me and I've never had a better birthday present. Listen, I feel well now and I've never thought a great deal about age. The years don't count if you're enjoying life and looking forward to what's ahead. I don't intend to spend my forties or even my fifties searching for wrinkles. What can you do about age? It's a condition, not a privilege."

The following year, Sophia helped Helen Markel compose an essay on this theme that appeared under Sophia's byline as her birthday approached. It was called "I'm Glad to Be Forty":

... I wouldn't be any other age. I have never felt better about myself. I wouldn't be twenty again for anything. At twenty I wanted desperately to have children and couldn't. I didn't know who I was or where I was going.

But thirty was the really hard birthday for me. I wasn't ready for that one. I had been in films since I was fifteen—always a woman, never a girl. ... So by the time I was thirty the world press descended on me to ask how it felt to be *middle-aged.* ...

Turning thirty is hard because it pulls the pillow of potentiality out from under you, and you're left looking at yourself for the first time. Accomplishments are simply *expected* and nobody says anymore, "and she's so *young,* too." At thirty there are no more advantages to be gained from simply being younger than other people. From thirty on you may be childish but you're no longer a child.

Thirty forced me to face the fact that I could no longer squander time and emotions and expect the well to be always filled. At thirty you suddenly know that you can't forever begin anew—failures are called by their proper names and you know regret for chances you never took.

The whole business of age depressed me for awhile. But now I know better. In the last ten years I have learned many things—about myself, about age, about love. I have no regrets. I've done everything I wanted to and taken the responsibility for what followed. I would rather do something than spend my time wondering what I have missed. Regret only makes wrinkles.

Forty is my most joyous birthday because I have finally found myself. I know who I am and what I need. I have never felt younger because I am finally fulfilled. I have two children, a miracle I prayed for all my life, and I love them with an intensity I never thought possible. Cipi and Edoardo changed my life completely and brought it into balance. I will never be unhappy again nor afraid of growing old, because I will grow up with them.

At forty I have learned to watch my detours, ration my enthusiasms, collect fewer experiences and more satisfactions. I am less cynical than I was ten years ago. I do not move as easily from ecstasy to despair. I have less need to see everything, fill all the silences and have everybody love me.*

*"I'm Glad to Be Forty," by Sophia Loren as told to Helen Markel, *McCall's,* Aug. 1974.

CHAPTER 20

Forever, Sophia

SOPHIA LOREN AND HER HUSBAND and sons and entourage (secretary Ines, nurse Ruth, and cook Livia) moved to Paris in 1974 while the actress was filming *The Verdict,* the late Jean Gabin's farewell film. In it, the great French actor played a judge. Sophia played a teenaged murder defendant's mother who sought to save her son's neck from the guillotine by kidnapping Gabin's wife and holding her hostage.

She received my family and me for tea on the last Saturday of May 1975 in the eighth-floor living room of her triplex in the Résidence George V. Each floor of the apartment measures some 200 square meters (240 square yards). One flight down were the kitchen, dining room, library, and bedroom of Sophia and Carlo with separate bathrooms. One flight above us were Ponti's Paris office and the quarters of Livia and, later, a chauffeur. On our floor were also the rooms of the children, Ruth, and Ines, as well as a playroom. Outside the elegant living room —all Louis Quinze and silk and damask with flashes of crystal— was a balcony with such a spectacular view of Paris that one wanted to sing the whole Maurice Chevalier repertoire on the spot.

"When we were ready to make *The Verdict,*" Sophia said, "we put Cipi into a private school here and he liked it so much that I decided: Next year he has to go to school anyway and if I have nothing special to do in Italy, it's better that he stays here. And my husband thinks French schools, with their formal educa-

tion, offer the best preparation for later life. So that's why we
moved to Paris."

Which was not what we had read in *Newsweek* a couple of
weeks earlier:

> "I can't live in Italy any longer; I'm afraid they'll kidnap my
> children," says actress Sophia Loren, who has moved to Paris
> with her two sons and visits with her husband, film producer
> Carlo Ponti, on weekends.

"First of all," Sophia said, "Carlo is here in Paris. We can do
our business here as well as there—so I don't have to fly anywhere to visit him on weekends. Second, we moved here before
the kidnapping epidemic broke out in Italy. I admit that, if
we'd been there now, we would have moved here. It's really a
war going on there—and nobody can tell between whom. But
the main thing is that I never said what *Newsweek* said I said.
Maybe they picked it up from some other place that invented it,
but they never asked me. I think it's because they have space to
fill and if they want a story on Italian kidnappings, my name
comes to mind. Now if they say we're living in Paris because we
like the school, that's truth, but it's not headlines. But if they say
we live here because we're afraid of kidnappers, that's news."*

I was surprised by the security—or the lack of it—in her Paris
apartment house. A disinterested concierge had simply waved
us to the automatic elevator when I'd told him Madame Ponti
was expecting us. It looked as if anybody could walk in off the
street and ring Sophia's bell. But Sophia once said that this was
a deception: "I'm more protected than you think. We have
bodyguards everywhere, but their guns are discreetly hidden.
I'm surrounded by very reliable people who would never be-
tray me. Cipi has a bodyguard who takes him to school. I worry

---

*In a November, 1977, interview with the Paris newspaper, *L' Aurore,* Carlo
Ponti disclosed two kidnapping attempts by what seemed like the same
band of armed, hooded men. In March of 1975, a car forced Ponti's car to
stop near the Villa in Marino, but the masked attackers were driven off by
bodyguards. A few months later in Switzerland, a similar attempt was repelled by bodyguards.

about the children all the time, but what can I do? We have to live like normal people."

Now Sophia, safely past her fortieth birthday, went on to tick off more malicious rumors, starting with almost-daily proclamations of pregnancy. I told her that, back in Vienna, one of our tabloids had a daily gossipmonger named Adabei whose virility was such that "he makes you pregnant in his column six or eight times a year." Sophia didn't think this was funny, but came up with a series of toppers:

"You know, I gave up smoking each time I was pregnant. Then, this year, I gave up smoking just because I was scared of smoking. As soon as they heard about this, they announced I was pregnant.

"Then they said I'd lost a leg! My own mother happens to read that kind of magazine and can you imagine her reading something like that? She would have had a heart attack!*

"Then they said I'd had a stroke while working with Jean Gabin and half my face was paralyzed.

"And that I'd adopted a Vietnamese or Pakistani baby from Danny Kaye [UNICEF's good-will ambassador]. Well, I just might have, but nobody asked me to. I haven't seen or heard from Danny Kaye in years. But they just went ahead and announced it. And always, always, whenever we try to trace one of these so-called reports, they originated in Germany."

In Vienna, our eleven-year-old had been using up her allowance to bring home alarmist German tabloids. And now my mother in Manhattan had clipped "The Gossip Column" by Robin Adams Sloan from May 6, 1975's New York *Daily News:*

ADDS FUEL TO FIRE

Q: A friend said she read somewhere that Sophia Loren and

---

*A couple of years later, Romilda Villani, well into her sixties, made the same gossip columns thanks to a romance with fortyish Sergio Saccho and photos showing her doing a wild rock dance in a Roman discothèque. And, for what it's worth, Sophia was quoted as complaining: "When Mamma wears skin-tight jeans, low-cut tops, and boots, she makes not just herself, but the whole family, ridiculous."

Carlo Ponti were breaking up. I figured I'd check with you.—
J.F., Tulsa, Okla.

A: We hear the eleven-year marriage is shaky, with Sophia
moving to Paris with the two children. To add more fuel to the
fire, actress Dalilah Di Lazzaro, who is starring in Ponti's latest
film, *The Gansgster's Little Girl,* claims she and the producer are
in love.

Even to the name Lazzaro, which Sophia had sported as a
starlet, the stories had sounded like some press agent's resurrection of the Pizza Pygmalion legend. Nevertheless, Sophia
bristled as she told us: "I don't want to talk about it. It's something completely ridiculous that started in Germany, of course.
I could tell you *how* it got started, but I wouldn't want to dignify
something that never existed with such a long explanation."

I told her my mother and daughter had been genuinely
worried.

"Of course, who wouldn't be? They must love me. But tell
them not to worry. There's no trouble." Later, in talking about
all the different kinds of rumors, Sophia said: "Listen, if I
would read something about somebody else, I would start wondering, too. And that's even knowing as well as I do that most of
these are invented. But, if you read anything, you're bound to
wonder whether there's at least a little smoke when they cry
'Fire!' It's not just being naïve, you know, particularly when you
read these rumors in a reliable magazine."

The place had changed but even in Paris Sophia was trying to
hew to her early-to-rise, early-to-bed routine from Marino.
"Here in Paris," she told us, "I lead a life that a woman can live
in an apartment. I can go out to the theatre and museums,
invite friends and visit them, but I can't just go out and walk in
a garden and enjoy life and be in the country the way I was in
Italy."

She would rise around six-thirty, have her coffee with the
children and, if not working, sometimes take Edoardo for a
walk in the Bois de Boulogne or Parc Monceau, but "I don't like
to go in the park much, so Ruth usually takes Edoardo there

and Cipi's class goes outdoors once in the morning and once in the afternoon.

"What has suprised me about Paris," she went on, "is that it's not as dressy as I'd thought it was. I wear pants all the time, unless I'm going to a party or a luncheon at Maxim's." She was in close contact with her mother and sister in Rome at the time, but mostly by phone. With Carlo Ponti jetting out to or breezing in from Tokyo, Milan, or New York, he and she hardly ever entertained at home. She had only "two or three good friends in Paris, but how many good friends does one need?" One of them was the actress Michèle Morgan; another was Madame Goffredo Lombardo, wife of the producer who named her Sophia Loren; still another was certainly her inseparable secretary Ines.

Rex Reed, who visited Sophia in Paris not long after I did, later wrote: "Sophia serves tomato juice swimming in Baccarat crystal. Her closets bulge with Balmains, Diors, Balenciagas, but she seldom wears them. The frescoed ceilings, the Louis XV furniture and the Picassos and Rembrandts on the walls are admired only by the nanny and the cook. The engraved invitations to fashionable parties and premieres remain unopened, like unwelcome bills. She has become a recluse in Paris." More realistically and relevantly, Sophia said: "I'm often invited, but I don't go out very much because I'm always afraid of being bored. When I go out, I like to have a good time, to dance. So I pick and choose. I go to the theatre, to cinema. I avoid premieres as much as possible because I am an early-to-bedder."

Sophia said that, on the sidewalks of Paris, "I'll be walking down a street and a passing stranger will see me, hurry back past me, and walk straight at me again, saying, 'Aren't youuu—?' And I'll say, with a smile or a laugh, 'No, I'm not'— and we'll both laugh, because then we'll both know I am."

This particular *meet cute*, she said, "happens everywhere— even in Switzerland, where they go out of their way not to notice you, and in Rome, where they're so busy admiring themselves, and in New York, where they're always looking down at the sidewalk. But it's bound to happen all the time in Paris, where people are looking each other over more than else-where." Wherever it happens, those who recognize her want no more than a word or two and perhaps an autograph.* Sophia is glad to oblige: "When you're a public figure, a big slice of your private life goes away. It's part of our profession. Success means popularity and popularity means being recognized in the streets. It's what we're fighting for. So I don't go along with actors and actresses who don't give autographs or interviews. Or give them, but complain, 'I don't like it' and act snooty. It's ridiculous! They'd really feel terrible if people didn't annoy them in the street."

One of Carlo Ponti's ploys to promote Sophia's lesser works is to premiere them in Japan ahead of Europe or America. Ever since *Woman of the River* in the mid-1950s, Sophia has been a Japanese sensation. By 1975 her cookbook had sold more than ten thousand copies there and *Brief Encounter* was being bought not just for TV but for theatrical distribution. Even weak sisters like *The Journey* and *Sunflower* had broken box office records in Tokyo, so Ponti had sent Sophia herself to the Land of the Rising Sun for the dawn of *The Gangster's Little Girl*: co-starring Mastroianni (not to mention Dalilah Di Lazzaro) and later reti-tled *The Gun Moll* and *Poopsie & Co.* in some parts of the world.

Sophia's first discovery in Japan had been that all the jokes about how Japanese reverse their *l*s and *r*s happen to be true and she was soon convulsed by what one of her interpreters termed *"clouds cramoling for Sophia Rolen."* Then she was taken "to see not just one movie studio, but every movie studio; not just one TV studio, but every TV studio."

"Didn't you see anything else?" my wife asked.

"The insides of three hotels in Tokyo, Kyoto, and Osaka," Sophia replied, "and I did get to one temple in Kyoto. But that was mostly for picture-taking, so I took off my shoes and put on

*On a recent publicity trip to the US, however, a young man broke through police barricades to thrust a religious tract at her. "Read it, Sophia!" he cried. "It'll tell you you're not just a body!" Carlo Ponti took it from his wife and threw it into a garbage can while shouting: "She already knows that!"

my shoes a dozen times and kneeled and bowed and saw mostly cameras."

Remembering our own glorious summer of 1973 in Japan, my family expressed pity at all Sophia had missed. But our hostess was philosophical. "I could have stayed longer and seen a few sights," she admitted, "but my husband wasn't with me and I just wouldn't enjoy wonders without my family. You know me: I want to share. So what you see of Japan if you're in a hurry is terrible ugly buildings, very commercial cities, and too many studios. Still, in Kyoto, I saw enough that I would want to go back. Next time, I would want the four of us to go there in calm and go where the Japanese go. . . . Yes, I know it's impossible for me to be a typical Japanese mother, but I mean we'd go as tourists and let our hosts show us the real Japan of beautiful houses and gardens rather than studios."

Carlo Ponti, Senior, was at home recovering from minor surgery in Switzerland, but when Sophia took us on a tour of the triplex at one point, her husband waved to us from the paneled modern kitchen, where he was watching TV with Cipi. On Sophia's night table during our tour, I was delighted to see a book, the Aperture Monograph 1972 collection of Diane Arbus photos, which I'd sent to Sophia after our 1973 conversation about photography and freaks. It lay right next to Tony Crawley's illustrated *The Films of Sophia Loren* and not far from Donald Zec's unauthorized, leering but relatively accurate, *Sophia: An Intimate Biography,* which had just been published in England. I was surprised to see Zec's book there, for Sophia had told me: "He's a tricky man. These things are always my fault: it's always my fault. Because it's always my good faith." Now, when I questioned her about Zec, she specified her complaint: "He writes very well, but how it was presented in garbage papers! They took headlines and made out romances with Peter Sellers."

Between that Saturday afternoon with Sophia and a return visit on Monday, my family and I paid a call on another Peter who has never, to our knowledge or his, been romantically linked with Sophia. No sooner had Peter Ustinov, who'd directed Sophia in *Lady L* a decade earlier, and his third wife Hélène welcomed us to their flat on the Rue Vineuse than our ample host began to expound upon the subject of the Pontis' marriage *(see chapter 3)*. After discussing at some length what Sophia may or may not have seen in Carlo, Peter added: "It's wrong in any case to imagine that very attractive women always fall for Adonises. That would be really a waste of both—and very bad for all the rest of us in The Ugly Majority."

When I replayed this line of Peter's for Sophia on Monday, she said an Adonis was never what she was looking for: "For me, what really counts in a man is his intelligence: his thoughts, his chosen way of being. I never just look at a man's exterior. I may notice, in a very abstract way, that he's handsome or has nice eyes, but that isn't how he strikes me as a man or attracts me as a woman. It takes more than that to awaken my interest. If he's very well-dressed, well, so is furniture."*

Later, Sophia told me what she looks for in people she befriends: "When I trust somebody, I give them anything they want. I never say no. Really I give of myself as they want me. Because I think they're friends.

"I believe so much in friendship and trust. If you came here *only* to make an article or get a story, I'm not interested. You have to have a relationship with somebody. Otherwise, you can't even have a conversation or say things you really feel.

"American women I like much. But some women over there who work, they're so much masculine sometimes. Particularly

---

*Less than a year earlier, Sophia had told transatlantic telephone interviewer Kay Gardella that she was rather naïve about men: "I'm not very practical and I'm quite inexperienced because I met my husband when I was a teenager, and that was it for me. I have worked for many, many years with actors, but that is different. When I met Carlo, I was only fifteen [*sic!*]. I thought he was the right man for me, and I still think so. . . . I like men when they are funny, when they are not boring. I like intelligent men who are good company. As for women, I think they, too, should be intelligent, but not look it. Otherwise, they can be boring, too." (New York *Daily News*, August 25, 1974).

when they have to deal with an actress, they treat her like an object. Which I'm not. We are all human beings. If you treat me like an object, maybe I'll react like an object—but I know that *you're* doing this to *me,* that I'm NOT an object. At the end, some women interviewers say goodbye as if they've never met me. They take from me in an hour whatever they want, without knowing that if they'd deal with me differently, they could have me forever.

"It's that way of doing things I don't care for. So selfish, it's terrible. I suppose it's not only in movies and magazines. The whole world nowadays is selfish. People take, take, take from you and give very little.

"But there are some people who give all the time. I am a giver. I don't take. That's a question of nature. I give, give to anybody. I'm happy that way. If you don't give back anything, it doesn't matter to me. But when you don't give, you lose something—and maybe it's your femininity or masculinity or your humanity."

Sophia thought it important that "a working woman shouldn't lose her femininity. A woman who works doesn't want only to be a mother, only to be a wife; she has a need to express herself outside of the home, not the need to lose her femininity. Sometimes, I suppose, if a woman is doing a job that's meant for men, she may *have* to be more aggressive.

"Women are fighting for emancipation. Yes, I agree with the right they make because they have a just cause. But sometimes they go too far. And they forget, for the sake of mere competition with men, all those wonderful qualities that are typically feminine—that make of her the right complement of a man.

"Women can be aggressive, too, like men are—because we are all alike, only a woman can be a mother and a man can't. That's too bad for him. He's missing out on something. But what would women do without men? Why, we wouldn't even be mothers! I think now is the time to liberate Man."*

*Other comments by Sophia on Women's Lib:
    To Nino Lo Bello (for United Features, 1970): "I find it is a serious

mistake when a woman is openly in competition with her mate. When a woman abandons her fictitious inferiority, which is part of her femininity, she does not know how many pleasant things she misses. And, of course, the husband suffers, too.

"I do not like the way women compete against men in America. In Italy women have always been the real head of the family—but the Italian woman has always made her husband believe he is the master. This is what keeps the family together.

"The only thing I like about Women's Lib is one of their clever slogans: 'Don't Iron While The Strike is Hot!' . . ."

To Helen Markel (in *McCall's,* August, 1974): "I am a liberated woman— in my own terms—which is to live happily with the man I love. I work. I make money. I could live very nicely without him. But I don't want to. I could leave any time I want without fear of being alone. But I don't want to, ever. The more years go by, the more I love him."

In a 1977 interview with the Brussels newspaper *Le Soir,* Sophia said that while she believes in women's liberation she personally likes to be a "slave" to the man she loves: "When one is in love, one becomes the slave of that man. I react like this: If I am in love, I choose to be a slave freely."

CHAPTER 21

The Vision of Ustinov as Seen by Sophia

WHEN I ASKED PETER USTINOV TO TALK about working with Sophia as an actress, he began by saying: "we've only worked together on two pictures."

"Two?" I said. "I thought there was only *Lady L.*"

Peter gave a Ustinovian chuckle and said: "Back to your musty film archive, boy! The first time was *Quo Vadis?* I was the Emperor Nero* and she was one of five or six thousand extras, so I doubt that we met. Like any head of state, I knew very little about what was going on among my people. And, being Nero, I shouldn't have cared less. While the extras were burning up in the midsummer heat, I was busy burning Rome.

"The only other time was with *Lady L.* By then we had met frequently and I had watched her work once or twice. I could guess—and I was right—that she'd be easy for a director to handle because she has something more valuable than intelligence, of which she has plenty, too. She has a kind of native sense. That's why she's at her most marvelous in Italian films or when she's doing Neapolitans—because she knows them inside out. Actresses from more sheltered backgrounds don't grasp situations so instinctively.

---

*Nero, Ustinov's first major film success, won him an Academy Award nomination as Best Supporting Actor, but that particular Oscar went to Karl Malden in *A Streetcar Named Desire.* Ustinov later won it twice, for *Spartacus* and *Topkapi.*

"I think Sophia's at her best in her country, with Vesuviuses belching in the background. True, she has always been a very clever girl and is now an international figure who can play almost everything. I'm always glad to see her up there on the screen, but we're making allowances when she's called Lady L or Princess Yasmin.* Her roots are still the best thing she has to offer because she doesn't have to think then of exactly who she is."

When I played this part of my Ustinov tapes for Sophia on Monday, she disagreed politely: "Not true. He makes philosophy of me." Though she had played everything from a Hong Kong countess to a nursing nun by then, she insisted that being a Neapolitan peasant on the screen required the most sophistication because you had to observe the human being beneath your own folklore.

Peter went on to describe our heroine to me as "a girl whose quality lies in the fact that she is still learning all the time. If Laurence Olivier weren't learning every day of his life more than a student is capable of learning, even at his age, he wouldn't be Olivier. It's a kind of humility, in a way, that's essential to all creative people. And Sophia has that. When you direct her, you feel that it's a mutual adventure you're embarking upon. And if I, as the director, make an absolutely outrageous suggestion, she'll trust me enough to at least try it. She's always quite ready to attempt to enter a higher orbit, which is not to say that she will willingly do something she doesn't think is right. No, she won't. And so anything she does consider undertaking tends to inspire great confidence in whoever's directing her.

"Perhaps the comparison to Olivier sounds presumptuous, but Sophia is one of the very few top people working who I feel may yet take everybody by surprise by doing something nobody ever thought of—including herself."

*A reference to her role of Yasmin Azir in Stanley Donen's *Arabesque* (1966).

"I like to suprise myself," Sophia responded when she heard the tape of this—and then, with her own special comic grace, added: "I'm flattered by Peter. What's more, in all humility, I agree. I am nothing if not 'umble."

More seriously, she elaborated: "Even with the easiest thing, I always approach it by thinking I'm not good enough to do it. But I'm only thinking that *before* I'm doing it, not *when* I'm doing it. So I never say no because I like to challenge myself. That's what gives me the drive to overcome this kind of timidity and shyness that really upsets me terribly beforehand. That's why I've always needed to be surrounded by De Sica or Peter or Carlo: people I could trust to push me beyond myself.

"Sometimes a director won't convince me, but if he has good reasons, I'll try—and only afterwards, if I've made a fool of myself and him, will I say no. But I'll say no positively. I'll say, 'Let's do it another way.' That's the advantage of screen over stage. You can undo mistakes."

As is so often the case, the discussion of Sophia's star quality shifted toward her innate personal traits. "There's an instinctive lady in Sophia," Ustinov allowed, "and yet what's so attractive about her to me is running into her in Rome when she was making *Man of La Mancha* there and going with her and Jimmy Coco to a small place to eat. Of course, Coco and I made it a smaller place just by being there. We had an inordinate amount of spaghetti and who do you think ate the most *pasta* the fastest? Sophia, in the hope that Carlo wouldn't come in and catch her at it.

"She is one of nature's truants, who does the Pygmalion bit very well with the teapot. But the sight of her really returning to her roots just by gobbling up the spaghetti is to me even more welcome than the sight of Professor Higgins' triumph.

"Another of her virtues is to make lapses of taste extremely elegant and amusing. This, too, is in the Neapolitan tradition because the things they shout at each other from under the washing is unspeakable, yet it's done with such fervor and purity that it becomes acceptable."

Concluding his eulogy of Sophia before focusing his analytical insights upon Ponti, Peter asserted:

"Sophia has an extraordinary ability. In awe, I call it stability; in admiration, I call it serenity.* But she takes obstacles like a thoroughbred. Her temperament is very sound. If she were a sportswoman, even at the very beginning, she'd have never cracked if Carlo left the stadium for a minute or two. She'd just say: 'Ah, he'll be back, and if I've won he'll be pleased.' And she'd go on scoring aces."

Continuing her dialogue-at-a-distance with Ustinov, Sophia's reaction to this was: "What does it mean to be lady? To be polite? To entertain people nicely? It's not a question of being a lady, it's a question of loving the others and being respectful to people you are with. Taste comes naturally and you add to it with traveling and the experiences you have in your lifetime. As for this business about 'nature's truant,' *Basta!* [Enough!] Next time I go to Peter's house, I dress up as a peasant in rags or show up in Neapolitan folk costume and eat off his floor."

Around that time, Sophia was bogged down in another cycle of undistinguished films. *Poopsie & Co.* would be followed by *Cassandra Crossing,* a bubonic-plague thriller with Burt Lancaster, Ava Gardner, Richard Harris, Ingrid Thulin, and Lee Strasberg, the Actors Studio guru. So I asked Peter Ustinov a slightly loaded question about Carlo Ponti:

"We hear so much about how Ponti was Pygmalion who made Sophia what she is today. But isn't it possible that, beyond the beginning, he limited her potential by putting her only in 'safe'

---

*In his book of interviews with notable women, *Femmes,* (the others were Indira Gandhi; the Maharani of Jaipur; Jeanne Moreau; Princess Grace of Monaco; *Vogue* correspondent Mary Russell; discothèque doyenne Regine; and Madame Claude the madam), Spanish playboy José Luis de Villalonga asked Sophia admiringly: "What makes you run?" And Sophia replied: "Stability. . . . Stability is for me the ideal of earthly happiness . . . a feeling more important and than any other . . . Without stability, love is just a whim, a caprice, or, all things considered, sexual attraction."

vehicles that fit his tastes but sometimes tend toward the trashy? I mean, the man is also the producer of *Ape Woman, Cocottes Anonymous,* and *Adulterer He, Adultress She.*"

Peter reflected for a minute and then said:

"Ponti surrounds himself with things of admirable taste: chairs and paintings and palaces. But, in point of fact, what he runs is a very commercial operation involving artistry. Sophia's accommodation to this is to keep working—on the assumption or hope that, sooner or later, perhaps the right vehicle will come to her.

"This may be more sensible than to say, 'Oh, God! This isn't very good' and not do it"—which Peter described as "The Joanne Woodward Approach," making it clear that, while Mrs. Paul Newman appears mostly in good movies, she doesn't appear often and is hard to make money on.

"I imagine," Peter went on, "Sophia gets twinges of conscience—I know I do!—when she must think or say: 'I should do something up to my own intellectual level.' But this isn't really fair. There are things which are commercial which are also extremely good, like certain drawing-room comedies or Coward or Feydeau. I think one is wrong to think that just because a work has a lot of thought in it, then it must necessarily be better. There are things which really have no particular thought in them that are hilarious."

Returning to Carlo Ponti, Peter continued:

"Carlo has various reputations in the business world, depending upon whether you get on with him or not. It's very difficult not to get on with him, except that he doesn't concentrate very much. When he's trying to get out of a conversation, he starts laughing at nothing or else daydreaming and you realize that you're at a danger point: he'll do anything to get out of the room *now,* even saying no to some project he wants to do. He just surrenders to the moment.

"Once, I allowed myself to be racial and I said to Carlo in the friendliest possible way: 'The danger with you Italians is that your weaknesses are your greatest weapons. You push your poverties in front of you the way soldiers used to push women across minefields in the war and advance behind them.' What I mean is that Carlo will say to you, 'We can no longer afford this' and, by the time he finishes that short sentence, you suddenly realize that you're no longer sitting in your seat, but on the floor, and Carlo is sitting in your chair in order to be in a better position to explain his penury further.

Peter Ustinov was alluding ruefully to the mutilation of his own *Lady L,* which Ponti had professed to love but did little to defend from dishonor. I myself had witnessed, in New York in 1966 and then in Prague in 1967 and 1968, Carlo Ponti's de-fanging of a Bohemian lion named Miloš Forman—then the up-and-coming young Czech film-maker of *Loves of a Blonde* and *The Firemen's Ball;* later the Oscar-winning director of 1975's Oscar-winning *One Flew Over the Cuckoo's Nest.* Forman had gone along with Ponti's embellishments and improvements of his final Czech film, saying, "I know I am playing very dan-gerous game, but the name of game is Art"—only to discover that the name of the game was rape. When Ponti withdrew his eighty-thousand-dollar investment in *The Firemen's Ball,* he put Forman in a "very severe and difficult position and in danger to go to trial" in what was then still Stalinist Czechoslovakia.*

I also knew that, back in 1966, Dora Jane Hamblin of *Life* had written an authorized biography of Sophia for Little, Brown and Company of Boston, but after Sophia had ap-proved the manuscript, Ponti had raised so many objections that he wound up paying Dodie Hamblin twenty-five thousand dollars (seven and a half thousand of which went back to Little, Brown to reimburse them for advances already paid her) NOT to publish the book. When I asked Sophia about this during our

---

*For details of Ponti vs. Forman, see "Watch Out for the Hook, My Friend" in the January 20, 1967 issue of *Life* and "How Miloš Forman Came to Amer-ica to Make a Film and Wound Up Owing Paramount $140,000" in the February, 1970 issue of *Show* Magazine. Miloš, who now lives in the Hamp-shire House himself, once wanted "to spill all my bitterness over the past with Ponti" to me, but, in 1977, he bumped into Ponti in a hotel in Switzer-land and later told me: "I was shocked. I met an old man, rather senile and pitiful and I felt sorry for him. I don't think that the man is dangerous any more to anybody."

1975 visit, she assured me that Carlo's objections had been her own, too, but insisted that these objections had to do exclusively with some financial allegations in Hamblin's manuscript that would have caused the Pontis great trouble with the Italian tax authorities. Sophia told me that when she and Carlo had asked Hamblin to take out the offending passages, Dodie "got on her high horse and refused," so instead, the Pontis revoked Sophia's approval and bought the book for themselves.

When I caught up with Dodie Hamblin in Rome almost three years after this conversation with Sophia, she confirmed that her settlement with Ponti's lawyers had required her to turn over all copies of the manuscript but denied that the taxing passages had been the bone of contention: "I had gone into a discussion of how I suspected the Pontis hid their money in Switzerland. But I think this was fairly common knowledge and always has been. . . . Still, Carlo objected rather strenuously to this and I agreed to take it out. I could see his point." She said Ponti later told her Sophia had killed her book because she was "so unnerved" by her 1967 miscarriage, but Dodie assured me, "You're not the first person who's seen Sophia and told me this version of hers." And this hearty, tough-talking, chain-smoking, but cherubic native Iowan—who has written a 1977 memoir called *That Was the LIFE* as well as half-a-dozen books on archaeology—also told me that at a point where she was "disillusioned, disappointed, and I suppose, a little bit hurt" and said so to Ponti, he responded: "Well, it's your first time, but in my business, it happens every day."

Thus, in 1975, Peter Ustinov knew whereof he spoke when he told me, more admiringly than grudgingly, that Carlo Ponti is "a businessman in the marathon sense of the word. He doesn't mind losing a lap or two so long as he's still running when the other man is retired to the pits. He plays a waiting game and doesn't get deeply involved in anything. That's what made his romance with Sophia slightly suspect to me at the outset.

"I think the last man on earth who will ever get an ulcer will be Ponti. Because he thinks life's too short and if he's suddenly stuck with an impossible situation, his solution is to walk away from it and let the bricks fall where they may."

Peter Ustinov had been amused by all of the previous year's "Sophia Faces Forty" headlines. Reminding me that, in parts of *Lady L,* Sophia had played a dowager of eighty, Peter said: "I knew her when she was twice her age."

On Monday, toward the end of my visit, I asked Sophia to reminisce about being eighty.

"I was a very funny and content woman at eighty," she began, "filled with humor, content with my age, with the life I'd had, with my children and nephews, and with being surrounded by relatives. That was how I was: a little shaky, perhaps. And I guess that's how I'd like to be at eighty, with Cipi and Edoardo and those daughter-in-laws and all the grandchildren and my sister and my nieces and their children—and, best of all, my husband still there, stealing the show from me because he will have turned one hundred a few months before. And when you ask me if it's really my eightieth birthday, I'll say to you twice what I say now about forty: 'I'm the age I look. I'm the age I look.' "

Taking the cue, I impersonated an eighty-two-year-old Codger: "Waahll, Sophia, what's it like and how's it feel to turn eighty?"

"Absolutely smashing!" Sophia replied in a voice that creaked but didn't croak. Then she invited me to come see her many times in between now and then, but to put down September 20, 2014 on my calendar for her eightieth birthday party. After some checking with Ines and an almanac, Sophia announced: "My eightieth birthday will be on a Saturday."

"Good!" I said. "Then I won't have to take time off from work."

"And you'll have all weekend to recover," Sophia added.

I can only hope the invitation still stands.

CHAPTER 22

Sophia Con Brio

FOR THE FIRST TWO WEEKS of filming *Cassandra Crossing* in early 1976, Sophia Loren would bar all visitors and press from the set in Rome—as she does at the outset of every picture. This is not temperament so much as her professional need to build up a family unit with which she can act and interact. A new film is "not just another film" (even though there have been more than seventy since *Quo Vadis?*), but "a new adventure with new people, new characters, a new story, a new world to put on the screen." On the first day of filming, the actors are still strangers to each other. Sophia may have to climb into bed with the man who plays her husband "and I don't even know him! I can't just say, 'Hello, how are you?' and go to work. I'm too shy."

In addition, other actors can be difficult—and those Sophia has worked with range from a volatile Frank Sinatra to a playful Marlon Brando to a cerebral Paul Newman who, in *Lady L,* would spend two hours discussing and analyzing a two-minute scene before playing it. She needs to get to know people and, without naming names, says, "I can find a way to like anyone within a week or two."

Thus, by the time outsiders are admitted to the set, Sophia invariably is the matriarch of one big happy family. She likes to compare this process, however, to the way a stage play evolves from a group of people working together in a room into a company performing in a theater. But Sophia herself has never performed on the stage, and only once in her star career did she ever yearn to. She wanted the title role in the Neapolitan comedy, *Filumena Marturano,* by Eduardo de Filippo, after whom Sophia's second son is named. Instead, the author's actress-wife made the part her own—until Vittorio De Sica gave Sophia the chance to play Filumena in the movie version, which was retitled *Marriage, Italian Style.* "Now I wouldn't care to do it on the stage," she told me, "because I already did it on the screen."*

We talked about all this on an early 1976 visit the week before Sophia was to start work on *Cassandra Crossing.* I found Sophia willing and ready to talk shop.

Elaborating upon Paul Newman's "Method," Sophia said: "This is *his* method. This is the way *he* likes to work. If he does that, I accept that he needs to do it. Otherwise, he wouldn't do it. He wants to be sure, he wants to feel secure in the part, he wants to know everything, he wants to talk a lot about it, to convince himself. It's not my way, but I give him what he wants because an actor is very vulnerable and certainly another performer should respect the way he works."

Sophia's method is to read a script three or four times in one or two afternoons "before doing anything. Then I start memorizing the lines because I believe they have to be so perfect that I shouldn't even have to think about them. They have to become really part of you and I spend a lot of time with them. Aside from knowing my lines, the only other thing I really care about at this point is that I truly understand what is going on in the script. If I have difficulty understanding some dialogue or it just doesn't sound right to me or the way I'd say it, I underline it and have a meeting with the writer and the director. They'll explain it or change it or cut it or add something to clarify it.

"Then I forget about the script. I like to live three or four

*In 1951, five years after its Italian stage premiere and a dozen years before *Marriage, Italian Style,* the play was filmed under its original title, *Filumena Marturano,* starring Tamara Lees and author de Filippo instead of Loren and Mastroianni. And such is the durability of de Filippo's comedy of a whore seeking to give her sons the name of one of their fathers that, in 1978 in English, *Filumena* was a London stage hit starring Joan Plowright and Domenico Soriano.

weeks with the part before I start work. I think about it as I lead my life and I reread it only once a week or so—and on the night before shooting. Carlo's always amazed that I don't start acting at least a little like the person I'm playing a few days before shooting starts. When I report for work, though, it's fully digested."

Sophia scorns the notion of Peter Ustinov and a number of critics that she is at her best in Neapolitan films because she is "playing herself" on the screen: "An actress plays a character and there is always something of yourself that goes into it, but you have to make a composition. The character comes first, but in it there is surely a little of Sophia Loren."

She is, of course, a director's delight. What struck the late Sir Carol Reed was "something terribly important to a director: She trusts you right from the start. She gives herself to you as an artist. During shooting of *The Key* (1958), she would ask me, 'What did I do wrong and what can I do to make it better?' I never knew her to pull an act—the headache, the temperament. Usually with such beauty, there is worry about how looks are. She didn't bother about looks. She was interested in acting." (If Carlo Ponti had had his way, Sophia might never have worked with Reed—the great director of *Odd Man Out, The Third Man, The Fallen Idol,* and *Oliver!*—in *The Key* as Stella, the somber mistress of a series of doomed tugboat skippers. Ponti admitted this in 1962, while claiming that "I am not, as most people believe, her manager. She makes her own decisions. I was against her accepting a part in *The Key,* for instance, but she wanted to. She went ahead and signed the contract and the film was made. As it turned out, she showed better judgment than I.")

Doing *That Kind of Woman* with her in New York, Sidney Lumet found her "totally responsive from the word go. She knew what to do right away and was a total joy from beginning to end. . . . She literally takes your breath away when she walks into a room. She's got wit, she sings bloody well, and linguistically she's extraordinary. What she doesn't understand in words, she understands in your eyes." Lumet worked with Sophia during the depths of her Marriage, Divorce, and Bigamy Italian Style crisis over becoming the second Mrs. Ponti. But Lumet could only admire the way "when some bad news got out to the location, she'd just sit in the back of the studio limousine, cry for twenty minutes" or so, and then, just as soon as needed, go right back to work.

Sophia was such an astute mimic of Sidney Lumet's East Side Yinglish (Yiddish and English) that, in one day, she startled several different interviewers, including Earl Wilson, by using *meshuggener* and *shmegegge,* which she defined as "two different kinds of crazy mixed-up kids." In his definitive dictionary, *The Joys of Yiddish,* Leo Rosten wrote—after defining a *shmegegge* as "an unadmirable petty person; a maladroit, untalented type; a sycophant, a *shlepper,* a whiner, a drip"—that:

> Miss Sophia Loren used the word with considerable *brio* in an interview with a New York *Times* reporter. The combination of great beauty, an Italian accent, an eloquent shrug, a tone of derisive dismissal, and a Yinglish word marked a high point in the life of this colorful epithet.

I found Sophia bubbling with *brio** on my brief 1976 visit to Paris. She served champagne instead of tea for our 2 P.M. meeting. The Pontis had just returned from three weeks of Christmas vacation in the French alpine ski resort of Megève, not far from Mont Blanc; Sophia had learned to ski, but Cipi had outdistanced her and earned his first star from the instructor.

Over champagne, appropriately, we talked about drink and the American penchant for mixed drinks, particularly martinis. "I think gin is terrible," Sophia declared, making a face of elegant distaste, as though she might spit out her champagne if a potted palm were handy. "Drinking gin is like drinking the perfume you put on. Vodka is okay, but I don't enjoy hard liquor anyway. I like a glass of wine.

"In America they drink down hard liquor faster than we

---

*An Italian, not Yiddish, word for vigor or vivacity, as in the musical instruction *allegro con brio.*

drink wine, and I can never keep up with them; I never try. Still, I think Europeans have a worse alcohol problem because they drink wine or brandy all day. You don't notice how drunk many people are in Europe because they're a little drunk when you first meet them, even if it's ten in the morning, so they don't change that much after you get to know them. You'd be surprised how many businessmen you meet in Europe who are drunk all the time. They mix up their wine and their apéritifs and their brandy with their coffee, just to stay afloat all day."

Coming from "a little *shnaps* in your morning coffee?" country, I smelled truth in Sophia's generalization and asked how she'd found this out for herself.

"Sometimes, in making films, you have to entertain people you don't much care for," she said, "but to be polite you do it. And sometimes because they are boring and nothing you came to accomplish is getting accomplished, you study them to keep from yawning. And you begin to realize *why* they are the way they are—and, often, it's the *grappa.*"

"Can't you be boring without *grappa?*" I asked her and, having put it that way, personalized the question. "Are you ever boring?"

"Nobody's ever told me so," she said, "but, of course, we all bore ourselves sometimes. I like myself best when I'm relaxed and merry, like right now. When I don't feel that way, it's not just my surroundings that are to blame, it's myself."

"Even when you're trapped by a bore?"

"Then it's my fault, too, because I've put myself into that situation. We are all responsible for our own uneasiness."

I asked Sophia if, when uncomfortable, she felt a need to fill silences.

"No," she replied. "I appreciate silence in my daily life and, unlike so many people I know—not just actors—I don't try to fill it in. Look, I enjoy my family, but sometimes I need to be left alone for my work. If I am reading a script, I like to be quiet for at least an hour alone. I cannot be called to the door or the phone because then I must start over if I am to grasp what the script and I have for each other. You can't just pick it up again.

I have to *go through* a script and I need the right thought of any story I'm reading."

Cipi came in from school, greeted me, and practiced a little of his now-French-accented English on me: "Excuse me for deranging you."

I tried hard not to laugh, but I did—and then so did Sophia and then so did Cipi, who didn't look the least bit disturbed when Sophia explained that the French *déranger* (to disturb) didn't mean quite the same in English. Cipi only laughed harder before wanting to know something else: "Can I go with you to Sleeping Beauty tonight, *Ma-ma?*"

Sophia was going to see Rudolf Nureyev dance that evening and had already invited me to join her at the ballet if I could promote an extra ticket for myself without using her name. She was going with her Italian friend Madame Lombardo, who had done the ticket-buying so it would not be known Sophia was coming. Now she told Cipi: "Oh, no, Carlo! The ballet here starts at nine-thirty. That's too late for someone who has school in the morning." Turning to me, she added: "It's too late for any human being, but what can I do?"

Cipi was easy to placate. "Then can I go with Ruth to the Eiffel Tower?" he asked.

"Tomorrow maybe," his mother told him before explaining to me: "Our nurse took Cipi there and he's crazy about it. He calls it "science fiction" and now he hardly collects matchbox autos: just Eiffel Tower key rings and souvenirs."

After a few minutes of chit-chat, Sophia said to Cipi in English: "Carlo, Carlo, listen, baby, I am having an interview with Alan, so you can go downstairs and listen to the new records. And don't come up very often while we are working, please."

When her son, who had just turned seven, had left without protest, I said to Sophia: "Cipi seems to understand your need to be alone."

"No, he doesn't," she said. "Oh, I put tempting things downstairs to keep him away from up here, but otherwise he'd be in here, singing and dancing and imitating everything he sees on television and turning the radio on and off. I don't lose my temper. I just leave and go upstairs. In this life, there are always enough rooms. So far, I don't need to lock the door, but I know that, sooner or later, I will."

"Would you yell at him then?" I wondered.

"I don't think so. Even with the children, I don't seem to raise my voice. Cipi yells like hell, so it's very effective to speak my side of the argument in a low, controlled voice. But sometimes he gets really bored with his brother or comes home from school annoyed and pushes Edoardo and so Edoardo falls down and cries and then I have to scream just to be heard when Cipi is yelling and Edoardo is crying. But Cipi is getting more and more of his father's character as he gets older. I mean, he's at his most dangerous when he laughs"—a truth about Carlo Ponti, Sr., that Peter Ustinov had discerned with *Lady L* and that Sophia must have discovered early in the relationship.

As usual, for my January, 1976, visit to Paris, I had packed the latest batch of clippings from my bulging SOPHIA file. By now, however, all the "authenticated" reports of romances failed to alarm or even titillate me, but apparently they still sold scandal sheets.

"I got the definite impression there had never been anybody else," Dora Jane Hamblin once told me. "She did say to me once that she was extremely attracted to Cary Grant the first time she worked with him. That's the only person she ever expressed any interest in—to me, at least. Of course, she liked Peter Sellers enormously. I saw him one day playing Ping-Pong with her in Marino. He was trying to make her laugh. He not only succeeded, but just having watched those two play Ping-Pong is enough to make me start laughing right now. Sellers would wait until the ball got clear under the table and was bouncing around down there before he'd return it.

"I'd heard tales about Ponti, too. I once read that Sophia said she had never strayed and, if he ever did, she would hit him over the head. I've never seen either of them in any compromising situation whatever and what little I've heard along these lines has sounded very inaccurate."

Collaborating on "I'm Glad To Be Forty," Sophia told *McCall's* articles editor Helen Markel: "I am a terribly jealous woman. Carlo knows I would leave him if there were ever another serious woman in his life. I am an absolutely faithful woman. Not from a sense of morality, but because I cannot conceive of another man's touching me unless I were in love with him. I have loved Carlo for my whole life, but I would leave him immediately if he were unfaithful to me. Because I don't deserve infidelity. I don't believe that men can do anything they want and women cannot."

And, moping amidst the splendor of the Villa Ponti in Marino, she once wondered aloud: "Can I be absolutely sure that Carlo might not one day be unfaithful. Can any woman ever be that certain? All I can do is try to be the wife he wants and the best kind of mother to his children."

The latest rumors linked her with an Italian movie star *(Emmanuelle II)* Umberto Orsini, thirty-seven, thanks to an evening out together at l'Ange Bleu night spot. ("They sat close together at a tiny table and shared the best champagne, Dom Pérignon," revealed the club's manager, Jacques Jacquemin, to the representative of the *National Enquirer*.) Sophia laughed and predicted: "Just you wait until we go see Nureyev tonight! If they discover I'm there, why, they'll have me running off to marry *him,* too." She laughed again.

Sophia's Paris masseuse, Michèle Chenu, had just given an interview to Hebe Dorsey of *The International Herald Tribune* in which it was confided on the fashion page that Sophia "can be touching because she is so insecure; it took her a long time before she would see Mrs. Chenu without full makeup."

"What nonsense!" Sophia exclaimed primly. "She never saw me without makeup in my life!"

I hit pay dirt, however, when I produced a news item saying she'd given five ruby rings to the Rev. Anthony Goossens, pastor of Trinity parish in Llano, Texas, for an auction to finance a new church building. The press quoted Sophia: "I don't really like to talk about it. It's just one of those things you do. Father Goossens and I have written each other for more than ten years. I learned he had a need and I tried to do something. It was a small but happy act of charity—just a very natural thing to do."

That's as far as the press took it. I knew that ever since her brush with violence in the Hampshire House almost five-and-a-half years earlier, Sophia was ready and almost eager to dispense with her jewelry. But I was intrigued by the idea of Sophia—after her difficulties with the Vatican—playing pen pal to a priest. So I asked how she'd struck up contact with Father Goossens.

The answer came cryptically: "Through Madame Léthien in Nice."

"Oh? Who is that?"

Now the real story came. Making *Lady L* on the Riviera more than a decade earlier, Sophia had taken sick for a few days. She was confined to her hotel room, where there was nothing much to do except watch TV. A regular program featured people who were in need—and that day's particular guest was "a woman so thin that, when she spoke, it was an effort for her whole body," Sophia recalled. The master of ceremonies explained that the poor woman needed heart surgery which couldn't be done in France. But one of the great heart doctors in Houston had offered to do the job free if Mme Léthien could just get there, so the TV program was trying to raise money for her plane fare and incidental expenses.

As the regular audience phoned in and the program's hour ran out, Sophia saw with alarm that "they weren't raising anywhere near what Mme Léthien needed." So Sophia phoned in to say she would give the rest, but didn't want her identity announced on TV. The producer came on the line, which was off the air, listened, and then said: "All right, my friend. But you hang up and I'll call the hotel back to ask for Sophia Loren's room, because it would be a shame if somebody played a joke on this poor woman."

Sophia notified the desk that she'd take the incoming call and, when it came, she invited the producer and Mme Léthien around to collect the money next morning. Mme L. went off to

America, "came back cured, and now she's fat as a horse," Sophia told me. "But while she was in the hospital, Father Goossens was making the rounds there and she told him her story. He wrote me a very nice letter thanking me and, since then, we're in touch."

When the pastor's church needed money, Sophia had figured those ruby rings would "do him good and, after the Hampshire House, only harm to me." Now Father Goossens had notified her that Mrs. Amelia Flores of San Antonio, who'd bought three one-dollar raffle tickets, had won the rubies and Trinity Church was now $25,000 richer, thanks to all the losing tickets that were bought—and his new Church that much closer to completion. To which Sophia added: "Every Christmas, I receive a letter from Mme Léthien, and if it doesn't come by New Year's, I start to worry about her."

Always, during lulls on the set and on location, Sophia can be seen answering such letters that she brings along with her. For her, fan mail is neither a statistic nor barometer, but virtually a family obligation to be met with at least a friendly, hand-written answer, however brief: "Because they already think of me as Sophia, this doesn't surprise them. In fact, if I take a little while to answer, some of them write to ask, 'Why haven't I heard from you?' If they thought of me as a movie star or if I'd never answered them in the first place, they would never expect so much of me. They only complain because, in spite of all I have to do in my life, I always pick up the pen sooner or later. But it gives me a warm feeling to have this kind of rapport with the public."

Sophia had a 3:30 appointment and I had to hustle up a hard-to-get ticket to Nureyev, so as I stood up to say goodbye, I asked her a perfunctory question about what would follow *Cassandra Crossing*.

"Oh, plenty of pictures," she said. "My husband has done a very good contract with the Shah of Iran to make twelve pictures anywhere in the world. So I am certainly going to have a few of them to do for their partnership. But most of all, I'm looking for the right story and a strong partner."

"What's wrong with Mastroianni? Or Richard Burton?"

"A female partner. Now that would be my contribution to women's liberation! I mean, who are today's leading romantic couple on the screen?"

Half of Tracy and Hepburn, Olivier and Leigh were gone, so I guessed: "Sophia and Marcello?"

"Wrong," she said. "Robert Redford and Paul Newman. Men and more men!"

As it turned out, Jane Fonda and Vanessa Redgrave in Lillian Hellman's *Julia* and Anne Bancroft and Shirley MacLaine in *The Turning Point* would beat Sophia to the punch, but hers was an idea whose time had come and Sophia was definitely looking. Wistfully, almost shyly, she told me: "You know, I'd like to be paired with Liza Minnelli, who's a real performing animal and Italian, too, like me. I've never met her, but I think I could persuade her. I know her husband* from when he directed two of my TV shows in Rome. Even then, though, my best argument would have to be a strong story—and I'm looking for a good director with whom I can work regularly now that De Sica is gone. I have one good Italian director who might be right for me. But the problem is he's Italian."

"What's wrong with that?" I asked. "After all, you were Italian once!"

"I still feel Italian," Sophia said with a laugh. But she went on to explain: "Barbra Streisand, Liza Minnelli, everything they do —the American market is very big and they can have a success the whole world over. But Carlo says if what we do in Italian or French is going to be just a success only in Italy or France, then it's going to be a disaster for us because pictures cost so much to make today. So we have to make pictures that we hope will go all over the world—and particularly America. Still, to find the right story, the right part, and the right director: if I have all three of those, I'd even make the movie in Russian."

---

*Jack Haley, Jr. *(That's Entertainment!)*, whose marriage to Liza Minnelli broke up in early 1978.

That night, in the Palais des Sports, a huge arena at the Porte de Versailles end of the Paris Métro, Nureyev leaped like a thirty-seven-year-old Russian gazelle, but more than met his match in the young ballerina Eva Evdokimova.* Perhaps his partner stole Nureyev's show, but one who didn't was Sophia Loren. She waited in her car until 9:40 P.M. and then, just as the auditorium darkened, she entered and hardly anybody around her noticed her arrival. Madame Lombardo took an aisle seat with Sophia next to her (the best I'd been able to buy was in a section behind them) and, at the first intermission, the two women fled to the car. By the time they re-entered the hall as the lights dimmed for the second act, the management knew Sophia was there and offered her an office in which to spend the second intermission.

All this, of course, meant that Nureyev had been notified, so instead of dropping him a note the next day, Sophia said she would go backstage to visit him. She didn't invite me to go there with her, so I dropped only one hint: "Will you need a chaperon if he invites you to supper?"

"If he invites me," she said wearily, "I'll go. But I'd just as soon go home instead of watch a tired dancer eat after midnight."

I asked her how she'd liked the ballet.

Her vivacity returned as she exclaimed: "Wonderful! I only wish Cipi could have come."

The next day, somewhere in the area of Radio Luxembourg, I heard that Sophia had not only dined with Nureyev, but was planning to divorce Ponti to marry him. Subsequently, there were similar rumors in the press. I didn't even bother to check this one out with Sophia.

---

*Despite her Slavic name, Evdokimova is Swiss: daughter of a Bulgarian father and Canadian mother.

CHAPTER 23

April in Paris?

IN LATE 1976, THE MANAGING EDITOR of *McCall's* Magazine dropped me a note that

> We'd like to make another assignment. Next September Carlo and Sophia will have been married for twenty years, and it will have been a couple of years since we last had her on the cover, so it seems time to go after them again. We would need copy in plenty of time to come out before their anniversary. I assume you'll be able to get it to us by the middle of May at the latest, and hopefully a little earlier.
>
> Twenty years is a long time to be married, particularly when a lot of people were skeptical about it in the beginning, and it has been rumored to be in trouble more than once, and that's what they should be talking about. How their marriage has changed over the years, what their biggest crises were, and how they resolved them, how children changed their relationship, do they imagine retiring and have they speculated on how they'd like to live if they did, etc. I don't know how realistic he is about himself (and I can't imagine quite how you'd bring it up) but he is not exactly the handsome young leading man type, and surely much of the curiosity about their marriage stems from the fact that people wonder how he was able to win and keep the love of one of the world's most delectable women. Will he talk about that? Will she?

Around the same time, I was approached by a Playboy International editor who wanted a "four-thousand-word interview, plus an introduction of maybe seven hundred fifty words, with your friend Sophia Loren."

Not just for contrast between "The Playboy Philosophy" and that of "The Magazine for Suburban Women," but to show how the media perceive her and the choices that are presented to her daily, let me further cite the guiding light emanating from just beneath the Bunny Beacon of Playboy Towers in Chicago:

> . . . She and Carlo Ponti passed through Chicago several months ago and dominated the front pages of all three papers for two days. I know people want to read about her; better, people would like simply to listen to her talk. Anything you and she would like to talk about would be welcome: her career, what it's like to be the world's most beautiful woman, the state of the world film industry, nudity and permissiveness, what men are attractive, women's roles. I trust you to grasp intuitively what would be interesting to our readers. . . . Soft-pedal why she's married to Ponti; I'm bored of hearing about that. Maybe query on what it's like to live in Sophia Loren's body.

When I reached Sophia in Marino in early 1977, she said the Playboy project sounded "very delicate, at least in my opinion" and asked for more information, but agreed immediately to the interview for *McCall's*. The women's magazine had already taken an option on some new Alfred Eisenstaedt photos of the Pontis, one for an August or September cover.

"I don't know how available Carlo will be," she said, "but I'm always happy to talk about my marriage and I'll be glad to as soon as this film is finished." ("This film" turned out to be *A Special Day*.)

"When will that be?" I asked.

"Middle or end of February," she replied. "And then I need to go off to Madeira for a fortnight with the children. I should be home in Paris around the fifteenth of March and, if you call me there then, we can set a date for the following month." After a little more conversation, she rang off saying, "See you April in Paris, dear!" and it sounded even sweeter than a song.

The Playboy editor wrote back, increasing the requested word count (but not the price) by a thousand, and offering the following clarification:

> I'm really not interested in hearing another time why a lovely young thing like that is married to a horned old thing like that. If Ponti has to come up in the interview at all, let it be in some other terms than those of June-January romance. Otherwise . . . as much sex and scandal as you can get in without betraying your friendship would be appreciated: gossip about the stars of the Italian movie colony, for example, and does she have anything to say about the late P. P. Pasolini?*

With little or no prompting from me, although I did paraphrase politely, Sophia declined the *Playboy* offer ("I just don't like my sons to see me in magazines that have naked women in them"), but our April-in-Paris date for *McCall's* was still on.

On Tuesday, February 8, ten agents of Italy's finance police, who enforce their country's tax and foreign-exchange regulations, raided and searched the Villa Ponti while Carlo and Sophia were there. Seizing several documents, the police indicated this was part of an investigation of currency irregularities that had been underway for a long time. And, even though Dodie Hamblin's problems with Ponti had started over where he stashed his money, I didn't fear that the latest flurry would affect me.

Exactly a month after the raid, however, Sophia went to Leonardo da Vinci Airport to catch a Rome-Paris flight now

---

*Pier Paolo Pasolini (1922–75), the Marxist director of *The Gospel According to St. Matthew* (1964) and co-author (with Basilio Franchina, Mario Soldati, and three others) of Sophia's first starring vehicle, *Woman of the River* (1954), had recently been bludgeoned by a seventeen-year-old boy to whom he may have made homosexual advances and then, while still barely alive, run over by his confessed killer. In mid-1978, however, a Rome court of appeals upheld a four-month jail sentence imposed upon the noted Italian journalist, Oriana Fallaci, for refusing to disclose her sources for a series of articles alleging that Pasolini was murdered by a group of young hooligans in a pre-arranged plot, possibly prompted by rightists.

that *A Special Day* was finished. She had booked her seat under
an assumed name ("Miss Entrice"), which her lawyer later said
was "a normal expedient used by actors and actresses." Rome's
ever-vigilant finance police, however, somehow saw through
her alias and took her into an airport room for what they at first
called "a routine customs inspection," which it clearly was not.
After going through her luggage, the police confiscated three
sealed envelopes pertaining to some banking transactions she'd
completed that morning and questioned her "in connection
with the inquiry regarding Carlo Ponti about alleged currency
violations." The police called the interlude—estimated by some
sources as four hours and by others as nine—"detention," although the three Ponti lawyers who rushed to the scene emphasized that "she was not arrested, . . . it's just a routine investigation into movie matters," and "nothing is going on." But, just as
clearly, something was going on.

When Sophia arrived in Paris a couple of hours after the
Roman police let her go, the press said she was still shaken and
devoid of comment. Thus, on a Friday night in March, when I
was traveling in Germany and had arrived at Dortmund's fit-
tingly named Hotel Römischer Kaiser (Roman Emperor), I was
not surprised to find a message, relayed by my family, waiting:
"Call Sophia in Paris. Urgent."

I dialed Paris and Carlo Ponti answered. "Listen, I want to
talk to you," he began. "Sophia wants to postpone the interview." I asked for how long. Ponti, whose English is never the
most precise, gave me three answers during our talk: "Three or
four weeks" . . . "three or four months" . . . and "indefinitely."

When I reiterated that April in Paris had been a fairly firm
objective, Ponti said vaguely: "Sophia may want to go to Brazil
some time in April." Flattery got me nowhere; when I reminded him that a story focusing on *their* marriage could con-
ceivably involve more of him and less of her time, he said: "Me?
Ha-ha, I am not so interesting, ha-ha-ha!" When I hinted that
he should at least suggest some new date to fulfill Sophia's
commitments to Eisenstaedt and myself as well as my own commitment to *McCall's* and a couple of other obligations, Ponti

laughed merrily as he told me "we all have our problems in this world keeping our word."

Remembering that both Ustinov and Sophia herself had said Carlo was at his most dangerous to others when he laughed, I said hastily that I'd wait to call until immediately after the schools' Easter recess ended in mid-April. Ponti welcomed the delay, but emphasized that he could promise me nothing. Laughing all the way, he concluded: "She is still very upset, doesn't want to talk to anyone, not even to me, ha-ha-ha! and when she does, most of her answers are no. *Ciao!*"

I hung up, shaken—but determined to get through to Sophia the next time and, if a man answered, hang up.

(Indeed, the only other time Ponti had ever answered the phone, I'd had trouble. That was in 1975, when my family and I had arrived in Paris for the long weekend Sophia had specified. I'd called her from a friend's home to say we were safely there and to set a time for the next day. Ponti, however, had answered the phone, denied Sophia was in town, and insisted she wouldn't be back for more than a week. When I'd called again an hour or two later, Ines had answered and put on Sophia, who'd laughed at—but not apologized for—Carlo's protectiveness.)

Soon after my Dortmund-to-Paris call, I wrote Sophia a note expressing my sympathy and outrage over the airport episode, reviewing my conversation with Carlo, and reiterating our commitment to each other. In early April I sent Sophia a new book of mine with a card saying, "This was the pre-anniversary gift I was hoping to hand you in person around this time."

Then, on Monday, April 18, 1977, I phoned Sophia in Paris. Ines answered. Yes, Sophia was in; just a minute.

Sophia came on the line and welcomed me warmly. Now she was fine, thank you, she said. When did I want to do our interview?

I gulped and said: "As soon as possible."

"I want to do it when Carlo is out of town," she said, "because I have more time then." Hearing no argument from me, Sophia went on: "How about Thursday April twenty-eight? . . . In the morning? . . . Is nine-thirty too early for you? . . . See you then!" It would indeed be April in Paris after all!

To see Sophia, I would have to interrupt a *Reader's Digest* assignment in Germany, but Pleasantville posed no problem if *McCall's* would foot my added expenses. Still, before I could see her the rollercoaster I was on had another twist to make.

Once again, my work brought me on a Friday night to the Hotel Römischer Kaiser in Dortmund, where I was still remembered from the previous month's message to "call Sophia Loren in Paris, urgent." This time, I was saluted by even wider eyes, a couple of open mouths, and at least one lecherous wink. The message awaiting me at both the reception and porter's desks read: "Frau Sophia Loren called at 1645 hours to say that her husband will be back on Thursday, so would you please come instead on Wednesday at the same time? She will wait for you to call and confirm, please."

I called and confirmed with pleasure and a bouquet of bright-red blushes.

CHAPTER 24

Twenty Years of Togetherness

"MY ELEVENTH WEDDING ANNIVERSARY was a few days ago and my twentieth will be in September, so I don't know whether you're early or late or just wrong," Sophia Loren greeted me after I'd crossed the Avenue George V from the Hotel George V, where she'd booked me at eighty-three dollars a night (single room with breakfast), to the Résidence George V, where she lives, to do what became "SOPHIA LOREN Tells the Story of 20 Turbulent Years of Marriage."

The proxy marriage in Mexico on September 17, 1957 apparently was still recognized by the McCall Corporation even though it had been nullified everywhere else. Or was it the value of a selling cover line? Sophia, on the other hand, saw the French ceremony in Sèvres on April 9, 1966 as the first time she and Carlo could relax in the security of calling themselves man and wife, Mr. and Mrs. Ponti, without fear of prosecution. "I don't really think in terms of anniversaries," she told me. "To me, it's just a bit more than ten years of real marriage and twenty years of togetherness. That's why we don't have any special celebrations; we wouldn't know when. Do you observe yours?"

I told Sophia yes; while traveling in America the previous August, Valerie and I had celebrated our own twentieth with a long rainy weekend indoors at the Hotel Concord in the Cats-kills. And I added that marriage being something I'd gone into at the age of twenty-four following the longest stints of anything I'd ever undertaken—four years of living at college and two years in the Army—I had, because I was young (or should I say immature?), thought it would be good if marriage lasted as long as either or both of those previous missions. Nowadays, I sometimes wake up amazed not only to find us the longest-married couple on our block—but to think that anybody's been able to live with me for two decades and more.

When I confessed all this to Sophia, she gave a throaty laugh and admitted: "I have to say I might have shared your feelings about marriage if I'd ever had time to think about it that retrospectively. Ten or twenty years is a long time to be married. But I think marriage is most beautiful when you're living it, not analyzing it."

Nevertheless, when I pressed Sophia about the particularly dubious risk of a performer marrying a producer more than twenty years her senior, Sophia burst out with:

"The difference between my marriage and yours—between most marriages and mine!—is that I was born married to Carlo. I must have always been looking for the father I never had, so Carlo means that much more to me. But I've never felt bound to him or him to me, in the legal sense. We are together because we like to be together, not because we have to be together. If it's a pleasure to be with someone, then your pleasure doesn't need papers or signatures: it's just your choice. And I think the pleasure is reciprocated."

I noted: "The way you're talking, you've been married to Carlo for double the twenty years."

"Well, I feel I've known Carlo since I'm alive," Sophia agreed. "The day I went to his office after the Miss Rome beauty contest, it wasn't what you could call love at first sight: it was a kind of easy familiarity, as if we'd always known each other, but had just met. Didn't life begin for me when I escaped the past and started having success? When you begin to work steadily, when you begin to have experiences of value in life that you can build upon, that's when you're actually born."

Sounding like Trilby talking about Svengali, Sophia went on: "I was terribly young, but I felt that, in joining Carlo, I was doing the right thing. And, because I was young, I *knew* it would last forever. When you do something as important as try to get married, you think it's forever—otherwise, you wouldn't do it."

Now I protested: "But the point I was making is that, in *my* marriage, I *didn't* think it was forever. In yours, you apparently did."

"That's because I didn't know the risks," Sophia said, laughing again. "Maybe because I was from Italy—and I'm still Italian in my nature and attitude, no matter if a piece of paper makes me French. In Italy at that time, marriages always lasted forever, no matter how bad they were.

"Nowadays, if you'd meet somebody when you're over forty or just see a couple falling in love, you'd ask yourself: 'Is it really going to last forever?' because you have much more experience of what can go wrong. If you're a little lucky, it's the experience of others, not your own.

"The other thing is that you lose your head completely in your teens or early twenties. But, when the years go by, you think differently. You start to wonder whether anything can be forever. Life changes. You change inside of yourself—from other responsibilities and experiencing new things. It's all so, so different from what you expected. When you're twenty or twenty-four, what does forever mean? It means the next two or three years—ten or fifteen per cent of your life. That's why *you* really *were* thinking of forever when you went into marriage, Alan. Forever just happened to be a minute or two longer than the longest amount of time you knew: six years of college and military service. Time is relative. I know this when I talk to my sons. If I say, 'Be patient,' what does it mean to them? They are four and eight years old and to wait ten minutes for something is forever because it is such a big portion of their lives.

"And when one is older and, for example, trying to have babies as I was in my thirties, and they say, 'Be patient,' they mean for five years, six years, maybe even ten years. Sometimes, it's dangerous to be patient. The same people who say, 'Be patient,' are the ones who tell you, 'Sorry, too late.'"

With this, the conversation turned to the Pontis' two sons. Cipi was growing "a little robust, like his father," Sophia reported, and Edoardo was "tall for his age." Cipi had just taken up the piano—and his progress had his mother both delighted and amazed: "You know, my mother was a pianist who gave lessons, so the flair for music must have skipped a generation. . . . Me, I like music, but don't understand it. Oh, I feel it. . . . I like Puccini. He's human and understands women; just listen to *Madame Butterfly* if you don't believe me. But when I tried to learn the piano, I was too impatient."

"But you're not ordinarily an impatient person?" I surmised.

"Oh, yes I am. You'd be surprised. I'm a very impatient person, but I don't show it. I get impatient when I have something important to do and the time doesn't go fast enough so that I can go right into it when I'm all ready to go. It's funny. When I like to do something, I get impatient. And when I'm scared to do something, I feel impatient because, once I'm able to do the best I can, I want to face it."

I told Sophia how, faced with a crucial decision that would take six weeks once all the arguments passed out of my hands, I had felt a terrible urge to go to bed and sleep forty days and forty nights.

Sophia laughed. "Your first reaction is to go to sleep," she said. "Mine is to get interested in other things. Some people can't sleep at such times. I'm more like you. I sleep more than usual when I'm impatient or anxious. But it's no escape, because then I dream about my problem. Anyway, I don't need to take sleeping pills or even aspirins when I'm troubled."

Back to Cipi went the chit-chat. Not only was he doing well at piano, but he was enjoying it and, like many another child, using music to express rage and soothe the savaged self whenever parents prove unbearable.

Sophia's youngsters must, of necessity, be sheltered—for they require more protection than yours or mine. Children of the rich and famous have to be guarded nowadays, but Sophia has done a good job of managing this without suppressing her sons' social lives. She always invited their friends up and accepted invitations which came their way. Whenever Tazio Secchiaroli came up from Rome to shoot her latest portraits, he was encouraged to bring his son David along to play with the boys while his father and their mother worked together. "David was his first friend and Cipi never forgets that," Sophia told me.

A few days before my visit, Sophia had given her sons the gift for which they'd clamored for a couple of Christmases: a new-born German Shepherd puppy named Nikko.

"Sounds like a Japanese camera," I remarked. "He's little now," said Sophia, "but he's going to be as big as a donkey."

Both boys were sharing responsibility for walking the dog. As they took turns walking Nikko, little Edoardo learned to tell time and Cipi became involved with other dog-walkers (not all of them knowing him for whose son he was) and the social life of his elite neighborhood. Always, boy and dog were accompanied by nurse Ruth or secretary Ines or some other grown-up, but the watchful adults would stay in the background. Sophia told me: "We make the pretense that the boys are on their own and don't let them shirk their duty."

Although Nikko came to the Pontis as an honor graduate of a Paris obedience school, apartment living and occasionally lax masters have resulted in a few training accidents to the triplex's wall-to-wall carpeting. But Sophia felt the cost had been worth it for the self-reliance and pride-in-accomplishment that the experience of looking after a dog had instilled in both boys. Nikko may well be a pampered pet, but Sophia's sons aren't.

Nikko hadn't yet come to live with the Pontis back when I was phoning Paris on April 18th to make my date with Sophia, and this made him one lucky dog. In the early hours of Tuesday, April 19, during the coldest night of a cold spring in Paris, Sophia had been awakened by "a very harsh knock on my door, but that's not unusual because now I close myself in and take a lot of awakening when my husband's away. Ines was screaming. There was the same shrill in her voice that she'd had when we were robbed in New York. But this time Ines said there was a fire in the building, and all memory of the robbery went out of my mind.

"You have to face new realities right away because fire is very,

very dangerous. You have no time to exchange old nightmares for new dangers: if you make that kind of comparison, you do so later on, like now, when you tell the story.

"I opened the door and smoke poured in from every place. We got panicky and tried to call the concierge downstairs to ask what was happening, but he wasn't there. So I phoned a friend of mine and told her to call the fire department and 'say that we have a fire in my apartment. I'm running. I don't know where I'm going, but I just have to go somewhere.' In my panic, it didn't occur to me that I could call the firemen myself.

"Then I went upstairs to where the children sleep. The nurse was already there. We put their blankets over them and each of us carried one. They both woke up a little, but I said: 'Don't worry. There's a fire and we don't know where it's coming from. It's not in our place, but we go up.' By then, we could see that the smoke was coming from below, so we had to head for the roof.

"We went several flights upstairs, but we didn't have the key to the door that opens onto the roof. There was a window there and I broke it with my shoe and we got outside. Already there were some people on the roof, but nobody had notified us: it was very strange and a little worrisome.

"I was in my nightgown and barefoot. The temperature was right down around freezing, so when the children were up on the roof, I went back down to the apartment to get something warm to put on—but also to open the door. I was thinking that *if* the fire is somehow from my apartment, then the firemen could come in. But the smoke was so heavy that I couldn't open the door the first time, so I went back up to the roof for some fresh air and then back down to open the door. As soon as I had the door open, it occurred to me that now I might be letting the fire out—or *in*. If there's a fire, you're not supposed to open anything, so I closed the door back again. That's what panic can do: a lot of wasted energy and unnecessary danger, but, in this case, thank God, no harm."*

---

*Somewhere in this commuting between roof and triplex, Sophia may have managed to dress up a little, for one of her neighbors, *Paris-Match* execu-

Meanwhile, the friend she'd phoned had panicked, too—and given the firemen a house number three higher than Sophia's. Thus, the engine company went to the wrong side of the broad avenue for a few minutes. Fortunately, somebody else had called in, so the firemen lost little time crossing the street. By then, Sophia was back up on the roof with the others shouting in vain: "We are up here! We are up here!" Then "we just stood and shivered and I began to look around in case we had to jump. There was another roof that some of us could have jumped to with a little effort. But what about the others?"

After an hour inside the building, two firemen had finally come up to the roof and one of them had informed the tenants: "Don't worry. The fire was on the fourth floor and it's spread to the fifth floor, but now we have it under control." Sophia—whose triplex rises from the seventh floor—had heaved a shiver of relief as the fireman continued: "We'll have to work for three or four more hours, but it is blocked. The danger is over."

"Still," said the other fireman, "you should take the children down to the lobby, Madame Ponti, because it's not good for them to be out here." With that, in Sophia's words, "he slipped a gas or an oxygen mask onto little Edoardo, who was awake, but like a statue: He couldn't speak, couldn't move, just frozen with fright maybe."

Sophia went on: "The fireman disappeared with Edoardo before I could say a word. The other one took Cipi and I told the nurse to go with them. They told the rest of us who had apartments above the fifth floor to go back down and open our doors and windows to let the smoke out. With Ines, I came down to the apartment and the smoke was so thick it was almost impossible to get in, but we did—and we opened up everything we could. When the smoke went out, it was about six-fifteen in the morning and the children came back up with Ruth. They

---

tive Hervé Mille, reported that her ordeal reduced Sophia to tears, but she remained a vision of enchantment in mauve robe, with sleeves billowing like wings in the wind, and matching turban. Mille marveled in print: "Imagine spending a night with Sophia Loren—under those circumstances."

were both a little annoyed because they hadn't been allowed to keep their masks, but the first thing Cipi did was to go directly to the piano and play a tune. For once it was okay for him to play the piano at six in the morning!

"I wasn't feeling too well, though, and a little later my head started turning and turning. I went to the hospital that afternoon and they said I had smoke intoxication. They had me inhale oxygen for an hour-and-a-half and sent me home.

"The good thing about the experience was that I'd kept too busy, even when I was doing panicky things, to pay attention to how cold I was. In that hour, though, after the firemen were in the building, I remember wishing and wishing that Carlo were here. We make our decisions about the children together— whether it's over school or just walking the dog—and any responsibility for them that a wife takes alone, well, she has to consider what her husband would think or do."

Back on April 19th, when I'd heard the news of the fire later in the day, I'd phoned Paris long-distance to ask how Sophia was doing. When Ines had answered "Fine!", I'd asked her to relay my joy and ended the chat fast before there could be any third or fourth thoughts about our forthcoming appointment. But I'd brought her one of my home-town tabloids as a souvenir with the headline: "SOPHIA LOREN ON THE ROOF IN HER NIGHTGOWN."

Sophia laughed and said: "You journalists have to bring sex into everything. Imagine! Maybe next they call it 'SEX KITTEN ON A HOT TIN ROOF.'"

Then, laughing again, but sounding a little more serious, she said: "Listen, if you think there's anything sexy about being up on the roof on a cold night with a fire below you, you try it some time."

And, even more solemnly, almost superstitiously, she added: "But I hope you never do."

Having raked the embers of recent memory, Sophia remained in a meditative mood: "I may be married ten years or twenty years, but I feel like I've been married for such a short time because our children are so young that they make me feel younger than I am. You start thinking differently, though, when your children are fourteen or fifteen and you dread the moment they will leave you."

My own daughters being twelve and thirteen at the time, I told Sophia a recurring dream I'd started having a few years earlier: *Erika is calling Monica, or else vice versa, and one of them is saying: "They stayed with me the last time they visited, so this time can they stay with you?"*

Sophia didn't laugh. Instead, she said: "It must be a very sad moment. It means a part of your life is gone, and you have to start and build a new life for yourself in order to survive. I think it's going to be the saddest moment of my life when my children leave me. Of course, it would be sadder if they didn't leave me, or if I didn't realize that they are grown and *must* go off on their own.

"I hope I can cope with it. It's not in my nature to let go of anything easily, but I know how people have to be free to do whatever they feel like doing and make their own mistakes in order to really understand life. My children aren't growing up in a cocoon now, so they won't have the problem and I'll try not to make any for them.

"I'll suffer maybe. I won't let myself go, though, in front of them. But I'll accept life as it is and turn to Carlo when it gets to me."

I asked: "And if your son starts going with a girl you don't approve of?"

"Then he has to do it," she replied with her *mamma mia* shrug. "It's much better to say to him, 'You can do anything you want. It's your life,' because if you stop and say no, I think that's the worst. Because then your children start competing with you, trying to spite you. You can say, 'I don't like her, but if *you* do, well, enjoy yourself! I have to say what I feel.' "

She lit a Muratti Ambassador cigarette, which took me by surprise. While I'd seen pictures (particularly some silhouettes by Irving Penn of Sophia the Smoker) and read her complaints that Peter O'Toole, while making *La Mancha,* corrupted her after she'd given up smoking ("Don't be chicken. Take one."), I had never seen her light up in the eight years I'd known her. I asked her: "Is that an after-effect of the fire?"

"No," she said. "It comes and it goes. But it has nothing to do with anxiety. I do it between movies and, when I go back to work, I can stop right away. I never smoke more than eight or nine a day."

If anxieties did play any part, early 1977 would have been enough to drive Sophia to smoking—and this was how I backed into asking about the February raid and her March detention by the Italian finance police. At home as well as at airports, Sophia refused to make any public comment or statement about it, and beyond "it's something I want to forget," she put our discussion of it on a not-for-quotation basis. Suffice it to say that while I, like Dodie Hamblin, just *knew* that no wealthy Italian was going to sit back and watch his or her lire depreciate, particularly with Switzerland next door, I came away convinced that her native Italy had singled out Sophia unjustly. Concerned about the decline of their currency (not to mention their economy and public order) and the flow of lire to neighboring lands for conversion, the Italian authorities had been cracking down on international wheelers and dealers of all sizes and shapes. A global mogul like Ponti and his world-famous wife, regardless of the merits of any case against them, were ideal media for signaling the severity of the law via headlines— just as they'd been labeled bigamists for the first decade of togetherness because the Vatican and Signora Brambilla wanted to make an example of them. Symbolism is one of the costlier prices of fame.

Back on the record, Sophia wanted to accentuate the positive. "This is turning into the morbid interview," she complained. "First fire, then my children leaving me, now taxes." So when I retreated to the relatively tame question of whether the tax crisis had brought her and Carlo closer together, she turned it aside with: "Marriage is togetherness, in good and in bad. If you're together in good times, you take care of each other in bad times, too. They say that adversity drives people together, but I don't think so. If they're fighting each other when things are good, they won't even know how to work together when they aren't."

I asked whether she could or would go back to Italy.

"Of course I can!" Sophia responded, eyes flashing. "They wouldn't have let me go if I couldn't come back, would they? Like I said, I'm still Italian, I still love Italy and the Italian people very much—and they love me. So there was an accident at the airport! I try to forget about it."

Thinking this over for a minute, Sophia added:

"If I went back right away, though, there would be so much rumor, so much publicity, so much fighting over me that I wouldn't be able to work well. Too many headlines mean you make no life. You have to be able to live your life. If I wanted to, I could go back to Italy tomorrow—but I think I'll wait until the day after tomorrow."

What she wanted to talk about instead was the movie she had just finished making in Italy when she was intercepted at Rome's airport. *A Special Day* co-starred Marcello Mastroianni and was directed by Ettore Scola, heir apparent to De Sica's mantle as Sophia's director. When I was visiting her, Sophia—who'd made the movie in Italian—had just finished dubbing herself into French for the Cannes Film Festival, where she would introduce it in person, and then the Paris premiere. Later in 1977, she would dub *A Special Day* into English and Spanish.

Ettore Scola, an Italian writer-director whose *We All Loved Each Other So Very Much* was hailed by New York film critic Judith Crist as a "delightful and deeply touching story of three men who met in the Resistance," first came to Sophia's attention when he "did a picture with my husband called *Bad, Ugly* and *Something Like That*, which I thought was very good. And I said to Carlo: 'Why don't you ask him if he has in mind some kind of story for me which is completely the opposite to what I've done with De Sica and in the other Italian films?' "

And Carlo Ponti said: "Why don't you ask him yourself?"

Which is what Sophia, anxious to arrest the creakiness of her vehicles, did. Almost like a shopper, she took her needs to Scola and told him: "I want a story that will fit Marcello and me, but something very different from everything else he and I have done together. We must present this couple, Marcello and me, in a new way. In all the pictures he and I made for De Sica, I am the strong one and he is the weak one."

Scola thought it over and, after two or three months, he came back to Sophia "with a synopsis which we all thought was very interesting. Carlo wanted some little changes, but the approach to the two characters was so good that we were all enchanted." Then Scola collaborated on the screenplay with Ruggero Maccari and Maurizio Costanzo.

Since it's often interesting to hear how a star sees her own picture, I asked Sophia to tell me the story of *A Special Day.*

"You can't really say it in words," she began apologetically. "It's a mosaic made of so many little things that you have to see and watch."

Trying to help her along, I spouted a writer's axiom: "You mean if it could be told in words, there'd be no need to tell it in film?"

"No," said Sophia. "It's a story that can be told very simply, but that won't do justice to it. I am the mother of six children. The film takes place in 1938 and I am married to a man who is not Marcello. And there is this big day when Hitler comes to Rome to visit Mussolini and everybody's getting ready for the big parade to greet Hitler. Almost all the people in the whole building go away, but the character I play stays at home all alone; her husband and children have gone to the parade. She takes care of the house and a bird, but this bird flies away and goes on another window. So she tries to catch the bird and she can't. Then she sees there's somebody at that window. She waves, but this person doesn't answer. So she goes to his apartment and that's how they meet. The film takes place on that one day, but it's a whole life in one day."

"It's a romance?" I guessed.

"It's everything! It's life. It's beautiful," she replied. "It's a very special film that nowadays producers don't do anymore. It doesn't have erotic or violent ingredients in it. It's so delicate that I almost fear for it." Which is why, from the outset, Sophia Loren had to mother *A Special Day* and Carlo Ponti had to husband the film to fruition. "We all decided," Sophia recalled, "that we would just make this film for us, Ettore and Carlo, Marcello and myself, because, for sure, it would never be commercial. In fact, it took Carlo a little time and trouble to find the funds to produce it."

"Wouldn't the Shah of Iran pay for it?" I asked.

"No, he and Carlo never completed that deal. Anyway," she added with a giggle, "it's not a picture the Shah of Iran would have liked. But we got an Italian-Canadian co-production."

"What's Canadian about it?"

"Well, my husband in the film, John Vernon, is a Canadian actor and so is the concierge whose radio keeps broadcasting the events of the day. But we made it in Italian. Even Vernon, he learned Italian and says his own lines in Italian. He and I will dub ourselves into English together. We didn't film any of it in Canada, though."

Sophia was already willing to go on record as saying that *A Special Day* was "the best picture I've ever done" and was quick to add that "Ettore Scola is one of the finest directors we have in Italy. . . . It's different from working with De Sica because Vittorio wasn't a writer. When Cesare Zavattini would write a script, De Sica would tell him his idea and then Zavattini would write it. But Scola is an author. He writes it himself, so it's something else. And if he has something he sees in his mind or wants to say or do, he knows how to put it in words and he knows how he's going to write it."

Despite Sophia's presence and an enthusiastic audience, *A Special Day* won no honors at Cannes. The "best film" prize, awarded by a jury headed by Roberto Rossellini and including Pauline Kael, went to another Italian entry, *Padre Padrone*. The *International Herald Tribune's* critic, Thomas Quinn Curtiss— who wrote that *A Special Day* "towers above other contenders" and "Sophia Loren, daring a non-glamour role as the faded wife, gives what is assuredly her most mature and moving performance"—later did a follow-up that reported:

> Due to the questionable verdicts of the 1977 Cannes Festival jury—in particular, its neglect of Ettore Scola's *Una Giornata Particolare,* generally regarded as the best film to have been shown in competition—future festivals may eliminate the bestowing of awards.

Apparently, there was initial resistance to Sophia and Mastroianni breaking their mold. Charles Michener's critical report from Cannes for *Newsweek* said the film "offered a sensitively felt, beautifully photographed study of a brief encounter. . . . But its two romantic protagonists were perversely miscast: Sophia Loren as a passive housewife and Marcello Mastroianni as a homosexual." ("Did he want it the other way around?" Sophia asked me at a later date.)

The phrase "brief encounter" recurred in the much more enthusiastic New York notices that autumn, for *A Special Day* conjures up comparisons to Coward's *Brief Encounter,* the pallid Burton-Loren TV re-creation of which proved to be an apt rehearsal for Scola. Vincent Canby wrote in The *Times* that Sophia was "magnificent" and, while "it's initially difficult to accept Mastroianni as the distraught, suicidal homosexual he is supposed to be . . . their brief encounter lights up the screen with the kind of radiance you get only from great movie actors who are also great stars."

Judith Crist, writing in The *Post,* said this "small and powerful film" about "a touching and true brief encounter between two unlikely people . . . re-establishes Sophia Loren as one of the finest of screen actresses and places Ettore Scola firmly in the first ranks of film-makers."

And Kathleen Carroll, a successor to the durable Kate Cameron*, declared in The *Daily News:*

---

*A journalistic trade secret here: "Kate Cameron" was invented in the 1920s by *Daily News* publisher Joseph Medill Patterson who thought "Cameron was an ideal movie critic's name because it sounded like *camera* and, for a

What makes their brief encounter so special is that Sophia Loren and Marcello Mastroianni have been cast in these unlikely roles. Now, one expects to see Loren in full make-up and wearing the latest Paris fashions, not stripped of all her glamor with dark shadows beneath her striking eyes and a run in her cotton stockings. And Mastroianni's off-screen reputation as a lover would hardly seem to qualify him for a role as a man who shrinks from a woman's kisses. Yet, surprisingly, it does not matter much that the leading man and leading lady of Italian cinema are playing against type.

Thanks to their long experience as actors, each is capable of the telling gestures that often reveal more about characters than words. In Loren's case, it's the way she curls a lock of her hair in a desperate attempt to pretty herself up for her male caller; in Mastroianni's case, it is the way he stares longingly at the telephone . . .

A Special Day becomes a tender duet between two performers who, after years of working together, have developed a telepathic ability to understand each other's moods and switches of personality. The electricity between them is of such a high voltage that one never tires of watching them.

All this new glory—and more—lay ahead, however, when Sophia and I sat sipping coffee in her eight-floor Paris living room on the morning of April 27, 1977. She was saying: "Everybody who's seen it says it's a very good movie. For me, it's a masterpiece. . . . You know, when you arrive at a certain point in your life, you don't do things just to make money. As a matter of fact, maybe sometimes money is the last thing you think about. But, of course, if you make money doing something you love, it usually means you've done it right—in the right moment, with the right people—and maybe said something that was worth saying. . . . So I begin to hope maybe our little film will do well commercially, too."

---

first name, Kate had a compatible sound." The first Kate Cameron was Irene Thirer, who later moved to The *Post* under her own name; the second, for many years, was a genteel maiden lady named Loretta King.

This wasn't such a longshot, after all, for Sophia's name on any picture guarantees an enviable amount of commercial success. In 1976, when she had nothing more notable to display than *Cassandra Crossing,* she and Robert Redford were voted the world's favorite movie actress and actor in a survey conducted by Reuters for the Hollywood Foreign Press Association. With that honor went a Golden Globe, Sophia's fourth.

Telling me how she went to Hollywood in early 1977 to collect it, she said "that made smaller headlines" than her tax and fire escapades, "but for me, it is already the biggest moment of the year—one of the most moving in my life. Maybe you saw it on live TV. I was the last one called to the stage and, after about two hours of presentations, I thought everybody must be a little tired. But when I came out everybody in that big place stood up. I didn't expect so much affection, so many people pleased to see me there. Nobody told them to stand up, but they did it spontaneously and with great grace. From the stage, the way they popped up was like a field of mushrooms appearing out of nowhere. It made me realize how much people—strangers!— love me. And they were giving me their love now not because I was *quote* Important *unquote,* but because of what I must have given to them over the years." Sophia doesn't like to be called an institution or a living immortal, though it was obvious, long before *A Special Day* was released and her artistic eclipse had ended, that she's passed beyond the phase of being only as good as her last picture.

She was forty-two going on forty-three the last time I saw her in Paris, but she had no fears of fading because "mine is now a career built on the work I've done, not on my looks." I asked her what would happen, though, if work she liked ever stopped coming her way. "I never think about it," she replied. "But if one day I should feel I no longer express myself in movies as I used to or I just don't feel the enthusiasm you have to have to make a picture the right way, then I would retire without telling anyone. I just wouldn't work anymore—and there are so many of my movies around all the time that people might not even notice I was away. Retirement isn't a tragedy—not if it's a decision that comes from you."

A minute later, though, Sophia was saying: "I don't understand the word retirement. Look at Carlo. He's in his sixties and he never thinks of retirement. He's from Milan, so he enjoys working hard and every day is just as though he's a youngster starting out on a job."

Despite the mortality tables, Sophia would never admit to contemplating widowhood—and when I raised the question, she warned me: "You *are* morbid today. First taxes, now death, be careful!" But she added: "Without ever thinking about it, I'm sure Carlo will outlive us all. Now please change the subject." So I reverted to the previous topic and asked her what else she might do if she could no longer act. Sophia curled a long double-jointed finger at me playfully as she announced: "I'd write!"

"Please don't" I pleaded. "You'll put the rest of us out of business. Why don't you open a boutique?"

I must have hit a nerve in our verbal fencing, for she took it seriously and squirmed for just a second as she begged: "Please, never a boutique, anything but a boutique! I'm not interested in that kind of thing. Fashions, clothing, they're all too *footy.*"

This was the only trouble I had all day with Sophia's English. "*Footy?*" I said. "I don't know what it means, but it sounds like a marvelous word to use around boutiques."

"*Footy,*" she clarified, giggling. "Useless. You know: *foo-tile.*"

"Futile," I corrected. "You make it sound like a Chinese restaurant." But Sophia, eager to escape from the futile frivolity of boutiques, turned her attention back to what else she could do if she didn't act:

"So many new interests can come to you if you don't have to think about your profession any more. I won't just die because I'm not an actress—any more than you'd drop dead if nobody wanted what you wrote. If you have the right temperament and talent, you may develop in some field you never thought of. But, please, not a boutique!" she implored me, as if only I could exorcise this bugbear I'd introduced into her future. "If you promise me that, I won't ever write, I'll read."

Under the circumstances, I gave my oath right away.

"The main thing to be doing is to nourish yourself," said Sophia, who knew starvation, "and to nourish each other. I'm not just talking about food but about marriage, motherhood, movies, relationships, retirement, everything. And you have to work at every single thing. Life is work. Without ever realizing it, you're working at life every day.

"For example, I've learned not to ask things of Carlo that I know will displease him. As you get to know your partner through the years, you just try to do things that will please him —though it hurts when you guess wrong sometimes. I learned early that when Carlo came home at night after working all day long, if he didn't speak, I shouldn't try to talk with him because it meant he didn't feel like speaking. But if he did speak, then I'd go at it, too. This took an effort, but it stops being work and turns to pleasure—and something very natural—if you're in love with somebody.

"I still think the job of a woman is to be very understanding: more so than that of a man. Understanding just comes naturally—or rather, more easily—to women. I think that's why I have such appreciation for women. I think they do so many things well—certainly where affection and understanding are concerned. I like them very much."

"Most of your friends are women, aren't they?"

"Yes. But of course it's very difficult for me to have a man for a friend."

Whenever Sophia went to a ball or ballet with a man who wasn't her husband, there were headlines in the tabloids that she held hands with him—which is hard to deny, of course, if you dance together in the traditional way. The major rumors since I'd seen Sophia last had her "visiting the penthouse of wealthy businessman Jean Barthet" and, when she took Cipi to catch singer Tom Jones' act at the Palais des Congrès, one front-page headline proclaimed:

TOM JONES SECRETLY
DATING SOPHIA LOREN

and, beneath a rather stiffly posed photo of the two together, the caption whispered:

Despite the fact that both are supposed to be happily married, Tom Jones and Sophia Loren are reported to be secretly dating and friends are wondering what will happen next. Other details on page three.

What happened next was that the reader who paid thirty cents and turned to page three felt cruelly teased.

"I don't care what they say," Sophia assured me. "If it's not true, you don't care about it. And if it *is* true, you try to hide it. You don't go to the opera with it, do you?"

I asked if Carlo and she had any policy about going out with others while they're apart. "Jealousy has no place in a marriage," she said emphatically. "The minute you don't trust, it begins to be finished."

I didn't ask Sophia *if* she and Carlo ever quarreled. I asked her what their quarrels were like. And she replied: "The big ones are the silent quarrels. If it's just a disagreement about work or a difference of opinion, we'll disagree, we'll argue—a look here or a word there, especially on my part—but not quarrel. But it's when one or both of us don't speak to each other that the fighting goes on for days."

"And what are these fights about?"

"Just things you say to each other when you're in a bad mood. Part of it is our work. Sometimes he forces me to make a movie because he thinks it's good for me. I do depend on him in this respect. But, y'know, between Carlo and me, there's more than twenty years of difference. You can't think of us as you are with your wife—what are you? three or four months different?— because years of difference do count in the relationship between a man and a woman. I think Carlo considered me also his daughter in a way—and our quarrels reflect this. When you quarrel with one of your daughters, what happens the next day?"

"She goes to sleep and when she wakes up it's usually forgotten," I replied, "and so I try to forget it, too."

"Exactly!" Sophia exclaimed. "Our quarrels aren't exactly childish, though. There's nothing childish about Carlo. I can be, but not Carlo."

I told her that, with my wife rather than my daughters, the best part of the quarrel was making it up. Sophia said:

"We never make up. Nobody ever says, 'I'm sorry.' One of us starts to speak normally at breakfast or lunch and the other eventually answers back in a friendly tone. Usually I'm the one who breaks the ice. I don't have Carlo's endurance. I couldn't carry it on for more than half a day if I had my way. I mean, I start to think of how childish it is: silence between two people who love each other. And life is so short, it's ridiculous to waste it fighting.

"On Carlo's part, it he wants to make up and we're really not speaking, he rings me up from wherever he has to go—and of course you can't stay silent to your husband on the phone, especially when it's long distance and you're starting to miss him."

The phone rang in another room and, a minute or two later, Ines poked her head in to tell Sophia her husband was calling from London. Sophia excused herself to take the call, but then as she made her exit, she stopped in the doorway to reassure me: "He's just calling to say hello. Don't think we're making up a quarrel."

CHAPTER 25

Meet Mara Danelo

IN EARLY 1978 A WOODMERE, LONG ISLAND, SCREENWRITER named Alvin Boretz and a British movie director named John Hough (pronounced Huff) were tinkering with Boretz's fifth draft of the screenplay of *Brass Target,* a four- or five-million-dollar World War II (or, rather, immediately postwar) Metro-Goldwyn-Mayer suspense film which had started out with an all-star, but all-male, cast that included John Cassavetes, Robert Vaughn, Max von Sydow, Patrick McGoohan, Bruce Davison, and Edward Herrmann. Based on a novel by Frederick Nolan and set in Bavaria and Switzerland in 1945, *Brass Target* was fiction about what it matter-of-factly called "a carefully conceived criminal conspiracy which led to the assassination of General George S. Patton," played by George Kennedy.

In Boretz's fourth draft, a woman named Mara Danelo had appeared in the cast of characters for the first time. In his fifth version, "the role got bigger. By the sixth draft, it looked like a cameo part for a big star. And by the seventh version, Mara was a major role and we were looking for an international star to play it."

Bette Davis, whom Hough had just directed for Walt Disney Studios in *Return to Witch Mountain,* was eager to appear in *Brass Target* and work with Hough, thirty-six, who directs women exceptionally well in an old-fashioned, straightforward, downright glamorous style. But Mara wasn't the right role for her, Hough explained:

"It was, by that time, the part of a younger women who did

certain things because of wartime conditions. In this case, Joe de Lucca, the character played by Cassavetes, told Mara when he went off to war that she shouldn't wait for him because he might never come back. But even though he told her not to wait, he can't forgive her for not waiting for him. Every relationship is a little like a summer romance: there is a time and a place for it and, if you try to pick it up later or elsewhere, it doesn't always work—even if you're still in love. So it becomes an uncounted casualty of war."

Hough and Boretz put their recruiting problem into MGM's hands and when Metro executive Frank Rosenfeld called back "to say Sophia Loren might be available, I dropped the phone —literally," Hough recalled. "When I picked it up, Frank was still saying Sophia Loren."

Recognizing that Sophia's name on their picture would raise its bottom at the box office higher than the highest ceiling they'd ever imagined, Hough and Boretz screened two of her movies, *Two Women* and *A Special Day,* to refresh their recollection of what she could do. Then the two flew over the North Pole to Paris.

Carlo Ponti was with Sophia when the two men entered the apartment in the Résidence George V. He greeted them with: "Why do you want Sophia Loren?"

Hough gave a good answer: "Because she's the best actress in the world."

"Then she must DO something in your film," said Ponti. He and Sophia had read the script—and while Hough and Boretz pleaded that it was a major part even though it could be concentrated into five weeks of *Brass Target's* eleven-week shooting schedule, Ponti meant something else. He was concerned not just with the size, but with the *validity* of the part: A star must always make a key contribution to the story. Boretz had written Mara some obligatory big scenes plus a few "Sophia touches," but her own role in the plot was not yet so crucial to its unraveling as those of her co-stars. Ponti told the two to do it over at least once more because "it's not enough to have a big star in your picture. The star has to mean something to the plot as well as the public."

Boretz and Hough flew over the Channel to England to work and were back in Paris within a fortnight. "What we came up with," Hough told me, "was to make Mara the only person in the story who is able to identify Patton's assassin and, with that particular clue, we can put the last piece into the jigsaw puzzle."

Sophia was alone in the Paris apartment when they came back to show the script to her. To Boretz's distress, she asked them to sit with her while she read their handiwork. This is one of the worst experiences that can happen to a writer: someone judging his brain child in his presence. And when the judge happens to be Sophia Loren . . .

"I've only let this be done to me three or four times in my life," Boretz told me later, "and even if they're crazy about what you've done, big stars won't show it because then it drives up your bargaining position. But Sophia must have known exactly what I was feeling because, as soon as she had read the first scene she was in, instead of keeping me waiting, she looked up and said to me, 'It's very good.' Softly, noncommittally, I mean, she still could have finished reading the script and said, 'It's not for me.' But it's not her way to leave anyone twisting slowly, slowly in the wind. Imagine that from an actress! I knew that no matter what else happened, I was in the presence of a real lady, an aristocrat with such a serenity as I've never seen before or since."

(Later, in on-location script conferences, wheneve Boretz felt ganged up on by Hough or MGM producer Arthur Lewis or even Sophia, she would pat him on the arm and murmur: "Keep calm. Don't worry about a thing. We're all on the same side.")

When Sophia finished reading, her earlier response still stood. And when Ponti came home, he, too, was persuaded. Sophia was signed and the *Brass Target* budget was upped by a million dollars.

Ponti was present at Sophia's wardrobe and hairdressing sessions in Paris, but after that, he jetted off about his business, sending Basilio Franchina on location to protect Sophia's script interests and watch out for her other needs. By the beginning of March, Sophia was installed at Munich's Grand Hotel Vierjahreszeiten (Four Seasons).

Filming began on Monday, March 6, 1978 in Munich, where Oscar-winning art director Rolf Zehetbauer (*Cabaret*) had recreated the blackened rubble and bombed-out buildings of 1945 amidst today's solid Deutschemark affluence of the postwar West German economic miracle. Then it moved some fifty miles east to a medieval fortress castle above Burghausen, a thousand-year-old Bavarian town right on the Austrian frontier. But the accommodations in Burghausen were not deemed suitable for Sophia and her co-stars, so they and the *Brass Target* brain trust were billeted across the border in the Upper Austrian lakeside village of Holzöster am See, some fifteen miles away.

Almost every day during a week's filming in Burghausen, a chauffeured MGM blue BMW ferried Sophia to and from the cozy rustic (Class A, but not De Luxe) Hotel Seewirt in Holzöster. Immigration and Customs formalities ranged from perfunctory to nonexistent to autograph requests—and the only eyebrow-raising event came twice a day when Sophia passed through the tiny Austrian village of Fucking.

The natives pronounce it *Fooking*. The first time Sophia spotted a boundary sign reading *"Ortsende von Fucking"* (the limit of Fucking) she gasped. The next time, she cackled—and, after that, she never failed to giggle at it. There was some talk about retitling the film with the road sign's message, but *Brass Target* remained *Brass Target.**

My first inkling that Sophia would be invading Austria came two days before she arrived. Through the Austrian mails, a press release from the regional tourist board proclaimed the impending presence of the world-renowned *"Filmdiva"* to lend new lustre to a landscape that had hitherto served as the setting for three German-language TV films: *In the Vestibule of Truth;*

---

*Connoisseurs of Austrian place names should note that Sophia was living between Rottenegg and Fucking and not too far from Windpassing.

A Winter That Was A Summer; and *Friedrich, Freiherr von der Trenck,* the true-life adventures of a Prussian nobelman who was guillotined in Paris during the French Revolution on suspicion of espionage for Austria.

I dropped a postcard to her at the Hotel Seewirt inviting her to visit us in Vienna if she had a day off. Since we were 150 miles east of her hotel, I also offered to come over with the family on Saturday or Sunday.

My postcard would have been waiting for Sophia when she arrived in the middle of the week. On Friday evening, when there was no response, I phoned her hotel and was told she wasn't there at the moment. I said I was "an old friend" and left my name and number for Sophia to return my call. When there was still no reply by Saturday, I called again. "I gave Miss Loren your message," I was told in German. "What else can I do?"

"Just give it to her again," I told the switchboard in German. "And tell her we're waiting for word when we can come there."

On Sunday morning, however, I was galvanized into action by a two-page spread in The *Kronen Zeitung,* one of Vienna's two daily tabloids. It purported to be an interview with Sophia by "People" columnist Peter *Kupfer,* whose last name in German means *Copper*—which once inspired his arch-rival Roman Schliesser (ao impregnanted Sophia several times a year in his "Adabei" column in the same paper) to coin the saying: "Speech is silver, silence is golden, and *Kupfer* is a liar."

Though many of my professional colleagues were convinced Kupfer never saw Sophia, he did write convincingly about how he laid siege to her at the Seewirt with flowers and a copy of his book of personality sketches before she granted him a brief interview. Very little in Kupfer's piece was so new that he couldn't have obtained his quotes from earlier clippings; in fact, some utterances I recognized as *my* material, but ours is a cannibalistic profession. Even the usual quote about how, while in Austria, she'd like to find an Alpine chalet to buy or rent—"I want my children to learn how to ski. For me it's already too late."—was an old "Adabei" staple. The only difference was that, this time around, Sophia was still in Austria when it appeared and the Seewirt's switchboard was besieged by fifty eager landlords that Sunday.

Less fortunate rival journalists were carrying such news as "the first spring weekend weather of the new year and the presence of Sophia Loren brought hordes of sightseers to the Holzöster am See, but even those who waited as long as six hours were unrewarded with a view of the diva, who stayed in her room all Saturday." So the press had to content itself with the insights of the local tourist director ("She was very nice, but reserved when we gave her our official greeting"), the hotel chef ("How does she keep her figure? She takes Wiener Schnitzel and French fries in her room, and for dessert, chocolate cake with whipped cream—and the plates always come back empty"), and the room-service waitress ("She drinks red wine, but she doesn't tip"*).

The Seewirt's number was giving out a chronic busy signal on Sunday morning, so I made a number of local calls instead. Finally, I persuaded Georg Markus, a reliable local journalist and editor of the weekly magazine *Hörzu,* the Austrian equivalent of *TV Guide,* to drive himself and his Jaguar and myself up to Holzöster am See, which was virtually inaccessible by public transport—and I don't own a car. Georg brought along a photographer named Peter Cermak and, shortly after noon on Sunday, March 12, 1978—the fortieth anniversary of the *Anschluss* with which Adolf Hitler annexed his native Austria—we set out on the road to Braunau am Inn, the very place where Hitler was born. And this was the symbolic day when the house of Hitler's birth was being ceremoniously re-dedicated as a home for handicapped children. Holzöster, where Sophia was staying, is a resort suburb of Braunau.

Georg's second-hand Jaguar (which used to belong to Niki Lauda, the World Grand Prix Champion driver) had a flat tire on the Autobahn and we lost another hour in the woods and

---

*Ten per cent for service is included in the price, but one generally leaves a fraction more. Sophia likely assumed that MGM was coping with this additional *"Trinkgeld."*

dialects of Upper Austria. Everyone we stopped for directions began with "Well, you know Gundertshausen; then you. . . "— but we didn't know Gundertshausen! Thus, it took us more than four hours to find our way to Holzöster and the chalet-style Hotel Seewirt, whose normally spacious driveway parking lot was a bit congested and *gemütlich* restaurant far more crowded than it had any right to be at four-thirty in the afternoon. Just a few fans stood around gawking, but the only sights to see were a couple of rented cars—with German license plates and MGM parking permits—standing idle and unattended outside the main entrance.

A very pregnant blonde receptionist-switchboard operator told me in cool English that she had given my messages to Miss Loren, who was having Sunday dinner in Salzburg, some twenty-five miles away, with some of the *Brass Target* brass. Then the owner of the hotel, a lively lady named Elfriede Maislinger, happened by and, when I introduced myself as an old friend of Sophia's, she added the information that Sophia and the others were eating in the Hotel Österreichischer Hof, which used to be US Army of Occupation headquarters. Elfi Maislinger advised us not to try to catch up with Sophia and her party there because then we'd probably pass them on their way back from Salzburg. She suggested we "just make yourselves at home" around the hotel.

We barely had time to wash up and take a little parking-lot air when two BMWs drew up and out of the first stepped Sophia—swathed, but somehow not sweating, in a svelte silvery white fur coat. She looked gaunt, almost hollow cheeked, as befitted a woman in Germany right after the war, but she has seldom looked more beautiful than she did that day at forty-three. Basilio Franchina, Ponti's deputy—a genial, grandfatherly, but a little younger and taller, version of Sophia's husband —and a young man in riding breeches (obviously, director Hough) had been traveling with her. From the other car, there emerged a couple of men in feathered porkpie hats so perfectly Tirolean that the wearers had to be from Hollywood: besides, they had a couple of English-speaking women with them.

Sophia smiled with surprise when she spotted me, but her mouth tightened a little when she saw I'd brought not family, but two journalistic-looking strangers, with me. So I kissed her on one cheek and, when she didn't kiss me back, I felt less warmth than usual and didn't try for two cheeks, our usual Parisian salute. Instead, I spoke the first words which came to mind, which were: "Well, here I am on the outside looking in."

"What do you mean?" she asked.

"Well, my calls didn't get returned, so I had to borrow a car and drive up here just to make contact," I said, using this excuse to introduce my friends. Sophia shook hands with them coldly and explained to me that she *had* told Basilio to invite me to come see her on Monday. (As it turned out, Basilio had turned the matter over to MGM's *Brass Target* production headquarters across the border in Burghausen and this was a real dead-letter office even when open, which it wasn't on Sunday.) "So I got here a day early," I said. "Better early than late."

Whereupon Sophia, who subscribes to this philosophy, introduced me to director Hough and the two porkpies: one of whom proved to be Al Boretz, the scriptwriter, and the other, Metro producer Arthur Lewis, who immediately told the expectant receptionist to give us three rooms. Then my three new acquaintances excused themselves for a script meeting with Sophia, who said she's be getting some new pages immediately thereafter and would have to learn them and go right to bed, but she would ring my room Monday morning.

CHAPTER 26

An Actress in Upper Austria

AND IT CAME TO PASS THAT SOPHIA was on standby for Monday, but was never called and did not leave the hotel. There was no room-to-room phone service within the Seewirt, but around 10:15 A.M., Sophia rang the switchboard and asked the operator to tell me to come up and see her in half an hour.

Sophia was occupying an L-shaped corner apartment directly below the two smaller rooms that John Cassavetes and I had on the third floor, which is called the second floor in Europe. (Cassavetes was a friendly neighbor who didn't want to talk about his work, including Sophia, when he wasn't working.) Basilio Franchina, who was just leaving, let me in the bedroom door and led me through a connecting bathroom that looked like a laboratory into Sophia's living room, which reeked of Peter Kupfer's importuning flowers. Clad in a purplish house-coat, her hair up in curlers, "the diva" was reclining in a chair. Yes, said Sophia, she had seen Kupfer and now she was sorry because she'd never said anything about a chalet and look at all the trouble his "quote" was causing the poor pregnant switch-board—"plus a few other inaccuracies, so say I didn't see him or, better yet, don't say I saw him."

Sophia beckoned me to a sofa at a right angle to her seat. Not satisfied with that, however, she stood up to remove an obstacle "so we can look at each other while we talk." It was a vase of flowers "from that man I never saw. They bother me," she said as she resettled them on the window sill.

I took out my cassette recorder, note pad, and latest collection of clippings. ("Sophia Loren created a minor furore by attending a Dior fur show with her hair a solid frizzle," and "she will be making her stage debut in the Broadway musical *Carmelina*" were the only new wrinkles.) When Sophia came back across the room, she laughed at what I was doing and said: "Always with piles of notes, Alan Levy comes. How can you still have questions when you know me so well? Already you have all the answers."

She lit a cigarette, but told me: "I'm smoking less than before. I really mean to give it up."

"What's stopping you from stopping? The movie?"

"There's always an alibi. But the truth is: I don't have the will to stop."

She was hoping MGM would let her take a little time off from *Brass Target* to fly to California for the Academy Awards in April. *A Special Day* was up for the Oscar as Best Foreign Film, for which it had already won a 1978 Golden Globe. While Sophia somehow had not been nominated for Best Actress,* she was rooting for her film: "If it wins, we all win."

"What a pity you weren't nominated, too!" I said.

"Well, it doesn't take away from the merits of the performance or the film, does it?" she comforted me.

By then, I knew a little about how Sophia had happened to Boretz and Hough, but not how and why she had enlisted in *Brass Target.* Sophia was quite candid: "I got fed up with not working. I hadn't worked since *A Special Day:* almost ten months off. So I asked Carlo to find me a part in some picture in Europe. He asked MGM and, when they showed me the part, with a little help from Carlo and some more work by them, it became very appealing, so I decided to do it."

"How would you describe the part of Mara?"

"Oh, it's a very nice role, very delicate, very human, quite romantic." Struck by the banality of what she was saying, So-

---

*That honor went to Diane Keaton in Woody Allen's *Annie Hall* (Best Picture) and France's *Madame Rosa* beat out *A Special Day* as Best Foreign Language Film.

phia smiled sheepishly and then tried a little harder: "Well, she's a very lonely woman. The only woman in the film, in fact. But that isn't what makes her lonely."

I tried to help: "Is she a woman in a village. A castle?"

Sophia picked up the cue: "In a castle. She's a protégée of many men. She can't live alone by herself: if she does, she dies. And so she goes from one man to the other, but not loving any of them. She only loves one man and this is Cassavetes, who comes back later on."

"Is she an aristocrat? Or a Neapolitan peasant?"

"Mmmm, middle class."

Rather than badger Sophia to describe with detachment someone she was trying to become, I switched gears and asked: "So what have you seen of Austria?"

"This hotel and the ride to Burghausen. I like this part of Austria; it looks like a little bit of Switzerland. And yesterday I went to Salzburg [which she pronounced Salisburg]. Very good food at the Österreichischer Hof, very good food." She had even partaken of a *Salzburger Nockerl,* the local bouffant meringue soufflé dessert specialty, and pronounced it *wunderbar!* "Then we went for a walk on the bridge and walked all around below the what-do-you-call-the-fortress?"

"The Höhensalzburg Festung," I said. "Did you take the funicular up there or did you walk?"

"No, we didn't go up to the fortress. I mean, it was our day off from Burghausen, which is a little like that, too. So we wandered through the city and there, on a little street, we saw Cassavetes with two Italian friends eating hot dogs at a stand, so we said hello and then came back and there you were."

She liked it when people stopped her for autographs in the stony streets of Salzburg. I asked her if she'd had any police protection there. "What for?" she said with a snort. "If you're not expected, you don't need to be protected."

"How do you like working in Germany and staying in Austria?"

"At first I was wondering. I asked, 'Why do I have to stay a half an hour away from the set and cross a frontier every time I go to and from work?' But they said this hotel was the best one around and now I'm very happy with it. As soon as I walked in, I liked this place better than the Four Seasons, my hotel in Munich."

"You do? Why?"

Sophia answered my question with a question: "Have you seen the décor in this place?"

"How could I have missed it?" was my reply. "You ought to be filming *Sleeping Beauty* here." For there were spinning wheels on every landing, wood-beamed ceilings, parchment lampshades, and in my room, a bearskin had been nailed to the wall. And on one's pillow at bedtime: a pyramidal packet containing a chocolate cherry with a pit in it.

"What I have here is much more *intime* than what Metro gave me in Munich. Only an Arab could afford such a place! It has kilometers of living room, so I stay always in my bedroom for fear I get lost. It must be meant for Arabs to give parties. But I feel so welcome in *this* hotel. The lady who runs it is so nice that she hired two or three extra people just to look after us. And they take very good care of us. You know, I don't ask for much. I stay in my room and don't demand anything fancy like *crepes flambêes* or *soufflé au fromage*."

I had already ascertained that Eva Richter, the receptionist mothering the switchboard, too, was a multilingual village schoolteacher on maternity leave. Well into her eighth month, she had come in to help out her old friend, Elfi Maislinger, by working from 7 A.M. to 10 P.M., at which late hour one or another of the Hollywood porkpies would buy her a well-earned draught beer and inevitably warn her not to drink it "for the sake of the baby."

Even with additional help on hand, however, it had taken one hour for us to get breakfast that morning and two-and-a-half hours for supper to be served the night before. When I hinted that the hired hands were too busy servicing Sophia & Company to wait on mere mortals, Sophia denied this:

"Not me, anyway, because I do my own breakfast. They don't start serving until seven and I'm up an hour or hour-and-a-half before then. Besides, they don't know how to brew Italian coffee. That's why I have an *espresso* machine in the bathroom and a mixer there, too. I mix eggs and sugar with it in the morning and drink it with the coffee and a little milk that they bring me the night before. So I don't have to wait one hour. I brought my own breakfast-making."

I told her I might have done the same if I'd known we were staying overnight, but I hadn't even brought my shaving kit. Hearing this, Sophia said: "Then I lend you my razor if you don't mind."

"Why should I mind?" I said. "I'd be honored."

"It's the razor I use to shave my legs," she explained.

"I'll take it!" I said. "And after I've used it, I may never wash my face again."

Around this point, my Austrian colleague and chauffeur, George Markus, popped in to ask if his photographer could shoot a couple of pictures. Sophia said: "Sure, but unless we're filming this afternoon, which I think we're not, it can't be today when my hair is up. We do it first thing tomorrow on my way out to the set."

Before going to the desk to extend our stay by another night, Markus popped a couple of "local interest" questions at Sophia, starting with: "Do you speak any German?"

Just as predictably, Sophia said: "I know how to say *Geh weg!* (Get lost!)"

"Only to journalists?" Markus joked.

"No," said Sophia, laughing. "No, no, the ones here are very nice, not like *paparazzi.*"

"But how much German do you really know?"

"Oh, I can make myself understood. I can make a long phrase if I have to. If I want to eat, I can say it. Or, if I have to say anything too much complicated, I just make gestures and everybody understands."

"What's the longest sentence you've spoken since you've come to German-language territory?"

"Oh," said Sophia. *"Ich arbeite den ganzen Tag.* [I work all day.] *Ich bin sehr müde.* [I am very tired.]"

"Brava!" I exclaimed. "Anyway, that's a much nicer way to put off journalists than *Geh weg!"*

Thus encouraged, Sophia persisted at her German with *"Ich liebe dich* [I love you] everybody knows. Another one—well, he taught me the phrase and only later did I learn what it meant."

"Who taught you *what* phrase?"

Sophia chuckled: "Well, I can't tell you who, but I can tell you what: *Wollen Sie mit mir schlafen? [Voulez-vous couchez avec moi?**] And then he said: 'Don't say it ever!' "

"Then why did he teach it to you?" I wondered.

"Because it was fun."

I told Sophia how, at the age of sixteen, I'd been detained and lectured by a village policeman on the Gaspé Peninsula of Quebec—not for a traffic offense, but for shouting the French version of her *verboten* German expression at every passing skirt: "It turned out this fell under a law against blaspheming."

"Oh, God!" Sophia exclaimed appropriately. "Well, now it wouldn't happen to you—not even in that part of Canada."

Saying goodbye to Sophia, Markus asked her if she'd found a house in Austria as a result of Kupfer's interview. Sophia snorted and said: "I never said it. I never saw him."

Joseph E. Levine, the movie mogul who might be presumed to have better access to the Pontis' plans than Peter Kupfer, had written in the latest *Ladies' Home Journal* that they were thinking of settling in Connecticut. When I asked Sophia about this one, she replied: "I don't know. My children both go to school in Paris now. I think they should finish this phase of their studies in France and then we'll see what happens. We haven't decided anything yet."

"But you *are* thinking of moving to America?" I persisted because such reports—which recur even more often than those of househunts in Austria—usually elicit immediate and total denials.

"Not really." Sophia responded. "I like America. I like how

*The highly formal, black-tie Euroversion of the proposition: "Will you sleep with me?"

warm and friendly people are there. But it depends upon what projects I have and Carlo has. We'll see. . . . Listen! What kind of a holiday in America is the Fourth of July?"

I told her all abut the Declaration of Independence and practically sang the score of the show *1776* to her. And Sophia professed such intense interest *("Ahhh, Independence Day, of course, Independence Day!")* that I asked her why she wanted to know. "Because I never knew," she said. "It's like your National Day, yes?" I said yes.

We made our arrangements for picture-taking the next day. I had the feeling she was a little lonely and wanted to be entertained, but rather than overstay my welcome, I made a brief overture toward leaving. Always bearing in mind her 1975 utterance, however, about interviewers who "take from me in an hour whatever they want [when] if they'd deal with me differently, they could have me forever"—from which this book takes its title—I obeyed as soon as she beckoned me to sit down. Sophia wasn't ready for me to leave: "It's a boring day and, unless I'm working this afternoon—which I doubt, because I would have heard by now—I'm just going to read the script and some poetry. Our meeting yesterday took so long that the new script pages didn't come until ten o'clock last night, but I stayed up to learn them and then practiced them again before I sent for you this morning. Now I won't need them till tomorrow, but I'll look at them a couple of times more today."

I asked what kind of poetry she was reading.

The answer was Pablo Neruda (1904–73) in the original Spanish. "It's so beautiful! What a poet!" she exclaimed. "He was married to a very rich woman, but oh, the way he died! You know, he was heartbroken about the death of Allende." The 1971 Nobel Laureate, Neruda (born Reyes, but having taken a pen name in honor of the nineteenth century Prague poet Jan Neruda) had been the Ambassador to France of Chilean Marxist President Salvador Allende and had died of grief and a heart collapse twelve days after his chief perished in a coup in Santiago.

The talk turned to more recent politics and the French elections, which were in progress. "What happened in France?" Sophia asked me.

It was virtually impossible to get foreign news in this corner of Austria, but, I told her, "I did hear someone in the restaurant say the Socialists aren't doing as well as expected. What are you hoping for?"

"For the best," Sophia replied.

"What's the best? Giscard? Mitterand?"

"I don't know. I wish we knew. Who knows what is best?"

"Now that you're a French citizen, don't you vote?"

"No, because right now we claim our residence in Switzerland."*

Sophia confessed to an avid interest in politics, but will never be an activist: "If you live in this world, you take part in the society and you have to have some kind of political direction. But you have to search for your own direction—and I don't think it's good for an actress to expose herself politically to such an extent that people who don't agree with her politics won't go to her movies.

"Not that I want to sound like a coward, but why should people resent my politics? And I am just not very much prepared to argue politics. With my instincts, I can follow what I think is the right direction or even the right leader, but I could never be implicated in any very profound political discussion. If I talk about something, I want to know what I am talking

*Early in 1978, the Paris right-wing weekly *Minute* published a 1977 internal document of the French Ministry of Economics and Finance on the subject of "Activities of M. Carlo Ponti." It was an edict instructing Customs officials to keep their hands off him and to clear any intervention with the highest echelon first. Among the six reasons given for this special treatment were Ponti's "possession of a Swiss residence permit since 1957," around which time Ponti had invested in a chalet in Bürgenstock, overlooking Lake Lucerne, and his "living only partially in France, having chosen our country for the scholastic education of his children"—circumstances which *Minute*, hardly the most respected French periodical, claimed were the same that resulted in a two-million-dollar penalty levied against singer-actor Charles Aznavour in December, 1977.

about and why. Many celebrities are no better prepared for politics than I am, but they talk too much anyway."*

After politics, we talked about family. When I told Sophia that both our girls, whom she hadn't seen for nearly three years, were now teenagers, she shook her head with amazement and made a hand gesture to show how little they'd been when they first came to Marino. And when I told her that after four or five years of steady quarreling, Monica and Erika had only recently "united against the common enemy: us," Sophia gave a laugh that was really a long rattle. (Later, transcribing from my cassette, I clocked it at eight seconds.)

Almost as if to toll the children's hour, the phone rang. Paris calling. Edoardo Ponti, age five, on the line. Sophia greeted him in English for my benefit: "Would you like to come here and see me?"

I could hear a loud and clear voice respond in English at the other end: "Nnnnno!"

"Why not?" Sophia asked.

"Because—I don't —want to!"

After bidding Edoardo *"Ciao!"* and chatting with his nurse and her secretary, Sophia hung up and felt obliged to give his big brother Cipi, now referred to as Carlo, equal time: "Carlo is so good with the piano—really beautiful! Now he plays Bach and Schubert. He made a concert the other morning. A jury examined him with some other children and one of them will win a prize. We don't know the decision yet, but I said to him over the phone yesterday: 'How did it go?' and he said: 'Very bad.' He always sounds pessimistic. It's a kind of defense. So I said: 'Then how come someone told me you were the only one that the audience started to applaud, but then the jury said, "Shhh, shhh, shhh, don't do that." He said: 'It's not true!' Well,

---

*Back in 1970, when Nino Lo Bello had asked Sophia if she opposed the war in Vietnam, she'd replied: "I am against the war. I am against all war. I am against so many people being still very hungry. I am against having too many babies when you can't feed them. When a baby is born, he should have a good life. I am *for* this kind of thing."

how could I argue with him? So I said: 'All right, we'll see what happens soon enough.' I don't want him to feel any stress about winning or losing at the piano—or even about practicing. Anyway, it's a kind of relaxation for him.

"He still doesn't like blood or violence. If he sees something violent on television or anything else he doesn't want to see, he runs away from the room and goes right to the piano. As soon as he hears the scene is over, he comes right back and says: 'What happened?' Then he wants to hear every gory detail, but he doesn't want to see it."

"Can't he just shut his eyes?" I asked.

"No, the sounds of these scenes are too frightening and the music that goes with them is so dramatic that he just has to go away. But our other one, Edoardo, just sits there sucking his thumb and saying, 'I'm not afraid. I'm not afraid.' But, of course, then he goes to his brother and says, 'It's finished' when it isn't true. Carlo comes back and gets frightened all over again."

"A boy is better off squeamish than insensitive," I opined. Sophia hadn't read of the recent murder trial in Miami where a fifteen-year-old boy's defense for killing an eighty-two-year-old woman was that he'd been so addicted to violence by television (and seeing actors die one day and turn up on the screen the next) that death (and therefore life) was relatively meaningless to him when he committed his crime.

"You mean he thought it was a scene?" Sophia reacted. "But he was too old for that! I could understand a nine- or ten-year-old—twelve maybe—but fifteen?"

I told her that's what the court thought, too (he received a life sentence), and then we talked about how so many of today's changes in perceptions and values can be traced to TV.

"There was a film festival of 'orror somewhere up in the snows of France," Sophia said, "and they showed little bits of some of the entries on French television in the afternoon. It was incredible! It was appalling! At just the hour when children are home from school and looking at television, they had to show this!

"There was one scene. A boy goes to a vending machine where you just push and a glass comes down and fills up with Coca-Cola. He was pushing a button and the machine wouldn't work. Then he pushed again and this time the whole machine opened up. There was a man inside, killed, with blood all over him. The boy closed the machine and just then the mother was calling the boy."

Now walking around her Upper Austrian hotel living room, Sophia started doing the whole scene for me—with almost as much performer's relish as mother's disgust.

"JoJo, come!" she said, mimicking the tired contralto of a shopped-out mother.

" 'Mama, Mama, come here!' " a little boy's squeak emerged from Sophia. " 'I saw, I saw a—' "

" 'Oh, come on, Jojo! You always with your fantasy!' "

Now, Sophia reverted to her own voice: "So they just go away. Then you see a very fat lady going to the same machine. She pushes the button. It works. The glass fills up and she drinks—*blood!*"

"And Cipi saw this?!"

"Yes," she said. "He couldn't even go to the piano he was so paralyzed with fright. He said: 'It makes me throw up.' But he didn't.

"Sounds like Roman Polanski running amok," I remarked. Sophia nodded and we got to talking about the director of *Rosemary's Baby* who was also the widower of Charles Manson cult murder victim Sharon Tate and who had just fled to Paris when a California judge was about to sentence him for having intercourse with a thirteen-year-old girl.

"He worked once with my husband on a mystery film," Sophia said.

"Which one?" I asked.

"*What?*" said Sophia.

Raising my voice, I elaborated: "I said 'Which film did he work on with your husband?' "

Sophia explained: "The name of the film was *What?*" Then she went on to speak up a little for Polanski. "You know, even girls of thirteen nowadays, you have to think whether they are really looking for trouble. Some girls of thirteen are not just thirteen. Who knows? They say that in America many girls do this. Sex, blackmail, and I think also television makes them know so much more at thirteen than I ever did."

Hearing this from one who matured early in wartime and who started the mating process with Ponti at a youthful age, I asked Sophia if she could relate in any way to Polanski's teen-aged "victim."

"Well, maybe she was upset when he tried to drop her," Sophia guessed, but then she shrugged off the subject with: "Who knows what the truth is?" We talked for almost thirty minutes after my hourlong cassette clocked off, but the only item worth noting on my pad was: "No, I still won't go back to Italy, but there are negotiations about the [tax] matter and I think a happy ending is in sight."* Then I borrowed her razor and promised to return it next morning when Peter Cermak would be taking her picture.

---

*In this, Sophia's optimism proved premature. On April Fool's Day, 1978, a Rome magistrate issued a warrant for Carlo Ponti's arrest on charges of illegally transferring money out of Italy and assistant prosecutor Paolino Dell Anno filed charges against Sophia Loren as an accomplice. The newspaper *Corriere della Sera* of Milan estimated the total illegally transferred abroad at twenty-two-and-a-half-million dollars: mainly to France, Switzerland, and Liechtenstein. The charges against Ponti are punishable by up to six years in prison, but France does not extradite its citizens for prosecution in other countries. Nevertheless, Italian law permits trials in absentia and the formal complaints were seen as a prelude to seizure, in lieu of heavy fines, of Ponti holdings in Italy, estimated to include the Villa in Marino and two other homes, a hotel, one hundred apartments, two hundred fifty acres of land, and four hundred valuable works of art. Dell Anno later accused Sophia of illegally exporting art works worth three-and-a-half-million dollars and failing to inform Italian authorities of her holdings abroad. More than two dozen others were accused by Dell Anno of complicity in the alleged Ponti plot, among them several Ponti employees and colleagues as well as Ava Gardner and Richard Harris. The two performers were accused of receiving several thousand dollars worth of credits outside Italy for working in *Cassandra Crossing* and other Ponti films. Closing in from another direction in 1978, a different Roman prosecutor accused Sophia and Carlo of appropriating archaeological finds, including seventy

That night, I drank gin and tonic with director John Hough, who studied film-making at London's Polytechnic School of Cinematography and apprenticed with Alfred Hitchcock, Fred Zinnemann, and David Lean before directing "The Avengers" TV series and the films *Legend of Hell House* and *Dirty Mary, Crazy Larry* and Bette Davis for Disney, among others. Hough was unfazed by having two experienced directors—Patrick McGoohan (who created the TV series, "The Prisoner") and Cassavetes (*Shadows, Faces, Husbands, Minnie and Moskowitz*, etc.)—acting for him, for he had already directed Orson Welles as Long John Silver in *Treasure Isalnd*. I told Hough how Sophia had marveled the most at De Sica taking direction from lesser directors. Hough said he could understand:

"Anyone who's acting thinks of himself totally as an actor—or as the character he's playing—and not as a director or author or anything else. After all, no actor will ever tell me how to direct. All of Welles' and Cassavetes' concern were on their own performances. One of the parts of movie acting is that you have to relate to somebody else—not to an audience, not to the crew. When you act in film, nobody in the world can tell you how you have done except the director. All the great directors I've watched have one technique in common: They *whisper* their directions to the artist. Privately. So, when the take is finished, the one person the actors look to is the director."

Hough, however, had not yet fully recovered from the coup of snaring Sophia for *Brass Target*. And he had naught but kind words for his superstar:

"From the minute I walked into her apartment in Paris, she

Etruscan vases that were found showcased within the Villa Ponti. Penalties for these offenses could total thirty years in prison. In the meantime, Sophia kept busy and in the limelight—turning up in such "locations" as Voice of America headquarters in Washington and Grand Central Station in Manhattan while filming her first post-*Brass Target* production: *Firepower*, an eight-million-dollar thriller directed by Michael Winner. Then, in July of 1978, she slipped into Italy by train from Paris for a quick costume-fitting session for her next movie—to be directed by Lina Wertmuller and co-starring Mastroianni. Its title, at press time, was *Love, Death Shimmy, Lugano City, Beautiful, Spider Dance and Sicilian Biscuits and Wine.*

confirmed in real life that she was just as emotional as she is on the screen. You can tell the way somebody greets you and talks to you even if she doesn't throw her arms around you.

"When we had been working together a very little while, she and I realized that we both share many of the same tastes in moviemaking. There's a big difference between European and American acting. Americans show their emotions on a very high level. Europeans, by inclination and tradition, show emotion on a lower level, but the explosion of it is therefore much more powerful when it comes.

"By virtue of the fact that I come from London, I could see that if Sophia plays certain scenes in an introverted way, they will have greater impact and so will her big scenes. In *Brass Target,* she has a shouting match with Cassavetes. Now, when two people shout at each other, an audience knows instinctively that *what* they're saying isn't as important as the way they're saying it. But if one of them lowers his or her voice, then his or her actual words assume meaning and you can even win an argument that way.*

"Sophia crystallized one such scene for me. It's one where she tells Cassavetes to go. She suggested to us that she put the word *please* in front of *go.* When you tell someone to *please* go, it's much more emotional. The whole key to Sophia's performance is how well she can lower her emotion.

"While we were filming a romantic scene, she came to me between takes and whispered one very simple idea. If, while playing this scene, she had a cigarette but couldn't find a match, it would add to the scene. We tried it with the unlit cigarette and it worked."

I asked John Hough if the inspiration to tell Carlo Ponti that his wife is "the best actress in the world" had come naturally to him.

Hough said: "I'm absolutely sincere about that. Many women look very good, but can't act to match their looks. Many more

*As exemplified by one of my all-time favorite bad-movie lines—Ava Gardner to Charlton Heston in *Earthquake:* "Don't you lower your voice to me!"

women can act very well, but don't look so great. Sophia's a rarity. I can't think of any star who has her emotional acting capability plus her looks. There's no woman in the world who comes close to her.

"The scene we're shooting tomorrow is a key one, so she's staying in her room again tonight and the set may be closed tomorrow. But I sent her a handwritten message saying 'Please cry for me tomorrow. And if you need help, just call.' But just before I came down to meet you, I got her handwritten reply: 'I don't have to. Just bring Kleenex.'"

"What's that all about?" I asked, a trifle mystified. "Are you in trouble?"

"No," said Hough. "It's a scene in which she has to cry. Now we always provide ammonia, glycerine or something or other to make the tears flow, but Sophia can do it without any aid. She just needs five minutes on the set. She'll go into a corner, turn her back on cast and crew for five minutes, and then turn around crying."

"How does she do it?" I wondered.

"I haven't had the nerve to ask her," Hough replied. "Maybe when the picture is finished, I'll ask her: 'What do you think about in the corner?' And I suspect her answer will be: 'I think about children. My children.'"

Silver Razor of Seewirt

That night, with photographer Cermak clicking away, I shaved with Sophia's Wilkinson Sword double-edged razor and blade. Now I am a chap of indelicate hand and sensitive skin who has been known to mangle himself with an electric razor—and to whom the words "safety razor" are a contradiction in terms. Nevertheless, using Sophia's leg razor, I managed to achieve a close shave of my face without so much as a nick.

If only Sophia had been that lucky.

Promptly at 8:45 A.M. the next morning, on her way out to the Burghausen location, she emerged all alone from the Hotel Seewirt's self-service elevator. She was already made-up for filming and swathed in a purplish fur coat that must have sent Gelett Burgess back to the Ouija board for a rewrite (*I never saw a purple mink*).

First, she posed for Peter Cermak and then with editor Markus and myself. After Markus had presented her with an article illustrated by one of her UNICEF photos of me, I told her I had a presentation to make, too. As formally as possible, I awarded her, in lieu of the acting Oscar she deserved for *A Special Day*, what I called "The Silver Razor of the Seewirt."

Sophia accepted her razor back in the same spirit and there was even a little applause in the lobby as she took the trophy from me. Then, to my alarm, she stuck it into her purplish pocket. The Jewish Mother in me prompted me to warn her: "Don't do that, Sophia! It's dangerous."

"What should I do?" she said. "My baggage is gone." This was the last day of filming in Burghausen and the unit would then go directly from the set to Munich.

"Give it back to me," I suggested, "and I'll give it to Basilio when I see him."

Just then, Basilio appeared and Sophia reached into her pocket to give the razor to him. In doing so, she cut her index finger on the blade.

It was exactly the situation I'd dreaded, but fortunately I had first-aid at my fingertip for her. Ever since I started bleeding from a fingernail while *shlepping* luggage from boat to train at the English Channel port of Oostend, Belgium, I have always carried a couple of Band-Aids with my passport and in my wallet. So I had one handy the moment Sophia took her wounded finger out of her mouth. Smiling she gave me the finger and trembling I bandaged it.

When my famous first-aid was finished, Sophia thanked me, but I kept apologizing for having caused her injury. Her last words to me then, were a cheerful: "Every time I see you I bleed."

I trust that will not be the epitaph for our friendship, Sophia.